THE BRIGHTNESS

Secrets of the Third Angel,
and
the Bridge at Kino Springs

SM NONA

Order this book online at www.trafford.com
or email orders@trafford.com

Most Trafford titles are also available at major online book retailers.

Printed in Victoria, BC, Canada.

ISBN: 978-1-4269-2748-5 (sc)
ISBN: 978-1-4269-2747-8 (hc)
ISBN: 978-1-4269-2828-4 (e)

*Our mission is to efficiently provide the world's finest, most comprehensive book publishing
service, enabling every author to experience success. To find out how to publish your book, your
way, and have it available worldwide, visit us online at www.trafford.com*

Trafford rev. 09/16/2010

*Photograph of framed picture of young man on Indian motorcycle by Anthony French. Cover image from
The Orion nebulae taken by NASA/ESA's Hubble Telescope. Courtesy of C. O'Dell and NASA.
Appreciation given to Raul Lopez of Radio Shack for his technical assistance.*

 www.trafford.com

North America & international
toll-free: 1 888 232 4444 (USA & Canada)
phone: 250 383 6864 ♦ fax: 812 355 4082

Dedicated to The American Library Association's marvelous program, **Born to Read.**

To the children who will one day conquer death,
And sing the songs of the Resurrection.

*   *   *

You who are holding this book. You.
And I, and all the others, every one.
We will die.
That's the way it has always been. That is our fate.
Until now.
We are crossing the threshold to the end of mortality.
We are in the gathering of belief.

(A Report to the Committee of the Safekeepers)

"No choice is uninfluenced by the way in which the personality regards its destiny, and the body its death. In the last analysis, it is our conception of death which decides our answers to all the questions that life puts to us."
-U.N. Sec. Gen. Dag Hammerskjold
(quoted by Ian Wilson, *After Death Experience*)

Think of the soul: I swear that body of yours
Gives proportions to your soul somehow to live in
Other spheres.
I do not know how, but I know it is so.
-Walt Whitman, *Poem of Remembrance.*

"WHAT IS important to realize is that 'mystical' experiences are not experiences of *another* order of reality, but insights into *this* order seen with extraordinarily clear vision and greater concentration..."
-Colin Wilson, *Religion and the Rebel.* 1984.

"I'm 80 and I hate it. I think about it ten times a day... I love my life and I'm not ready to give it up.. We've got to do something about death, Larry."
-Andy Rooney, to Larry King, Feb. 1999.

"They that dwell in the land of the shadow of death,
upon them hath the light shined." -Isaiah 9:12.

"Nothing is too wonderful to be true, if it be consistent with the laws of nature."
-Michael Faraday.

...IT cannot be possible that all that we know, and all that we were, evaporates into nothing,
-Prof. Lloyd Man Foglesby.

Don't forget, Zorba, we shall meet again and who knows, man's strength is tremendous. One day we'll put our great plan into effect. We'll build a monastery of our own, without a god, without a devil, but with free men; and you shall be the gatekeeper, Zorba...
-Nikos Kazantzakis, *Zorba the Greek*, 1946.

"Papa, will they ever find a cure for death?"
-Eric David, age 4.

Contents

WHAT FOLLOWS NOW is an attempt to portray in ordinary words the experience of another reality.

CHAPTER ONE

THE LETTER

Sometimes we almost make the connection. We almost understand...
And so powerful is the reality that its mere shadow cast upon us for an
instant lingers bright as the sun, because for a brief moment we feel the
power and presence of the Source, and know that it is within us...
-Lloyd Man Foglesby, Nobel Address, 2005.

MOST EVERYONE called him Fo, a strange name for so complex a character, and this is how he would introduce himself, just "Fo".

In the mechanics of speech itself, unlike mathematics, there is no number smaller than one. A certain quantity of vowels and another of consonants, and single syllables, but no fractions of them. The fractions and increments and subtleties come in the expression of speech, and not in its mechanics- in what is spoken between the words, and beyond them, and through them, in infinitely discreet shades of thought and emotion. This is how he once explained it... The simplicity of his name appealed to him, a *naked singularity*.

His students- and there had been many- called him Doctor Fo.

It has been said that all things that come into conscious experience are beginnings, as all things noted change the observer. When our attention is called in even the slightest way, we are turned from what it was we were toward what we may become.

And so it happened on that summer day out of shadows changed into a brightness which never recedes, because we are turned irrevocably from what we were toward what we will become.

THE LETTER which began the telling of this story came by express carrier, by the brown van which slid silently across the countryside a mile away, its image shimmering in the summer warmth. As it made the turn its windshield caught the angle of the sun and erupted into a bright burst of energy which just as quickly faded, leaving the van to skim forward before its trail of light dust, steadily growing larger in its approach.

Although few visitors had come in the fleeting weeks of my retreat, and none were expected that morning, something caused me to leave the porch at the rear of the little frame house where I sat reading and savoring a cup of coffee, walk around the old wood tower of the windmill with its flowering trumpet vine, and continue down the entry road to the post and wire gate held taut by the leverage of a singletree.

Just as I was opening the gate I looked across the mile of pasture to see the little truck moving quickly and soundlessly towards the turnoff which leads up to the farmstead. Perhaps, I mused as I leaned against the gatepost, something subliminal had alerted me to the van's approach, a disturbance of the atmosphere below the range of hearing. Still, I wondered why I had sensed, not just the approaching van, but its driver as well, and yet such occurrences now seemed almost natural, and hardly out of place.

A young man with sandy hair jumped down from the truck and handed me the envelope, and then the tablet to sign for its receipt. He was whistling a tune under his breath and his body seemed poised energetically to spring back into the van at the earliest moment.

"Beautiful day," I commented, noting his happy nature and trying to get a better look at his face.

"Yep, sure is," he agreed. "I'm trying to get done early for my twin daughters' birthday party." Now I understood the source of his enthusiasm.

I offered congratulations and asked a couple of questions about his family. He mentioned that his own birthday comes a week before that of his two young girls, and that today was the celebration for all three birthdays.

"How many for you?" I asked.

"Thirty," he answered cheerily as he turned to leave. "About the same as Alexander when he conquered the known world!"

"You've done better than Alexander," I called out as he boarded the van. He grinned broadly and raised his arm as he sped away.

I walked leisurely back up the road toward the house and passed by the windmill, stopping within the caliche stone wellhouse to have a drink of fresh water which rhythmically spurted from the three-quarter inch pipe above the cooling trough within which had sat containers of milk and eggs in times gone by, before the arrival of the refrigerator.

Encased in cement on opposite walls and covered by damp moss was a one-inch bar of iron from which still hung a forged meathook by which were suspended sides of beef or pork in times when the air was free of flies and the meat could be kept relatively fresh within the cool shadows, even through the summer. A name, a signature etched into fresh plaster on the day of completion a century ago spoke its immutable greeting across the generations, the familiar curl of its letters warmed by a shaft of sunlight through the open door. Out in the yard a bed of yellow and orange iris bloomed within a circle of the same white stones which composed the wellhouse, and may have been older than any structure remaining here, as pioneering families brought the bulbs with them from wherever they had come, passed down through the generations, some brought over from the old country as a living reminder of homes forsaken for the dream of a new beginning.

Pulling the dotted strip from the express envelope, I drew out a linen paper envelope within which was a single page.

"Would you consent to tell us your story?...Kindly respond at your earliest convenience. Many thanks," was all the note said.

It was written upon fine stationary under letters set above the image of a sky blue lotus flower with a yellow calyx which simply read:

SAFEKEEPERS.

At the bottom of the page in small letters was a list of names which included some I immediately recognized as prominent individuals, including a former head of state.

Below the note was the palindrome: OTTO.

I looked over the letter several times as I sat at the table, and noted both a satisfaction and a lack of surprise at having received it. The stillness of the air was broken by a sudden breeze which stirred up within the old elms back of the corral and reached over with just enough force to nudge the windmill wheel and send a knock reverberating down the well pipe and back up with that unique and soothing sound which is so musical to those who know it. The Aermotor vane creaked and adjusted its setting with the subsiding breeze, and then all was quiet again, except for the humming of the bees within the flowers of the trumpet vine.

Although there would be much to say about this adventure beyond mortality- beyond all comparison- and much to tell about the strange and real journey to the other side and its true meaning, I had no idea at that moment how to begin.

Through an intense period of reading and study, with long interludes of deep reflection, I had barely begun to comprehend the implications of that future- and yet, present- reality, or of the revelations of knowledge poured out upon humanity in the annunciation of destiny which would affect every life.

What was revealed there was literally the salvation of mankind, and yet how do you put such a thing into words? How does one with unpracticed thought explain the visionary?

In seeking the manner in which to prepare, I had heeded the counsel of the esteemed teacher to his students: "Find the quiet of your life, and listen to your thoughts. The mind breathes thought as the lungs breathe air."

In the moment just before rising to walk down the entry road to meet the express carrier that morning I came across the lines again, noted in one of the spiral notebooks which were stacked before me on the table, and set by a student's hand on center page. Below the lines were written what may have been a continuation of the same quote of the famed professor, or may have been a notation of the student's related thoughts, reminiscent of Thoreau:

"Life is reclaimed in quiet places; thought, from the silence. The senses come alive in the peace of solitude..."

Some days later I am answering the invitation to come and discuss the experiences which will be related in this book. I am reluctant to break away from this place so covered by invisible footsteps, so alive with the voices of memory, with the music of nature unchanged by the strange and silent passage of time.

But home *is* the silence, and I knew I could return.

THE VIEW from the air was familiar, as I had made the trip on many occasions, but in reverse, flying northeastward from my home in the desert of Arizona, over the spectacular mountains of New Mexico to descend onto the broad, flat plains of West Texas across which I would drive by rental car two hours back toward the setting sun which often translated itself through the dust-laden atmosphere into a surreal and ornate splendor which could wrest a soul from its moorings. No doubt that ancient spectacle, cast upon the firmament in its intricate variations since creation day, and witnessed by the living creature since antiquity, has played no small role in painting the landscape of color and beauty within the developing consciousness, inciting the senses to emotion.

Wouldn't it be a providential irony, the teacher whom you will come to know once spoke poetically of these occasions, if human emotion had been first wakened, not into fear, but by the kiss of beauty to possess thought and from this to know love, and if this was the purpose of creation from the beginning! How else can one explain, he asked his class to consider, why beauty inspires a sense of the infinite, and love, of the eternal, except that this is their source, and through the experience of them the human senses its purpose and destiny?..

A jarring of the aircraft broke my train of thought, as the engines were throttled back to begin the descent to Tucson, bringing a momentary heave of lightness as the plane nosed downward. Only an hour and a half of flight separated the world I had left behind the gate of posts and wire and the world below, within whose setting there occurred the extreme events and happenings of the last years, for whose reason the letter had arrived. Worlds of the past, the present, and the future in the strange coexistence of experience converged into one, and how do you express in mere sentences the reality of it!....

Just minutes before taking his last breath, before he entered that tunnel of light through which I was to travel and return, my father carefully lifted his frail arms and removed the tube which fed him oxygen, freeing himself from the science which held him to this earth. Seated at his bedside I watched at eye level as the arms, summoned by the last of his noble strength, guided themselves back downward to slowly place the aged and beautiful hands together upon his breast, in the last personal gesture of respect.

We never really return from any journey, do we, or from any experience, because we bring the journey back with us. We absorb it, and it becomes us. And so the journey shapes itself as our own creation, as does the miracle of life itself.

*   *   *

CHAPTER TWO

A TRIBUTE TO MAN.
THE SAFEKEEPERS

IN THE imagination are born memories of the future.
-purple Spiral notebook "11", p8.

AN ELDERLY gentleman, almost slight in build, with a distinguished air, answered the introduction and made his way to the lectern, holding a paper in his left hand.

He looks at the audience as he walks across the stage, and smiles a broad, infectious smile. His face is creased in the manner of someone who has long smiled easily, his eyes are dark and intense and set beneath bushy eyebrows above which rises a large brow made even more prominent by a rim of wavy white hair which flows backward and over his collar.

I know him already.

He is the man at whose invitation I am making this visit: one Ottolin W. Narstedder, Professor Emeritus of History at the university where he is speaking, and long a friend and colleague of the subject of this tribute hosted by the Alumni Association. The auditorium is filled to overflowing and people are standing in the outer aisles along the walls. I arrived just in time to occupy one of the last seats available and am seated on one side near enough to the stage to clearly see the speaker.

The appreciative round of applause subsides and the speaker thanks his audience and begins to speak in a clear, baritone voice recognizable to a dozen cycles of students over the last half-century. Typically, he dresses his speech in what he calls historical raiment, without which, he reminded his listeners, all mankind and all thought is naked and unashamed because it has not that with which to compare its impoverished state. A mirthful smile spreads over his face as he glances at his notes, and begins:

THIS IS *a story about Man.* [Spontaneous applause breaks over the auditorium, as much from anticipation as from the mention of the honoree's given name.]

This is a tribute to a man named, Man, made heir at his birth in the first half of the 20th Century to a most unusual name, although every human who has ever lived lays claim also to the same, in the title of family, of whatever time and place, beginning a thousand millennia before writing was devised to pass down to unborn generations the author's version of history as he or she saw it and wanted it to be known.

Although there is little physical difference between one member of the human family and another- unlike other species, like dogs, or even cats [the speaker smiles broadly at the light laughter, and continues to embellish his point]*: some big, some little; floppy-eared, pointy-eared, elongated with short legs, long-legged and fast; pug-nosed, long-nosed, shaggy-haired, hairless, of all shades and descriptions- humans are pretty much the same everywhere, except for those differences imagined and conjured up and magnified by misbegotten insecurities of which the world is full, divided into nations and religions and mythical races and territories which make masters of some and servants of the vast majority.*

This is a story about Man, of whom you know, and man's inhumanity to man, and about the love that can redeem one and all, and erase in a final deliverance the illusions of separation.

It is a story about the Dream, which was first born close to the time when the species, still in swaddling clothes, peered out of the manger of its birth by the virgin mother and saw that innocence was lost, having been replaced by knowledge, some said; by sin, others said; or by both knowledge and sin, their being one and the same, avowed still others [again, light applause and laughter ensue as the speaker pauses and smiles his bright smile].

And the baby wailed once long and loud before it crawled out of the crib and began the great adventure for which both heaven and hell could wait, as indeed they would, until the child determined what each should be, and chose her paths accordingly.

For the great differences which have divided and bedeviled the human family have been of the heart and mind, differences of understanding and of knowledge, differences of freedom.

Knowledge is freedom, and for this reason the greatest challenge for those so blessed is to be both learners and teachers, and guardians of the freedom of knowledge to light the paths to mankind's betterment.

Knowledge is reality unfolded before man's understanding, granted at the wish of a question diligently pursued for as long as it takes to receive an answer, for every knowledge finally learned has been ages in the revealing, bought by untold sacrifice throughout the conscious experience, and paid for in some part by every curious soul who dared to question and wonder why, to challenge the rigid powers of convention.

Among these wonderers and questioners are history's sublime and splendid heroes, most unknown and unheralded, who are the true saints in the gallery of human advance.

Every free thought was, at one time, forbidden, because in every age the powers knew that freedom of thought was liberating, and challenged their control. These powers devised their own doctrines of truth, which forbade dissent and froze into crime all matters of question which might arise, even from simple curiosity, so that man fell into ages of darkness from which the birth of freedom was immensely slow and painful as the real truth could only be spoken in whispers or not at all, and even a glance misread could unleash the cruel and ignorant forces of repression.

Every true and noble thought- does this not astound us?- was bought at the price of blood!

Every freedom, even of the ethereal thought, was an escape from chains; every true expression in art and science a strike against convention.

And yet for all, the spirit of knowledge survived, but only because it could not be chained, or crushed underfoot, or beaten into submission, or tortured to death. The spirit of knowledge is human, and, like the human, belongs to a greater destiny, and a greater time.

Within knowledge itself is guarded a hope and an assurance that man has a future, for it always asks the question, For what?... For its own sake..? No, my friends, knowledge can never be for its own sake, for to be so would imply that it is meaningless.

Knowledge is the bridge to unity; it is the connection to greaterness which brings us to the central meaning inherent in creation, to the destiny toward which the child, free of the cradle, ineluctably makes her way.

NOT MANY of us are given to personally brush shoulders with heroes, or to have known great minds and seen them in their mysterious work. Most are invisible to their time, because history takes time to catch up to them, and by then they are gone.

And fewer of us have had the fortune to be present at the moment when a great pivotal discovery is made which has the potential to profoundly shape the way mankind views itself and the cosmos of its belonging, to define explicitly and universally the nature of the conscious presence in time, and the human's place- each person's place- in the panorama of existence. We who are here in tribute to a friend and colleague have watched with an astonished world the making of modern history, and wonder at our fortune in being witnesses to these events.

There are some humans, walking among us in any generation, who possess extraordinary gifts, and an unexplainable presence which sets them apart, and imbues forever the lives of those whose privilege it was to know them.

They are not many, so that in a lifetime one may count their number on the fingers of a hand, but their unassuming power and influence is such that it far disproportions their rarity.

Their image is unforgettable, and lingers within those affected by them throughout the course of their lives and into new generations, undiminished by the passing of time and experience.

Something about them, beyond their great intelligence, carries an almost childlike wonder and naturalness, a neotenous spontaneity which lights their lives, and the lives of those touched by them. They are above all fully awakened to life, and they have the ability to awaken others into a perpetual awareness.

Theirs is a consciousness which seems not wholly of this world, but of something immensely greater, transcending the ordinary realities of their sisters and brothers in the human race.

They are personalities of great power, and yet they are humble, and true to friendship.

They are extraordinarily illumined, and yet they do not shine a light upon themselves, but rather before others who stumble in the lesser light.

Their home is the province of the mind, and their place is wherever thought takes them in the cosmos of being. They are denizens of time and space, and creators of realities conceived in observations of their quickened minds.

There live within them the spirits of imagination and memory, which speak to them and through them in the images and voices of time, beyond the mortality of the day.

They are heroes in the truest sense, who quietly inspire in ordinary souls a sense of grandeur.

Lloyd Man Foglesby, beyond any doubt, was one such human.

EVERYONE stood for an ovation which seemed to last minutes and was sprinkled with shouts and whistles and waves of applause. Many had not personally known the man in whose honor they came, though many had, but all felt that the words were spoken for them also on this occasion, in celebration, not just of a man, but of a new vision of life.

The shadows had grown long beneath the glow of evening sky as I stepped out into the fresh summer air. I had just pulled a note out of my pocket upon which was written an address and a phone number when I felt a touch on my shoulder and turned to see a statuesque young woman who spoke my name as a question and introduced herself as "an assistant to an acquaintance of yours." She said her name was Anabel Rhee and that she had seen me enter the auditorium, and asked if I had had a pleasant flight out. Then she explained charmingly that she was sent to be my escort if that was okay, and that we would be going over to an informal reception where I would be able to meet some people who were very interested in meeting me. I assumed that she was fully aware of the context of my visit, so made no further comment.

After a ride of perhaps twenty minutes in her little car we arrived at a rather impressive residence surrounded by a tall wrought iron fence. My chauffer tooted her horn as she pulled into the circular driveway and parked behind some other cars. As we walked up the brick driveway in the deepening twilight an array of yard lamps suddenly flicked on and bathed the house and its grounds in a welcoming glow. Through the large windows some figures could be seen inside, engaging in quiet conversation as their silhouettes weaved lightly among the pleated curtains.

The door opened and the man I had known simply as Otto stood smiling as he reached his hands out to shake mine. Then he reached around in an embrace and slapped my back heartily, as I had seen him do when greeting another friend in the time of a world past.

It was a most illustrious group assembled there on that evening, and I could not help sensing my presence among them as anomalous, which of course it was, although the events of the past years had served to radically shift the priorities in my own life so as to steer it, through no professional merit on my part, into a confluence with people who would have considerable power and influence to direct the implications of my experience to some greater understanding and good. For this reason alone I was there, to simply relate as best I could the unexplainable happenings which had intervened in the affairs of my life.

I continued to feel, and remain convinced to this day, that the journey through a portal in time is not so unusual, so that many have made the journey and returned- often in a time of great crisis and intensity in their lives- to carry throughout the rest of their days, if not the direct and vivid memories I was offered, then an unconscious residue of calm and assurance that none can explain, but which is in fact a direct gift in love from the children of a future world who know us intimately, because we came before them.

When I was asked by this committee of distinguished individuals what I considered to be the salient lesson of my experience, I would tell them that it is that the future is a calling.

*   *   *

THE DESERT is replete with the soft singular call of the mourning dove in that interlude just as the light breaks.

Only one with its lonesome cooing seems to serenade you with the same nostalgic call every morning when you rise early to write a story such as this, although in reality there may be more than one individual singing which only appears to the untuned ear as one.

There is a magic time which lingers in the changing of the watch from darkness to light, when night has left the womb and the day is not yet born, when a surrealness seeps out of the still air and through the pores of your skin, and it is then that you notice that we do not merely see light but are filled by it as well, as even those physically blind to it are not really blind, but construct within the mind's senses the intimate worlds of sight.

The reception at Otto's house was remarkable, and I was relieved at the degree of understanding and kindness I found among the people who call themselves the Safekeepers.

I had questions of them as well, but waited first to see what they would ask of me, and was surprised at the personal nature of their questioning, aside from their scientific and academic interests, although it would be central to inquire of the personal in such matters of the afterlife.

The man with the famous birthmark upon his forehead and the intense and riveting eyes which never lost a certain twinkle was most curious, quietly exploring for answers with a deep personal interest. I knew that he had lost his mate some months earlier, and answered his inquiries as forthrightly as I could, without elaboration.

Their questions during the pleasant hours of our meeting dealt not so much with a passage of events as with the picture of that future reality and what relationship its inhabitants bore with the present time. Questions which I considered more academic or scientific probed the significance ascribed by the future ones to matters relating to the Discovery itself and the history it would set in motion.

These were valid questions as the time that I visited was indisputably a child of the Discovery, and so it was essential to understand who the descendents were and what their personal and intellectual connection was to us.

Did the future play a hand in scientific and spiritual revelations as a way toward its own fulfillment and if so, how?

Who was the entity known as the Third Angel, the being of enlightenment and knowledge, and how did he relate to the convergence of knowledge completed in the professor's discovery?

Was the future reality a creation of the present, a creator of the present, or both, and what elements were involved?

What did the children say, what may they have implied, what was their look, their manner? How did they seem to relate to the patriarchs and matriarchs among them who bridged the present of our time and theirs without the knowledge of death?

Who were the 'beings in Time', who came from the future's own future, from 'nearer to the Omega'?

My charge would be to relate these things as best I could, and I took the task gladly as it was a matter of urgency for me to divest myself of all secrets. The experience was not mine alone, but belonged, I felt, to others as a phenomenon which was greater than the personal level of one's own experience. Unexplainably, it was my lot to have been given memory of these events, so that the story could be revealed opportunely at a time of great developments upon a diverging and weakening planet.

I wanted to be able to speak well so as to speak for others, while challenged by an immense theme and modest talents to portray it, and so I began on the dawn of the first day by receding into a deep contemplation connected to the present only by the thin pure and mystical string of a dove's cooing which seemed to be of one creature but may in fact have been more.

Here is the story they asked me to tell. It is only one voice, although there are most probably many, many others.

*   *   *

CHAPTER *THREE*

LETTY.
THE BRIGHTNESS

All experience is ordinary, until it is transformed
By love...
-small red notebook "6", p47.

YOU MAY WONDER how I came to know him, how the two of us would ever meet, and this is a fair question, since I was a marketer of fruits and vegetables from a warehouse situated on the border, a few miles from the land inhabited by burgeoning descendents of the natives and *conquistadores,* and he was an astrophysicist, philosopher, and teacher, known and esteemed in circles first punctuated in the lives of the many individuals he touched, and rippling outward from those affected lives in ever widening circles, as when many sparkling pebbles are scattered in a handful upon a placid lake. A man whose domain of thought stretched throughout the cosmos.

It was by chance fortune, or by providence, however one sees it, as our paths would not have crossed ordinarily. The simple truth is that I knew his wife for some years before I met the professor, or realized who he was, and we formed one of those friendships that can transpire between a man and a woman and not trespass upon the carnal, which more than the other is the nature of the man. If you are a man, and have known such a special friendship, you know that it is an irreparable treasure which gives you far

15

more merit than you deserve and so humbles you into a worthiness which dignifies your soul and makes you a far better human.

Leticia was her name, though she was known by, Letty, and she worked those years as director of a university program for the border community, designing and organizing classes and programs for senior citizen students which were based at the hotel in whose restaurant I sometimes had lunch or morning coffee. There I would see her from time to time as she busily attended her duties, and upon occasion we would have time to sit and visit enjoyably, often about our parents, and about the strange passage of years which changes all things. "Worlds without regret," is how Letty characterized the past, "the uncompleted history."

I did not know what she meant by this until much later, but I recall exactly her words and the expression in her voice and eyes. She had large, dark eyes, full of expression and mystery, as is the nature of beautiful women, in whom so much is contained- always more, one felt, than was expressed, in a reserve and depth which was invisible to words.

She sometimes closed her eyes when she was thinking hard, and it was then that I could study her features, in those brief interludes when her long eyelashes rested still beneath the shapely contours of her eyes as she retreated into the volume of her thought to define or clarify something she wanted to say. Some seconds would pass in her repose during which I would note the detail of her face: the strength and fineness of its conformity, the intelligence shaped into her forehead and cheekbones, the curves of her cheeks, drawn slightly in to accent the cheekbones and jaws in teardrop-shaped cups which angled down from below her temples towards the corners of her mouth, which protruded somewhat in a sensuous way with full, expressive lips slightly off-centered, favoring one side when she smiled, and inducing a dimple to fold itself into her cheek.

Her hair was black, with a luster of cleanness and health, worn shoulder length when I first knew her, or pulled up on her head, then later shortened somewhat, befitting her age, its waves pulled back sometimes on one side or the other to frame more of her face, and show her ears. These she sometimes adorned with small, pretty earrings which might have been gifts from someone special in her life.

She had an exquisite neck, noticeable not because it was longer than is normal, but for its graceful proportions, as if it had been perfectly fashioned to suit her shoulders and head.

Delicate lines sometimes showed themselves across this neck, depending upon the light. Natural folds in the soft skin carried over from babyhood, which curved partially across the front, depending upon the position of the head, would melt away as she lifted her head back, as she sometimes did when laughing.

Her smile was easy and radiant, and her eyes sparkled with her smile, as if it came from a true happiness within. A gentle music sang in her laughter, and continued echoing in your brain from the thoughts of her, setting aglow something within the soul which took delight in her joy. Letty was simply strikingly attractive, whether you first glimpsed her gliding walk a block away, or turned to see who it was that brushed against you as she passed, her appeal the more enhanced because she seemed unaware of it. Her beauty was graced by her inner vitality, her intelligence, and goodness of heart.

She was to remain the same throughout the years I knew her.

"Does your husband admire you?" I once asked before I knew the man to whom she was married. She knew I was speaking of her physical beauty.

"He calls me Fancy..., but he's the only one," she answered, smiling coyly.

I was to hear him use that name once, among the last words he would speak to her in this life.

HER EYES opened suddenly, as she looked at me thoughtfully for a moment, as if measuring her words.

"Can you fix it?" she asked simply, condensing the range of her thought into a direct, concise question which was far from simple.

As I studied her four words, which implied the clearest solution available to me even as they stripped away the circumlocutions I had carefully built like rock walls laid from refuse of things past, across the horizon of my emotional life in zig-zag patterns peremptorily made piece by piece in the raw labor and sweat of emotions over twenty years, I felt the calm of a loving truth, so sincerely offered by this thing of beauty which sat before me. My thoughts swirled around me, reaching in to touch with healing fingers and awaken the powers lain dormant by a pain so common to generations in the family of man.

As I look back now, across the lightyears as they seem, which connect that moment and this, through a journey across and beyond death's moment, and into a future which shall be ours to fulfill, I realize that it began for me, in that wondrous and magical way that great journeys have of beginning, with a turning.

They were my eyes that she opened, even as I watched her open her own, after pondering in her clear thought a view beyond the obstructions I had vaingloriously composed throughout the loss of years.

With the eloquent architecture of her four words, uttered with intimate concern and the sweetest gestures of her mouth, she pointed my life into a new direction, a mere look away from that past which held my objections, and into a future which knew no bounds of understanding and love.

She took a leave of absence not long after the meeting I have just described. Someone said she was away traveling, perhaps on a world tour with her husband, and I noted her absence with a particular regret, as those minutes of our last visit lay fully awake in my thoughts, as if what they contained were something apart from, and beyond my consciousness of self. They agitated me, even as they soothed me with an assurance that everything was going to be well. I did not so much need, as wanted to hear her counsel further, even though I had already decided to loosen the straps which bound me so unreasonably to lost opportunity. And having done so was half of my freedom gained; the other half to be enfolded in a response so eagerly wanted and given, so long in the waiting.

*   *   *

LETTY WAS born in Magdalena de Kino, a small town seventy kilometers south of the border. It is a pleasant village of some twelve-thousand souls, some of whose families can walk the same dusty streets, and relax in the central plaza where did their ancestors through centuries.

The old church stands at a corner of the plaza, its thick adobe and plaster walls enshrouding the cool interior in an earthy quietness, save for the trickle of muffled sounds peculiar to these historic churches: the creak of a wood plank over in the corner, worn shiny and cupped out by countless knees of the faithful through generations; the rustle of an old woman's clothes as she shuffles by to find her place upon a pew near the front, in the same spot where her mother and grandmother, and the mother before her had sat to count their rosaries and say prayers for loved ones, souls living and dead, and in times of difficulty, to ask the Virgin's grace upon themselves.

A low cough somewhere. The almost inaudible shudder of a heavy door opening back of the vestibule, letting enter a momentary shaft of sunlight. A trickling of water at the basin in the entry way.

In such old churches, scattered throughout Mexico, one can sense the spirits of history. In a sense, guarded by an almost changeless tradition passed over generation to generation in faith, time stands still, some part of the human retained in original form by the centuries, passed forward like the wine and the bread at the boundaries of life, in an endless benediction.

But more so, perhaps, one feels it at this church. It is not the oldest to stand at this place: the oldest was obliterated and paved over by cobblestones so long ago it is not remembered, after its structure failed from the effects of time and the Indian wars. And even the graves of the old padres, buried under the altar, were lost.

Somewhere there in the plaza they lay, under the shade of the great sycamore trees which arched above the stones over which young women promenaded with their mothers on Saturday evenings through the generations, around and around the plaza in one direction even as the young men promenaded around in the other direction, so as to be able to view and exchange smiles and greetings with the girls, and cultivate the approval of the mothers.

Among these lovely young women, some with beauty that could melt a statue, with their coy smiles and furtive glances, would most probably be found one whose smile and sparkling eyes would wrench the heart of the young man, who would vie with others to win her approval, then her lasting love.

Thus would begin another cycle in the mystery of mysteries of life upon this planet. The old church would be witness once again to the celebrations of weddings and christenings and, at the end of the cycle finally, to the somber ceremony of farewell which would lead across and up the hillslope to the cemetery, for the eternal reunion with the family of the dead.

On this hillside overlooking the town, scattered in moments frozen in time, whose voices forever whisper in stone words etched into memories of the living, lie the communities of generations past.

Therein at some hallowed spot, bounded by an old wrought iron fence, under wild roses and lilac, were laid to rest among ancestors in turn, Letty's father, Don Benito, and by his side, a score of seasons later, his own beloved. And next to them, a little grave of one older in death, of whom they silently spoke, throughout the years that Letty remembered.

PEOPLE OF Magdalena de Kino would say that providence has a hand in all things, including chance. They would tell you that there is an All-knowing, and that nothing happens that is not ordained somehow to happen. And that all mysteries are revealed in time.

So that, not many years ago after some fifteen generations of the living had appeared and passed on- a mere instant in death's sleep- some workers were digging in the plaza to install a water line and came across, buried a meter within the sod, a band of stones angling across the ditch, and some dozen meters farther along, another line of stones.

An excavation was conducted which easily exposed the boundaries of the old church walls, and then, in a careful excavation of the area beneath the old altar where the mission priests had performed the weddings and christenings and ceremonies of farewell throughout those early years of European settlement, there were brought to view of living eyes the bones of the old padres themselves, who had been laid to rest beside one another in turn.

The smaller skeleton was of the best known and revered, who left his native Italy in the service of the faith to live out adventures matched by few of his time. He left a string of monumental churches in the intrepid wake of his dedication, laid out in an arc like pearls on a string, their lime-white walls gleaming in the desert sun. Their great bells, hauled out of the Old World on the westward winds, and then inland on ox-carts, pealed out their soundings within earshot on still days, one from another, of the missions built at intervals of a day's ride, in places with sonorous names: Caborca, Tubutama, Pitiquito, Tumacacori, San Javier.

You can stand there now, within the plaza of old Magdalena de Kino, beneath the arched dome which covers them, and peer through the glass into the silence of the tomb where something of them, some presence, lays sleeping still in recognition of memory. Many changes have intervened since their passing, and many things have remained the same. Of all, the most changeless, linking in an unbroken arc the era when these skeletons were dressed in the glory of life and the present day, is the spirit of faith which lies in the open tomb of mortality, proclaiming, beyond mere hope, the day of resurrection.

*   *   *

LETTY'S adored father, don Benito Delani, died tragically the day before his daughter's tenth birthday. Although he was a horseman without peer who loved his animals and could do anything with them that a man and a horse can do together, on that eventful morning some things conspired to upset this synchronous relationship. A state of nerves, perhaps, in the animal, or a fever, and against this disability the horse perceived a threatening movement, a smell, perhaps the sudden alarm of a rattler beneath its feet. In a reaction as much to protect its rider as itself, it instinctively reared, then bolted right, throwing the veteran rider into the unyielding bough of an oak tree.

There were some hours after consciousness returned, and before the inevitable swelling which brings on the blackness, when the man she knew as Papa was lucid enough to hear the fervent prayers, and squeeze the hands of those two souls dearest to his heart, and to express in the words which had always been most difficult for him his great love and appreciation. He had always told them of his love, daily, in his looks, in his gentle and sweet manner, and his fond caresses, *los abrazitos,* in which he would urgently hold those loved ones to his breast for a time longer, like a wordless punctuation of his special love.

The years which followed were of great sacrifice for Letty's mother, although she never once complained. She had thought it best to sell the small ranch where her husband had worked his livestock, and moved north over the border where a day's labor fetched a living wage. The ranch was too small to produce a living under her management, having been divided over the generations to sons, and then to their sons, as is the tradition. The great ranch which once extended north for many miles, and over east to the range of mountains, was now reduced through expropriations of the government down south, and the divisions among heirs in succeeding generations, to many parcels, few of which were sufficient in area to yield through the pasturing of livestock a generous life.

Anyway, they spoke of it in those last hours, and Don Benito thought it would be best. Letty could be schooled in the north, and attend college there, as had always been his desire for her, to open opportunities that were not to be found in her native country.

He had always been aware of her intelligence, and enjoyed seeing her countenance brighten as she turned through the books he kept in his meager library, which revealed to her worlds beyond the little ranch set within the familiar hills which had cradled her family for generations.

For her part, Letty, for years after her father's death, wondered at this extraordinary man of the earth, unschooled in formal ways, who kept his books upon a carefully-hewn bookcase set into a corner of the living room, and poured over them assiduously well into the night, by the dim light of a kerosene lamp. Books on philosophers, and artists, and statesmen, and scientists, and their lives, and what they thought and dreamed. And now she knew that "Papa", this proud man with his cracked and calloused hands, was also a thinker and a dreamer, and that he found, within the worn volumes of his humble library, an escape into history, and into the limitless possibilities of the future.

*   *   *

Leticia liked to think that she had her mother's eyes, and she did have the inheritance of her mother's mellifluous voice, her intelligence, and of her sweet, feminine touch.

They were, she considered in later years- she and this noble woman who gave her birth- soulmates connected by a common spirit, perhaps sisters in a previous existence. At least it was fun to think of it, and certainly they were equal in their regard for one another as individual persons in this adventure of life. They talked for hours at a time, and her mother listened to her, and she listened to her mother in those admirable ways that are more difficult and rare between sons and fathers, though the bonds of love be just as strong. As the years turned, and the silver-haired Dona Elena grew frail, there were opportunities for Letty to ask questions, about her friend's view from that quixotic and sacred place near the end of life, and what it was like.

Whatever wisdom and secrets there were to be understood, the daughter felt, would grant her powers of accompaniment, to share in the mysterious transition which would separate their bodies, but not the spirit which bonded them.

Dona Elena took employment where she could find it, for some months after arriving in the United States- albeit only a few miles north of the border with her native Mexico. She cleaned and cooked, and ironed, and cared for the children of busy people, and stitched the worn socks of men of the house.

For a pleasant interval she lived with Leticia in a little cottage within the headquarters compound of a large ranch north of Sonoita which had once been part of a Spanish Land Grant and was won in a fabled card game by an Englishman around the turn of the last century. It changed hands once again in the 1930's, and these owners were the people for whom Letty's mother worked.

Besides the housework there was a garden to tend, and canning to put away in the cellar beneath the kitchen. Her employers were kind, and there was the unforgettable smell of that first spring when the apricot, and peach, and apple blossoms filled the air with perfume which drifted through the open windows on still mornings moist with dew.

There was, as well, the familiar noise and bustle of cattle roundups, when the vaqueros would leave their bases in the line shacks miles away to drive the herds down the mountains to corrals of the headquarters for branding and culling. From there, those animals ready for market would be herded overland to Tucson, for boarding on the outbound cattle trains.

The first two seasons after the passing of Don Benito were spent here in this tranquil setting, held in a kind of embrace within the ordered world inside the stone and adobe walls which once served as protection against people who had called this land their home for many thousand years, and could not understand the vast conspiracy of events which signaled the end of their ancient universe.

To have the immense panoply of their existence in a unity with nature and her eternal spirits upended by invaders who seemed devoid of spirit, and so had to stake out and fence their claims upon a piece of the great Earth, must have been maddening and incomprehensible for these indigenous souls. But for now the conquerors had left their legacy of fences and walls, and among the latter, adorned in ivy and morning-glory, was this curious and antiquated relic of another time, over which Letty and her mother could view the ever-changing hues and shadows of the sierra, over and beyond the great valley below.

Something about the distance, and the long, long view consoled Dona Elena and her daughter as well, for it is always the greaterness which consoles and inspires us in this mortal life.

WITHIN THE second year, at the end of the summer, and before the cottonwoods in the valley turned golden, Dona Elena decided to take her daughter nearer to a town which had a fine school. It was essential for Letty to be grounded in English, to assure her place in the culture which would adopt her.

Letty enrolled that fall at Lourdes Academy, just three miles or so by winding road from her mother's new place of employment, which was on a picturesque ranch set within the basin of Kino Springs, near the intermittent Santa Cruz River, and whose headquarters sat cupped within this lovely setting above a lake ringed by cottonwood trees and cattails, upon whose waters floated lily pads and visiting ducks.

It was almost as if it all were nestled within the palm of a great hand, edged by the ridges and mountains of the Coronados which changed their shapes and colors dramatically during the daylight hours, depending upon the angle of the sun and the resulting shadows which fell into and over the ridges and canyons of the upper slopes. And at night the hills and mountains reflected dreamily the magical light of the full moons.

All kinds of birds nested in the cottonwoods, palo verde, pine, locust, and mesquite trees that grew about the lake, including a remarkable variety of hummingbirds of various species who, on certain warm and delightful days could almost have sucked nectar from the air around this sweet and tranquil place.

For many reasons including those I've just described, as well as many others hidden within the topography of a human's life and experience, a man from another world, an actor from Hollywood named Stewart Granger, came and bought the ranch from its owners- bought it, they said, for his bride, Jean Simmons. And there they lived for a number of years in the 1950's, except when they were away, making films.

They built a beautiful home there near the lake, with walls of earth, and knotty pine trim inside, with an ample kitchen, extra guest rooms, and a large swimming pool in the back, by a great patio shaded with vines. There were also guest cabins, and horse stables.

A large dining room with a long table provided for the many guests who visited periodically, to enjoy the company of good friends and the peaceful and panoramic setting which extended across the horizon from dawn to dusk, and into the regions of the stars at night.

Those were the halcyon days, the precious days of an era which would surely pass, as all do, never to return, because all things are subject to change within the arrow of time.

It was during these colorful and emotional years that Letty's mother, Dona Elena, worked in the household of these people from Hollywood, just down the curved and winding road from where her daughter attended school at Lourdes and was taught by Sisters of the Order there her lovely command of English, as well as the disciplines of the Three R's and the teachings of the Holy Church. It was, all in all, a good time for the mother and daughter.

Letty recalled with humor the time when Elizabeth Taylor spent some days, "between husbands", with her friends, Jean and Stewart, staying up late, sleeping late, riding, and swimming in the pool, surrounded by red bougainvillea. For Letty, just barely a teenager at the time, the fame of the splendid actress was just a mere fact. So when Liz took leave of a bra and a nice Panama hat, found in her room after her return to the West Coast, Letty was happy, with the permission of her mother's bosses, to acquire the two items: the one, amply sufficient for Letty's comfort; the other, lending a charm and practicality in the hot sun to her pretty head.

The black bra she wore until it was frayed and frazzled, after which it was simply discarded. The Panama hat was loaned to a girlfriend who wore it to a Sunday bullfight, and then compulsively threw it into the bullring after the spectacle, from where it was caught in the stampede of fans, and was not recovered.

Robert Wagner, Paul Newman and Joanne Woodward, the young Marilyn, William Holden, Janet Leigh, and many others visited this refuge among the quiet hills, bordering on another country and culture, and yet far south of the northern reaches of the original Mexican Republic, whose great areas were ceded to its northern neighbor in the settlement of a conflict wherein, as in all conflicts, power prevailed.

These extraordinary and gifted personalities, who worked and lived in the tradition of the ancient Greeks and of Shakespeare, and of every human who has told a tale of myth and legend in books, on stage, or around the ancient campfires which sent their sparkles upon the night sky since the dawning of human time, pass their traditions over to the generation of children who succeed them, so the stories can be told anew from the perspectives of a living present steeped in the passage of history and lifted by great dreams of the future.

Throughout the years to come Letty was to recall with a particular fondness that passage in her and her mother's lives, wherein they brushed so casually with the rich and famous, and witnessed, most interestingly in retrospect, their humanness.

Granger built for his wife, at a high point of the ridge of hills near their home, a little gazebo of sorts, though more like a shaded deck, to which, it is said, she would often ride alone to look across the expanse of the valley and over into the descending hues of four ranges of mountains which revealed themselves in stair steps of blue: the light powder of the farthermost range, darkening in increments into the deep, almost black shade of the nearest. And when the setting sun cast its descending rays upon this favored landscape, then the sky and hills conspired to absorb and emit in eerie scintillations of beauty a mesmerizing panorama of ever-changing hues and colors, subtle and brilliant, of burning yellows and flaming reds, and golds and blues, crimson and magenta and rose, distinct, and combined into that infinite spectrum which throughout immeasurable time has beguiled the awakening brain into a sense of wonder, and civilized into love the human form.

$$* \quad * \quad *$$

LETTY HAD been away now for several months, and since her name was still on the door of the school offices, I could assume that she was on leave, or perhaps had taken a sabbatical after some ten years in her position as director.

I inquired of no one, and simply noted that she was away, until a succession of coincidences resolved themselves- or so I thought- into an event so strange and portentous that it jolted me, not so much from my reality, but into another reality which bore no comparison to the normal, but was indisputably more real, and from which one could in no way return unimpressed and unchanged, having seen as it were into a promised land which lay beyond, and yet, I was certain, within the dreams which possess the heart and soul of the human race.

I fancied in retrospect and with sufficient reasons that somehow that last counsel Letty offered in the form of four words posed as a question, and the subsequent turning of my life toward a willful recognition of the miracles of love and acceptance, and the immeasurable rewards of moments grasped and held in the anticipation of memory of those things kept so dear, which in every greeting whispers a same goodbye, bore directly upon the visitor in time, of whom I shall tell, and of the revelations in his embrace.

For some months before the dazzling and profound events of that summer evening- signaling no less than the birth of a new humanity- which played themselves out just down the road from the fine house overlooking the lake which is visited by many birds whose clear and ancient melodies are danced to by golden butterflies, and still within the deep, sweet passage from childhood which finally came on a quiet morning in midweek on that eternal day made ready by love, some ethereal veil which surrounds us just beyond the touch of the senses began lifting in that unexplainable way which answers the silent and intense voices of deep emotion with a resonance of the infinite.

In that room filled with the silence of music and light, with space drawn into a ceaseless moment from the infinity of time, with the taste of salt of the last tear, with the moist cooling of the beloved form, and the ceremonious closing of the eyelids with a cupped and honored hand, there arose a message clear and audible, from out of the sublime peace that wrapped itself about all judgment and thought, out of the stillness which remained throughout, out of the joyous yearning, and the strange repose. It was a voice more clear than any other, which spoke wordlessly a message I understood in a language which had been too personal for me to speak:

"Don't be afraid of the brightness."

I sat forward, and turned my head toward the closed door. A deep sense, like a great and timeless blessing, came over me. An infinitude, an understanding of all that had been in my life, and in the lives of the others, as if our love made us into one, to reach fully that near and distant moment and its priceless grace.

As I turned my head, as if to capture the sound of an external voice, this voice, with a resonance clear and lovely, repeated itself from within, from that space around, and yet from no place I could ascertain, but from forever, and from all places that ever were, and from all times that have been, and will ever be. I knew it to be a message to the human, a kind of song of the infinite, resounding, though I knew not how, in a promise:

"Don't..be..afraid..of..the..brightness."

NOW THAT I can look backward- across the sunlit meadows where children play and sing, across the fields of joy unspoiled; across the deep forests; upon the rivers of life on whose banks grew orchards whose sweet fruits are picked on sunny mornings amid ripplings of laughter; upon a circle of friends in joyous celebration of past and present unknowns; upon the reunions infinitely dreamed as the divine and immortal supper, upon the hallowed history, and the gleaming future- it all has meaning, and each and every grain a complete and full significance in a world created, as all worlds must be, in the image of its inhabitants, and of their dreams of the future.

And most surprising and poignant of all was to find that the angels who could save us were of our children, the creatures of our own creation.

*   *   *

CHAPTER *FOUR*

THE MAN ON THE BRIDGE

A thousand years will come, as will a day...

THERE IS nothing extraordinary about the bridge itself. It is a common design, a standard structure built to standard specifications for its span, load bearing characteristics, and foundation. Its plans could have been pulled out of a drawer marked with a reference number for this type of bridge, built numerous times in numerous places.

It could not boast an upper structure of wood or iron crisscrossed in trusses which retain the charm of an era gone by, no symmetrical skeleton through which trotted teams of horses drawing wagons loaded with freight, and buggies in which rode family members bound for Saturday business in town, or courters heading home from a dance. No Model "T" chugging over wood planks amid clatter and smoke at breathtaking speed, its radiator cap whistling out a tune exhaled in steam.

No, this is a modern bridge, of common design. A platform of concrete a hundred meters long edged by steel railing, set upon four rectangular bases of reinforced concrete poured into place above the bedrock which underlies a sandy riverbed which has changed little in fifty centuries.

All this long, long after the Pacific seafloor had lifted upward to expose Arizona and Sonora to the sun and sky, its great white beaches inexorably slipping southward over eons to where they now lie curved round the scenic bays and peninsulas where Father Kino landed in the New World and unloaded his livestock and goods three centuries ago, a hundred and fifty miles to the south.

But physical things, though they be unremarkable in themselves, have a way of changing their character to become places. A place is a thing remembered, having borne witness to events which memories recall, which wishes assign it.

Just how a place can become infused with human feeling, breathing emotion as a living form; by what process it absorbs a significance and acquires a kind of soul is a mystery, even though artists and poets have labored for centuries to reveal it. And so it is likely to remain for a long time to come, for the mystery is always greater than the known, lying out there in the beyond, in the tantalizing realm of possibility, enticing and beguiling the willing traveler to follow its distant light.

In the months and years preceding the world shaking events which inexplicably relate to this ordinary bridge I had crossed it many times, usually going to and from work, little noticing except on days when the sun's light, conspiring with the senses, caught it in just a certain way, accentuating the shadows below it and illuminating its base and railings as one rounded the curve leading to it, and caught the angle of its side in a glimpse. Old cottonwoods on the upriver side framed it just right on these occasions, and some quality about this unremarkable bridge, bathed in the afternoon light which created contrasts in sun and shadow, announcing its angles and straight lines, changed its appearance to make one suddenly slow and remark to oneself about its strange beauty.

Otherwise it was just a bridge, sturdy and durable, over which one could cross easily at any time day or night, whether the riverbed below was dry, as it usually is, or swollen with waters rushing out of the highlands on the Mexican side.

Now the Santa Cruz River, which you will reach if you go just past the house there by the lake, defies all expectations and flows northward in the seasons of rain, out of Mexico and under the barbed wire fence which separates two nations, around and toward this bridge some two miles away on the ranch of Kino Springs where, at a time within the end of the Twentieth Century and the beginning of a new millennium there occurred the most extraordinary events which I shall now relate as best I can, having been a fortunate witness to some of them, and a beneficiary, as I have said, through chance friendship with those who were at the center of developments so astounding that they seem miraculous, so encompassing that every life will be changed by them.

IT HAD BEEN one of those days my brother calls, "pretty woman days", on which for no particular reason you feel "in tune", when beauty resonates to you and you notice it, when you sense reality touching you, caressing and stimulating in a way like your mother did in your just-born days before life somehow and with capricious regularity allowed space and distance into the odd scheme of things which constitute personality. Some have called it *aloneness...* But, as many will tell you, a pretty woman day is a day when life and wonder dance lightly, a full dimension away from self-doubt.

On these rare and vivid days people smile and remember your name, and you happily remember theirs. There is an energy rising out of the earth and pervading everything caught within your notice. Casual occurrences appear surprising and new. Reality is alive with symmetry, and intimations of greater realities shimmer within the order of your thoughts.

You enjoy unexplainable coincidences in this charmed alignment of nature in your behalf. A letter arrives from a long-lost friend, and someone of whom you have been thinking calls to say hello, and loved ones draw near. Concerns fade into insignificance, and the scheme of things makes perfect sense, and you marvel that you had not seen it before, this joyful reality that was there all along, awaiting your notice.

It was on the evening of one of those days of unusual symmetry that I noticed the mysterious figure, just as the bridge came into view around the last curve.

He stood almost at its center, his hands resting upon the railing, and first caught my attention simply because it is rare that people will stop upon this solitary bridge, its use being reserved for vehicles, cars and trucks, and an occasional biker or jogger, passing rather quickly and directly across it.

As I approached to within a short distance I noticed his striking appearance. He had a demeanor unlike that of anyone I had seen before, intense, and yet deeply at ease. He was dressed in loose clothing, a billowy shirt open at the neck, and trousers of the same color and texture covering his feet so that I could not see what shoes he may have worn. His garments were near white, though they seemed to emit colors, perhaps those absorbed into and reflected by the material itself as he stood looking westward at the unusually brilliant spectacle of a summer sunset unfurling its fiery canvas upon the skies in almost mythical splendor, painted even more wondrously by the artist of sight within the living brain, tingeing exquisitely in emotions the hues and colors smoldering within the panorama of light. Illuminations of oranges and yellows within embroideries of silver and gold, translated out of cosmic energies and rendered into inner beauty by the soul of thought.

His age was indeterminable, neither young nor old, and yet not in the category we would define as middle age. His hair was white and flowing, his face clean shaven, his lips full, cheekbones set high, handsomely like those of a Native American, although he was of no discernable race or nationality. Creases of a smile curved upon his cheeks. His chin was rather angular and dimpled, his jaws strong.

But most striking, as he turned his face toward me, were his eyes. They were magnetic, burning with intelligence and intensity, immensely serene, and they looked directly into me as he smiled broadly as if in recognition.

Without thinking, I braked the car and came to rest within a few meters from where he stood. I sat looking over at him, not knowing why I had stopped so uncustomarily in response to this solitary stranger who still held me in his gaze, his white teeth showing slightly in his easy smile. I may have been trying to ascertain just what about him was so familiar: The distinguished aspect of a revered uncle of long ago? A kind of composite of those men favored in my life? That special one who called me his son?

Perhaps. And yet his presence was beyond that.

Something occurred to me just then. And it was that he stood there as if this were his place. As if it were a part of him, and he had always been there, only I had not noticed until now.

This would seem a logical explanation for a person who had sped almost unconsciously back and forth across the bridge in a daily routine, and had gradually accumulated rings of keys, including some to locks long lost to memory, retained, nevertheless, out of deference to that inscrutable rule which says that if you throw a thing away you may need it thereupon. For whom the years had been passing at a quickening pace, Januarys merging into Decembers with seasons compressed unaccountably into a somnolent rush punctuated by intermittent awakenings in time to witness astonishingly how trees had grown, or acquaintances aged.

Just now the stranger turned his head back toward the west in a way which invited me to look also. The sheer marvel of colors, changing by the moment in their profusion, now cast itself over the whole sky to immerse the world in its glory, burning orange and gold in the flowing waters below, and infusing the hills around with an eerie luminescence which shimmered as if in pouring back, transfigured in color, the light of the day.

Unconsciously, I opened the car door to stand outside for a better view, placing one arm across the top of the low-slung car, one foot resting upon the threshold of the door. My eyes swept over and across the brilliant scene, then back to the figure standing there at the railing, shoulders erect, fingers lightly touching the rail. The hues which I had seen reflected upon his clothes now seem to have faded, leaving him dressed in pure white which was heightened more by its contrast with the colors spilled over from the evening sky. He continued his gaze westward, absorbed in contemplation, as I studied him from the corner of my eye, wondering how his incongruous presence could seem so natural to this place and moment.

Just then, a movement down at the end of the bridge caught my eye.

Something had appeared directly in my line of sight as I looked past the white-robed stranger and down to where the single railing turned to anchor in the ground, some fifty yards away. I narrowed my eyes to make out what it was- an animal, no doubt, and cat-like. Dark, maybe black, and too large to be a domestic creature.

Suddenly, as the animal flicked its tail and began calmly to walk toward where we were standing, it dawned on me that this was indeed a cat. My heartbeat quickened, for I knew that the mountain lions, or cougars, were very rarely seen in this area, having been decimated by shootings, and by the mere presence of humans who had supplanted natural wildlife with themselves. It was a thrill just to see a big cat, even from a distance, but this animal seemed bent on approaching us, moving casually, head somewhat lowered, shoulders rotating left and right as it walked.

The surreal quality of the scene numbed my reactions as I stood transfixed in amazement, forgetting this was a creature which might not perceive that it was entering a potentially dangerous scenario by approaching members of a species which had been antithetical to its survival. Perhaps it had not even seen us, the visual images within its brain not corresponding with information known.

I began to fidget, standing upright in beginning alarm and motioning to the stranger by a hesitating movement of my arm. He exhaled slowly and shook his head slightly in an expression of wonder at the beauty of the sunset panorama, then calmly turned, cupping one hand lightly over the back of the other as he looked over at me, smiling.

My eyes may have shifted nervously in the direction of the phenomenon approaching silently, now within a few yards of where we stood. He held his glance, relaxed, then casually shifted his attention to his right, where he calmly watched as the animal took three or four more steps before stopping.

It was jet-black, its pelt rippling with a sheen impossible to describe, translating all colors now radiant upon the waning sky into a unity of the spectrum, melding one single expression in the form of a color which is not a color, but a rainbow painted in a single stroke.

Two large eyes, emerald green, looked across as the head lifted slightly and fixed upon the stranger as if the creature knew him. Not a hint of alarm was evidenced by its manner. It blinked once slowly in that casual way that cats have, and licked its upper lip with its tongue, then flicked its tail upward and back, still looking at the figure turned towards it with perfect calm.

I did not know what to make of it. The hypnotic eyes, a liquid green, gazed, not at me, but directly at the being in front of me, who had merely turned his head in the animal's direction, his shoulders still aligned as they were when he looked at me, smiling.

I was stunned by the improbability of what I was witnessing. The man on the bridge, whoever he was, seemed obviously connected with the creature who had joined us, and yet I could not imagine why, or how. It was already obvious by his manner that this was no ordinary person, and not being ordinary, he might well be accompanied by a pet of this type, however rare and exotic… I remembered seeing, many years ago in Los Angeles, a woman walking upon the sidewalk with her pet ocelot. It was a sensually exquisite sight, these two beautiful creatures who were both feline in their grace, moving like lovely apparitions in a young man's dream…

But however dreamlike the scene was, those two creatures had been definitely connected by a leash, white and sparkling, as I remember it: This animal is free of any restraint, and moreover, I had seen it appear from the roadside down at the end of the guardrail, and had watched its approach, and my sense was that it was not a pet.

I knew that the black panther, or jaguar, is native to the forests and jungles of Central America, and is now exceedingly rare, and is never known to wander two thousand miles out of its territory, north to the semi-arid region of the Sonora Desert.

A roommate and friend from my freshman year in college was from Belize- then called British Honduras- and often regaled me with tales of the jungle, and voodoo superstitions, and the burning eyes of the black panther reflected from the pitch-black darkness of the forest by a campfire's light. The creature was invisible in the dark: only the eyes appeared, and shot eerie green shafts of light which could enter and hypnotize the fearful visitor who did not understand the spirit world... I enjoyed my friend Arthur's rich imagination, one generously tended by the influences of the cultures and setting of his tropical upbringing, but I learned to appreciate his use of metaphor.

As I watched the uncanny drama before me, which seemed like a recognition between acquaintances, having nothing to do with my own presence, I could hear my heart beating excitedly in the pulsing of blood through my inner ear. My vision, however, remained steady and my thought processes crystal clear as they had been all day, from the moment of awakening to the first light of morning.

It had been months, I remarked to myself that day, since I had felt so sane and alive. In the frenetic sleepwalk called modern life, which I had inadvertently joined, my daily activities seemed to have been taken over by an automaton, whether friend or stranger to myself I could not ascertain, although I remained confident that nature had her ways of protecting the creatures within her domain.

What I was witnessing here before me, unlike the blur of past months, was starkly real.

Just at this moment the cat turned her head and shifted her gaze forward to the opposite end of the bridge from which she had come. Her interlude with the stranger simply ceased, and she stepped forward to resume her passage.

But not before the strangest, haunting glance she cast at the other person, serendipitously present, who stood in a state of wonder, leaning against the door of his red car. In that one look I imagined things completely unjustified by reason. I thought she spoke to me.

Nothing heard, not even really seen, but something silently transferred in her glance. An archive of life passed over in silence between two souls of different species, yet differing in no important way one from the other. I felt my illusions of separation crumble, and a reality expand outward like a shockwave from the center of my ego, drawing into itself in a perfect and natural unity the entire universe of knowledge assembled into the family of experience, of whatever species and degree, of matter and energy and spirit.

The creature, ghostly beautiful, glided past me, effortlessly and silently continuing the walk it began before pausing before the man in white. As it reached the guardrail at the opposite end of the bridge it hesitated for just a second, a glistening black sculpture, then lifted upward in a graceful arc, over the railing and out of sight where the embankment descends to the river's edge.

I gazed after it in astonishment, overcome with imageries which continued to pour into my senses as I tried to absorb and rationalize what had just transpired. I gasped excitedly and turned back to the stranger, exclaiming silently the words which wouldn't come out of my mouth. He had been watching me, and as our eyes met he nodded to me and laughed wonderfully, a low and carefree laugh which seemed like a celebration of things far beyond what I had ever known.

"What a day!" I continued to say to myself, shaking my head. "What a day!"

"Yes, what a day!" he repeated. "A unique day, indeed!"

I fell silent, after uttering the only words which came to me from this chamber of reality which, beyond all human expression, grew outward into an infinitude. Only that ineffable awe remained, which the soul is capable of, but which so seldom overtakes us in our busy world, except when we are shaken by great loss, or great miracles.

HE SEEMED in no hurry for further conversation, as both of us turned our gaze toward the dark ridgeline of hills outlined against the deep red of the setting sun which cast streams of its color through clouds which spread outward from its descending furnace and over the deepening canvas which would soon become night, inhabited by a million suns to other worlds turned by time and remoteness into the presence of twinkling starlight.

We stood in silence for some time. The waters flowing beneath us emitted a gentle, steady resonance, as much felt as heard within the perfect calm of the evening air. I scarcely breathed, listening to the faint liquid wind below as it brushed across its ancient bed of sand. Coyotes sang out in the distance in a chorus begun by a lone voice over towards the mountains, then taken up by others behind the hills and across the valleys to the west, sounding like the call and answer music of a gospel church, in a cryptic melody as old as the hills themselves. A mockingbird warbled a lullaby from a tree behind us.

A full moon was rising from behind the mountains to the east, alabaster white and resplendent, her featured countenance magnified by the earth's atmosphere as if drawn into proximity for her voyage across the ocean of night. She would soon cast her borrowed light upon the landscape of the world she has watched over since the beginning, laying a velvety luminescence across its sleeping face. As night fell over the valley, the stars appeared one by one at first, Mars and Jupiter in close adjacence, sister planets of the earth, who like the moon, communicate by reflected light, and then hosts of burning suns and galaxies of them, resolving themselves into countless needlepoints upon the palimpsest spread out across the canopy of sky.

Nothing more had been spoken between us as time suspended its measure against conscious thought. As happens when we become lost in the wonder of creation, I had completely forgotten my self, and the tick-tock sound to which we set our lives lay silent within a sense of the eternal.

"I've never seen anything like it..," my voice broke the spell at last. I looked over at the tall figure, whose face, outlined against the moonlight, was lifted slightly as if he were tuned to mysteries I could not fathom. He opened his eyes and smiled, in lingering reflection, waiting for me to continue.

"Although I have no explanation, I felt that she recognized you," I offered tentatively as a question, feeling that somehow the elegant creature in her sable coat represented something, some dimension or symbol which I needed, and wanted to understand, before the opportunity was lost.

"Yes," he answered, "but only because recognition is everywhere. At all levels throughout nature...Each atom, and each star, and each world recognizes every other in a universal language throughout all space and time, The heavens have no walls.." He held his arms outward, and laughed that low, melodic laugh.

Suddenly, I understood something which I had not fully grasped until now, something incredibly basic which had escaped me. I had seen beauty, and, through beauty, the mortal recognizes the infinite.

"Another day has slipped into eternity," is how my father would describe those heart-wrenching sunsets which unfurl themselves over the vast New

Mexico prairie, and the child would listen and remember the words, until the moment would come to experience their meaning.

"Why is it when you experience beauty, you think of the eternal?" I thought out loud.

"Because the source of beauty is infinite," he answered simply.

I repeated the words to myself, measuring each one. *The source of beauty is infinite...*

I made the connection. They are the same! And come from the same source!

So this is how the infinite speaks to us in the universal language...

"When we are in love, we talk about forever," are the words I was to find in the voice of another during my studies in the months to come, in a gradual self-awakening to realities which bore directly on this day, in ways I could never have imagined.

Throughout the succession of events on this incomparable evening I had found myself repeating in my thoughts an adjective which has fallen from use in recent times.

Magnificent, I had breathed at the sunset sky. "Magnificent," again, as I stood paralyzed at the stunning presence of the black creature who seemed as much a spirit as an animal. And again, the only word which seemed appropriate to describe the living silence into which poured the wonders of that summer night.

This is why we sense their magnificence (the stranger is saying), *because that piece of beauty, or of love that we feel, is passed over to us from an infinite source...*

The being before me waited as if to let me absorb these thoughts, and then offered a remarkable summation about the mortal entity who has it in her power to contemplate such grandeur.

"The greatest failing of the human," he declared thoughtfully, "is not to recognize his own magnificence."

I did not begin to understand until much later the significance of these words. They seem strange and incongruous when applied to a species still caught within the shadows of its past.

But the stranger was not speaking of a past, I was to learn, but from a vision of the future.

"I'm afraid it will be awhile," I offered, sadly. "We've got a ways to go yet."

"Oh, there's time enough," he carefully assured, smiling his bright smile. "A thousand years will come, as will a day."

*   *   *

IT WAS LESS than two minutes' drive up the rise and around the curves which lead from the bridge to the lighted porch of my house. But this evening the time was lost in a strange dilation which occurs within intense experiences wherein the events of thought become transparent and so time, which is measured in conscious events, loses its frames of reference.

By losing consciousness of time the illusion of time is lost, and so we have entered into that timeless dwelling of the soul wherein the instant loses its boundaries with forever, and true and exotic secrets long hidden within the maze of counted moments are opened to conscious view.

Suspended in this state as I closed the car door and turned to the house, I heard seemingly from a great distance the sweet voice of my daughter, whom I hadn't noticed sitting outside on the porch swing with a friend, as she called out a happy greeting and then, noting some difference in my behavior, asked if I was okay.

"You look like something has happened, Dad..."

"What a day!" I repeated. "You won't believe.."

I sat down on the swing opposite that where she sat with her friend and proceeded to relate the strange and surreal experience at the bridge.

She and her friend, who was a graduate student in psychology, listened attentively as I told what I had seen, and tried to qualify it with possible explanations as I went along. The young man began shaking his head affirmatively as I was finishing my story, a smile fixed on his face.

"That's awesome, Man!" he exclaimed. "Do you know who you've got to meet?...He's definitely got to meet Dr. Fo," he said, turning to my daughter. "Definitely!"

At that moment I did recall conversations about the popular and controversial class, but not the name associated with it.

"Has he seen the man on the bridge, too?" I asked, momentarily relieved.

"I don't know... Well, maybe," the young man answered, hesitating. "Anyway, he teaches some far-out stuff that sounds sort of connected to what you saw... I took his class two years ago, but I still have my notes. I'll bring them for you to look at, and you can decide."

The psychology student then launched into a recitation of thoughts and ideas that I found astounding, and had never heard before. It was obvious that he had been deeply affected by this one class he had taken as an undergraduate, and in fact he referred to it as seminal, affecting his view and understanding, having taught him to 'observe knowledge,' and 'to observe the observer of knowledge,' to assume the power and history of the human, who has 'the potential of ultimate answers.'

Whatever those words meant I could not fathom at the time, but I was, with the delivery of the first notebook, to be sent on an odyssey in search of the meanings, as I grew to believe there was indeed a connection between such deep matters and the happening on the bridge at Kino Springs that illustrious evening.

*   *   *

CHAPTER *FIVE*

THE NOTEBOOKS.
INCIDENT AT TOMBSTONE

The whole of creation speaks from infinity in
the still, small voice of the living soul.
-red notebook "9", torn cover, p71.

THERE FOLLOWED DAYS of distraction wherein it was difficult to conduct business as usual.

Nothing had changed, really, in the physical world: The same familiar names and faces, the same hum of the forklifts which scurried about the warehouse floor unloading and loading the mangoes which sent their rich and sensual aroma throughout the big room. The same voices over the phones; orders for two pallets here, for twenty there- this size, this quantity, what's your best price. Hurry, hurry.

It began to seem strangely unreal, this world of physical things assembled and pronounced by the senses in a tenuous construct of sight and hearing, taste and smell into shapes and actions and odd juxtapositions of people and things.

For the first time the newly born observer began to smile at the symbols which had throughout the years evoked no question or reply, and little curiosity against the conditioning of past experience.

Are you prepared for new worlds? Are you prepared for your own rebirth?- the new voice would challenge resoundingly- for the former things will surely pass away!

One morning only some days after the event which had radically altered the balance of my life my daughter Anna appeared at my place of work and happily delivered a brown spiral notebook filled with handwritten notes taken from a class whose name was boldly marked upon the cover: DESTINY 101.

My daughter laughingly passed on a message from her friend that I was free to read, study, or copy, but not to misplace the tattered notebook, as it came for him somewhere between Carl Jung and the Bhagavad Gita.

Other notebooks, on loan from different former students, were to follow, arriving in the mail, or hand delivered in a package with a return address and sometimes a note inserted within the pages, explaining the circumstances of the offer.

In the days and weeks following the happening at the bridge I found myself dropping by Letty's office rather often to see if she might have returned. Her secretary informed me that she was expected to be away for some time longer and referred me to the assistant director, who repeated the same information, saying that the director had taken a leave of absence to attend to personal matters, but did check in from time to time, leaving me an opening, it seemed, and so I simply requested that he say hello for me in case she called.

He took my card and assured me that he would be glad to do so.

I HAD NOT made copies of the notebooks, even though it would have been the practical thing to do from the outset. What I found was that the original copies, set in the hand of each student, entered and noted in the realtime of lectures and discussions, then marked and underlined in subsequent study, contained a certain quality that copies do not have, a genuineness that some would call an aura, or essence, from which I fancied a more direct relationship with the thoughts contained therein.

I did not add my own marks or notations, as I had customarily and irreverently (though some would say, reverently) done through the years to books checked out of libraries, although it might not have violated the spirit of the personal favor granted me in the loan. I carried the notebooks with me everywhere, even when busy with the trivialities of business, with no time to review them, as if their mere proximity granted me some access to the greater realm of their concern. They were guarded in a leather carrying case, and placed in my vault at night, and treated as priceless artifacts because I thought that in them I had heard a voice, related mysteriously to the melodious and transcending voice of the stranger on the bridge. I held open the possibility that the connection might be an illusion, but it was exceedingly important not to be mistaken.

One day I arrived at work early, peered out the large window which overlooked the warehouse floor where the activity seemed like a video replay of the same moment on the previous day and the day before, and left my assistant a note saying that I was gone for the day.

The mere act was exhilarating, and I walked out the door, dropped the leather case into the seat beside me, and drove away.

A leisurely and scenic drive, thoroughly enjoyable, took me to the historic town of Tombstone where I visited the world-famous Banks Rose Tree, planted in the 1880's from a cutting brought to the courtyard of a frontier hotel by immigrants from Europe.

Its trunk is a yard in diameter and its vines reach out to shade a quarter acre with cool foliage, and at the time of my visit, to fill the atmosphere with the intoxicating perfume of its white blossoms.

I wandered the streets steeped in history where the ghosts of another time replay their desultory roles to the imaginations of tourists as far-off echoes of a reluctant past: The gunfight at the OK Corral, errant child of tribalism and masculine egos glamorized into shameless pathos for the price of admission; the office and belongings of the lawman, Wyatt Earp, in the courthouse overlooking the gallows. The artifacts of dogged and often brutal labor in the mines carried out by hardy souls who had little voice against their lot in life. The haunting pictures of women and their children who bear in their tired countenances the weight of the world-although one is never sure about the old photographs:

It is as if the photographer, ready to squeeze the shutter, exclaims from behind the box, "Look somber. Do not smile. If you smile then we will have to retake the picture!"

On the east end of Main Street which once hosted a hundred bars and dance halls in the heyday of the mining bonanza sits the museum which is my favorite, because it remains largely intact after a hundred and twenty-five years, preserved in much its original state through the misfortune of a mining disaster one fateful day when a vein of water burst into the subterranean tunnels and flooded the big mine.

Thinking the flooding would be contained within a short time, the hundreds of miners stayed around town, spending long hours and their money in the dance halls and saloons, waiting to return to their jobs. But the days turned into weeks and months, until finally the people left town in wagons, on horseback or train, and mainstreet was boarded up.

The grand Bird Cage Theatre, which hosted the rich and famous as well as the miners and cowboys on their payday celebrations, boasting the finest entertainment by artists and performers anywhere between St. Louis and San Francisco, fared no better than the rest when the money no longer came in, and so timber planks were placed over the windows and doors, sealing within the interior the memorabilia of a lost world- cards of the last game left upon the felt of the tables below the stage, glasses and half-empty bottles, personal belongings of the ladies left behind in the rooms below, drawers left open, here a comb, there a shoe or mirror.

A world came to an end, the world they themselves had made, and the people moved on.

In the front saloon still hangs the imposing portrait of the famous Fatima, a bullet hole piercing her exposed abdomen, her alluring smile still promising an evening of pleasure.

Below her, by the narrow stairs which lead to the upper rooms once known as the Gilded Cages, there sits the old music box, and for a token you can hear played from the large brass slotted discs the same music which came to life on that last night two decades before the century's turn, a museum-piece of sound passed forward in a nostalgic serenade to the living by the long dead. The wistful emotion of the music they knew and loved still wafts undiminished into the ears of the most modern, emotion touching emotion, and the lady Fatima's smile still stirs up a response within the living soul, as if she, too, even now hears the music of life playing.

I WAS STANDING within the old theatre room with its empty stage, its faded curtains hanging open for the next act which never came, the great piano which traveled around the Cape and then overland by mule cart sitting in its long state of rest, its last performance given; the curtained bird cages above empty of spectators; the wooden ceiling still pockmarked with the bullet holes made by rowdy frontiersmen who armed themselves because other rowdy ones were also armed, in a curious vestige and harbinger of war lodged in the male brain.

It is said that each place on Earth holds the memories of what took place there in times past, and if you look for them and listen, you will find the images and sounds of a world which is not dead, but only sleeps until it senses the ear and eye of living thought within its midst. The celebration of life is impossible, we find, without the past, and any knowledge hollow without the wisdom of the ancestors.

Upon the wall near the entry door to the theatre I noticed a circular or bill which had announced the program of an evening in the final days of the old theatre. As I leaned toward the small billing sheet, its aged paper held by a glass within a frame, and studied more closely the names and details on the program of that night long ago, the present fell away and I began to feel the event unfolding in this very room thirty years before my father was born, even before his parents had met, two decades before the turn of the 20th Century.

The gas lamps are glowing yellow-pale, their saffron light wavering across and about the air made visible by the smoke of tobacco. The stage curtains are about to be drawn and the pianist, dressed in long coat, sits just below the stage at the big piano playing the prelude. There is noise and chatter within the theatre room; people can be seen behind the open curtains of the upper rooms known as Bird Cages.

The brother of Czar Nicolas II, as is his evening custom, occupies his box just to the left of the stage, his bottle and glass upon the table, coat hung upon the coat rack, bearskin draped over the wallpaper as a reminder of his Mother Russia.

Within weeks he would be lynched on a mistaken charge of horse thievery, but tonight he doesn't know that.

Behind the curtain the performers prepare for their entrance upon the stage. The master of ceremonies moves nervously among them, repeating the sequence of their appearances and assuring each one that this evening's event would go down in the annals of history as one of the best ever at the famed and elegant Bird Cage Theatre of Tombstone, Arizona Territory.

I can feel the silent vibrations of souls, see the look in their eyes, sense the brush of their ghostly forms moving about me, the stirring of their emotions on this day which, like all days of a lifetime, is momentous.

There is a tapping, and the piano signals the opening of the performance as the curtain begins to rise:

Suddenly I feel a breath upon my neck, and a simultaneous scent, sweet and familiar, jolted the lost consciousness back to the present.

A woman's voice, whispering behind my left ear, said, "What would you give for a ticket?"

Even before I turned I knew it was Leticia.

Her eyebrows were raised slightly, signaling that she was expecting an answer. She was smiling.

"Oh!" I reacted. "For a moment it seemed like I was really *there*..., or that they were here!" If the ghosts of the past are so easily summoned, then must they not be present still..? I felt a shiver, and smiled. "... But what would you *really* give for a ticket?"

"You mean, to actually be there?" I asked. "As a visitor, or to be one of them?" I was making an important distinction, although of course her question and any answer would be strictly rhetorical.

It would make for an inconceivable experience to enter this room holding the powers of prescience and perspective that a visitor composing a century of history yet to come would have!

Who would that visitor be? How would she seem to those present? Would the eyes, something of her aspect, the memories of things to come give her away? Would the presence of the future in their midst be eerie, unsettling, fearsome to the citizens of that world before the future came to change it so irrevocably?

Would the visitor's knowledge be too dangerous and alien to tolerate, unwelcome as a dark witchcraft?

Or in going to the past, would I relinquish the present?

What price would one have to pay for a travel in time?...

MEETING LETTY was always a stimulating experience, and more so this time for the sheer coincidence of seeing her here at the very time when she was most on my mind.

The influences of my experience on the bridge some weeks before had expanded with time as I continued to ponder their implications and to immerse myself in study to try and divine their meaning.

"What are you doing here, Letty?... I've been thinking about you!" I exclaimed in a low voice. "Something has happened, and I've wanted to talk with you about it."

"Yes, much has happened," she answered with a bit of strangeness in her voice, "very much." She paused for a moment, then patted my shoulder and said, "How about a hug?"

Then she turned slowly and gracefully and raised her arm to point a finger toward the stage.

A man is standing in front of the faded curtain which has not heralded the opening of an act since the close of the Nineteenth Century. The piano just below where he stands, its varnish darkened with age, the ivory keys grown yellow and brittle, sits heavy in its silence, while the bones of its player rest somewhere in the comfort of their grave, the ending of those musical nights. Everything returns to silence after the music has been played, someone has said, who believed things truly do come to an end.

"My husband," she announced as she tugged at my sleeve. "I want you to come and meet him."

She waved to the man as we approached across the wood floor. He stood unmoved and relaxed, hands in his pockets, a 1940's style felt hat upon his head. He seemed rather tall, although his slender frame and the fact that he was standing some three feet above floor level made it hard to tell. He wore casual slacks and a dark shirt that seemed too big for him.

I noted to myself as I stood by the piano looking up at him that he seemed the quintessential scientist, as if he could be related to an Oppenheimer or Feynman, Sagan, Lanza or DeGrassi, although of course any stereotype simply derives from the prominence of these individuals.

He had a remarkable presence. A pleasant, most interesting face which held something mischievous behind its intense, yet tranquil countenance; coal-dark, reflective eyes, almond in shape, like deep pools of intelligence which drew everything into their gaze, but twinkled serenely as little creases appeared on the outer corners, the signs of a good nature, people used to say.

Prominent eyebrows which moved like agile cantilevers with expression. Thin lips fixed in a straight line which easily lengthened somewhat to make a wry and humorous smile. A gentle and good face.

As we reached the stage, standing just above the old basement door which led down to the poker table whose felt top is strewn with the cards of the last game, whiskey bottle and glasses left as they were on the final closing of the curtain, two bullet holes still visible in the door frame where they passed through on their way to oblivion, diverted from their mark, so the story goes, by the strong and quick arm of someone sitting next to the drunk miner who was not amused by a performer on stage, the modem man had already approached the edge of the wood floor and bent down, hand extended, the look on his face just as I have described it.

Letty spoke my name, then, rotating her upturned palm slightly toward the man who already held my hand in a firm grasp, announced simply in her informal and engaging style, "Lloyd Man Foglesby, my husband and friend..."

He had removed his felt hat, which he held in his left hand, a habit of courtesy, and as he was bending down a shock of thick straight hair fell across his forehead. As he released my hand, having expressed his pleasure at our meeting- it seems that he had heard of me through his wife, though I doubt he would have remembered a name- he brushed back the black hair with a casual movement of his hand and rose to stand, his pleasant face holding the same, straight smile which pushed on either side against a crease in the shape of an arc across each cheek, one of those physiological details that have no common name in our language, though it be considered a handsome feature.

It occurred to me that in my conversations with Letty we had not spoken much of our personal lives, and that I had not heard the full name of her husband. We would often visit about 'the old days' our parents knew, which, one could note, were only a generation or two removed from the era celebrated in this unique museum, locked away in time when the planks were nailed upon her doors and windows in the wake of a disappointment long ago.

Although my habit of work had precluded for me a generous sweep of general knowledge, having afforded little time for reading or reflecting upon current affairs beyond a cursory interest, the full name of my friend's husband, Lloyd Man Foglesby, when I heard it pronounced, pegged a memory in my brain of having heard or seen the name before. I was still trying to sort out this mild perplexity when Letty's musical voice shaped a word among the others of her introduction which was nothing short of startling:

"...known to most students and friends as Doctor Fo."

I was scrambling mentally to regain my balance- Did she say, Dr. Fo!- and I must not have succeeded in concealing my reaction, as Letty read my surprise and laughed lightly, adding, "It's a name his students gave him long ago as a short for Foglesby- some students have called him, Fo Man... Since I was his student too, Dr. Fo is the first name I knew him by."

I did not have time to go into an explanation of my reaction when hearing the name, as Letty suddenly changed the subject of conversation by saying, "Say, we're on our way to meet an old friend in Bisbee. Would you like to come along?..., if you have time, that is."

Oh, I'm afraid I might be in the way- Oh, no. Actually Fo has business to take care of...you can keep me company while he's busy. We can catch up on things..., there's something you wanted to tell me- If you're sure I won't impose, great. I've nothing really planned for the day...

"Wonderful. That's settled, we're going to Bisbee!" Letty beamed.

At their insistence I left my car where it was parked by the old freighter wagon under a grand cottonwood tree, and began the short ride south to historic Bisbee. The half-hour or so seemed to pass in a quarter of the time as we engaged in conversation mainly occupied by the professor and myself. He had not had the occasion before to talk with anyone about mangoes, and so asked a litany of questions which gave me the sense that he would very soon know more about the fruit than I did after twenty years of mating my fortune and misfortune with its perishable and wanton charm.

I was happy to let the conversation proceed in this manner as any line of questioning I might have about astrophysics was severely restricted, and about philosophy and metaphysics- well, my perspectives were being challenged at a maximum rate just by studying the notes taken by students of this same man, and I had a long way to go before my questions could be beyond mere repetition, or even sycophancy.

And so I sat in the back seat of the moving car answering questions about mangoes, of which I knew something, as my peripheral vision caught the outline of Letty's willowy hair to one side, and the dark, sincere eyes in the rear view mirror noted my answers with genuine interest.

*   *   *

CHAPTER SIX

BISBEE.
THE CODE

By visitations of thought history extends into the future,
and the past claims its presence in the now.
-Pen-Tab notebook, plastic cover, p43.

Discoveries of knowledge, once made, are as enduring as the universe.
-brown notebook "5", p88.

THE CAR EASED to a stop in front of the steps leading up to the renowned Copper Queen Hotel. I had not even noticed our turn onto the narrow street that climbs steeply to its entrance.

The chauffer offered to find a parking place and return if his wife and their guest would like to debark here where it was convenient, and so Letty and I climbed the broad steps to the entrance doors where we stood waiting for her husband, who soon was to be seen walking leisurely down the old brick street toward the picturesque hotel, car keys dangling in his hand.

After relaxing for some minutes in the grand lobby and drawing room with its curved oak staircase which had known the footsteps of guests for a hundred years, we were carrying on light conversation when Letty's husband recognized someone in his field of view and excused himself, stepping quickly across the carpet toward the entrance doors.

"It's our friend," Letty smiled, then added, "We're having lunch here.. I hope you're hungry!" just as the hostess appeared, to say the table was ready.

As we made our way across the lobby room and around the staircase to the screened entrance to the dining room which had served its diners every day since the old hotel was built, I could not help but notice Dr. Fo and another gentleman standing just outside the elevator doors, engaged in conversation. Letty, catching her husband's eye as we crossed through the lobby, discreetly signaled our intentions as he smiled and nodded.

The table reserved was in an ideal spot near the corner of the dining room whose windows opened on one side to the brick-floored terrace, and on the other side facing the old Presbyterian Church to an abundance of blooming roses which wafted their perfume through the open windows. Lace curtains moved in light undulations with the cool breeze which crisscrossed the corner where we sat, and old things in the room lent the flavor of history to the place and to the moment.

Even though there were to be only four persons, the hostess had ushered us to a long table which held some eight places marked by comfortable high-backed chairs, perhaps of the same vintage as the hotel. Candles wavered within transparent globes, and a vase of flowers decorated with color the white brocaded cloth upon which were already placed the four settings- one at the end and another beside it, where Letty and I were to be seated, and the other two across from each other two chairs down, where Letty's husband and the friend would soon be seated, to continue in low, earnest tones an intense conversation as they hardly touched their lunch. This would allow Letty and I the occasion to visit, an opportunity I took in order to briefly outline the drama of my recent experience, and to solicit her reaction in the light of the part her husband now seemed to occupy in that matter, though the exact nature of that role was far from certain.

Letty listened attentively as I talked, and I thought- in fact, I was almost sure- that her reactions indicated a perception which in itself was mysterious to me.

She evinced no hint of surprise, at times she nodded in concurrence, or would make her funny, rather purring sound which indicated that she recognized what was said. Her eyes, deeply expressive, registered subtle responses that her face didn't show- a dilation of the pupils, a narrowing of the lids, or a length, or distance, opening up in her view, deepening her glance.

Her reaction to my tale was rather mystifying, though I wasn't sure what actually I had expected. She was neither credulous or incredulous, not at all dismissive, and seemed to simply understand what I had told her.

As to the coincidental referral by a student to her husband's teachings, there was no proof of a direct connection, only that the professor's thoughts were irregular and expansive and so was such an event as occurred upon the bridge.

Perhaps I was reading too much into it, and yet there was just now the strange, elusive sense that with Letty's reaction I had confirmed some unknown dimension. That I had found an ally.

*   *   *

THERE IS something unique about conversations of moment.

They are not the opposite of trivial conversations, of course, but they are only distantly related to common talk through the mechanism of thought and voice, while yet as far removed as is the human from his mammalian cousins which still leap from branch to branch in the dwindling forests.

Conversations of moment, of reason and heart and conscience, are a higher species of communication, closer to the soul, closer to love, to death and birth, to the divine, and are a highway to meaning through an otherwise lonely expanse. Their occurrence in an increasingly cacophonous world seems increasingly rare.

It was this rare species of conversation that I witnessed that day between two colleagues and old friends who sat leaning toward one another two chairs away from where I sat with one of the most beautiful and intelligent women any man has been graced to know.

In the culture in which I was raised, a community of rural families living on humble farmsteads which dotted the landscape settled two generations before by pioneers who ironically and perhaps by necessity respected and even revered the privacy of their neighbors, one was taught not to listen to private conversations of others, or even to contemplate matters which were not of one's business.

Such regard was, in those days, elevated to a common courtesy, and most everyone abided by its elemental principles as an ancillary contract of the Golden Rule: Do unto others...

Someone requested the placement of the tableware two chairs down.

It was most probably Letty herself who, in her quiet wisdom, foresaw the interchange of thought in the messages passed back and forth between her husband and his old and cherished friend about a matter of enormous urgency. This is how I see it today, after all these things are passed into memory.

I've thought about the silly admonition, told by someone to their lover as they said goodnight: "Don't think about pink elephants." This is how one's childhood training in its rural setting can prepare one for the rare conversation of moment which so overshadowed common thought as matters of history unfolded their primeval wings at last to take flight.

Never did the two men try to exclude us from their conversation- there would have been more appropriate settings and occasions for complete privacy- and from time to time I would even notice one or the other glance at Letty in an acknowledgment that she was included in the matters discussed.

There was some humor expressed between them, and digression, of course, as they were also in the process of eating their meal, but it was the urgency which sometimes broke the surface of their conversation, and indeed seemed to flow beneath it which one could not help but notice, despite the reminder to oneself not to consider the pink elephants.

From time to time as we carried our own conversation I would notice a look in Letty's eyes, not that she was distracted or concerned, but that her thoughts occupied more than a single plane, and yet her eyes yielded that deep serenity I had noticed about her husband, which settled upon you with her look.

There was something exceedingly true about the both of them that I found remarkable to a degree that I have not seen again.

The other gentleman, the "friend" they had come to Bisbee to meet, who listened in deep concentration to the words spoken in a low, matter-of-fact voice across the table, was in fact a colleague who had long been considered family. In the world outside of mangoes and other tropical fruit he was a well known and regarded scholar, now a retired professor, who had written many books, including textbooks, and noted publications on subjects of history, politics, sociology, and ethics.

Perhaps in his late seventies, Otto, as he insisted I call him, was a grandfatherly type, of rather slight build but with a bearing and aspect which made him noticeable anywhere. One would assume that he had grown more handsome with age, as some men are given to do, and it may be that thing they call character, and not the clean, chiseled face or the snow white hair which he kept long and combed backward on the sides to where it had long ago receded from the tanned dome above.

Most of the talking was done by the younger man, bracketed by the noticeable reactions of his friend who could be overheard asking, "Are you sure?...How can you know for sure?", to which Letty's husband said, "Because everything fell open."

"What do you mean, fell open?"

"It was a code, Otto. The knowledge was folded into a code. The equation is a key, nothing less."

"What kind of key?"

"Well, a key to what intelligent life has been searching for. A key to understanding, to future evolution, to the secrets of oneness with creation-how mystical do you want to get?.."

A long silence ensued, during which the elder professor slumped somewhat in his chair and just studied his friend's face, looking through the silence for some clarification, or admission of an intellectual prank..., who knows?

The silence dominated, and the conversation I was having with Letty abruptly ceased, as I sat looking at my plate and Letty quietly studied the two men.

"Fo, that's the Grail, that's the Holy Grail! Do you realize what that means?" Otto finally spoke.

"Not entirely. Do you?" Fo answered, a sardonic smile pushing at the creases which arched over from the corners of his mouth which have no common name. It is one thing to study and teach the dynamics of philosophy and science, and yet another to live them.

Another silence.

"When will you publish?"

Fo rocked forward and back, his elbows braced on the arms of his chair.

"That's the problem." Otto's bushy eyebrows raised.

"They won't let me do that."

"Who won't?...Who?"

"...Is that an owl I hear?" Fo turned to Letty, and smiled, his deep black eyes twinkling as he winked at her lightly. Otto was deeply serious.

"Well, the powers that be. The Corporation. The Cartel. The Estate. The Establishment... Whatever you want to call it."

"And how do you know? What did they say?"

"Thou shall not publish this 'item'... We regretfully ask that you refrain from disseminating this information."

"What gives them the authority?"

"What is their pretext? National Security."

"Oh, yes. That elegant catch-all. It serves best to bury their screwups and perfidies... But what gives them the right?"

"They have badges and guns."

"That's license, not right." Otto looked aside for a moment, deep in thought.

"Where do you stand legally on this thing?" he advanced the dialogue.

"How does the department stand?..Can't say. Only the head knows."

"Fo, you are the head of the department."

"Oh yes. Well, like I say, only the head knows.., and a superannuated teacher of history and other old stuff."

He could have added, a wife and an itinerant mango salesman, but didn't.

"And I did have a word with the president."

"With Clinton?"

Fo smiled. "No, with Simons."

"What did you tell him?"

"That I was going to publish the proof of the unified field theory."

"How did he react?"

"He thought I might be having delusions of grandeur."

"That's probably because Simons has delusions of grandeur."

Fo laughed. Not so much a sound as a contagious expression which spread over his face, somewhat flattening his ears in the process as if they as well recognized the humor.

Otto continued.

"Is the NSA demanding that you turn over your discovery to them?"

"Oh, no. I gave it to them. The complete hundred pages up to and including the key equations. I was going to give it to everybody- not that everybody would understand. They're just saying that I can't talk with anyone else about it."

"So the U.S. Government is now in possession of the solution to the unified field, and they want to put a lid on it."

"The University will back you up." Otto had a further thought. "The people up there will defend your right to publish."

"I once assumed so," Fo concurred, "but now Simons is as slippery as a snake in oil. He's beholden to a lot of people for grants and contracts, discretionary funding, et cetera."

"He's beholden to the NSA." "Sure."

"Great." Otto rapped his knuckles on the table. "Great." And then he had another idea. He leaned toward his friend. "Fo, this is your development, is it not? You've been working on this for years. You weren't under contract, were you?"

"I see what you're saying, Otto, but that's not the problem. It's not a question of intellectual copyright. I'm ready to give the solution to anyone with half a brain and a dull pencil... It's not my property. It does not belong to me, it does not belong to the department or to the university, or to the National Security Agency. It does not belong to America, neither to the time in which we live. I don't even think it belongs entirely to the human species. It is of Mind, of intelligence itself."

"You're saying it's cosmic."

"Yes, my friend. Read it in the universal language of mathematics and you will know for a certainty that such knowledge is not of this race or of this earth. For want of a better description, it is cosmic in origin, and cosmic in purpose. It is wonderfully given, and it doesn't belong to us."

"Are you saying that all thought is on loan, a trust?"

"Makes you wonder, doesn't it?" Fo answered quickly, the mischievous smile lengthening his lips.

A jazz and blues trio by the name of The Soul Senders played in a far corner as a portly gentleman in a light blue shirt and bow tie, a white straw dandy hat upon his head, as if in a trance, pulled the feelings of his music out of their deep bed and gave them life in his rich, mesmerizing baritone. The sounds, recalled from generations of artists nurtured in the deep South, filtered out the open windows and onto the street below.

All four of us walked slowly up and around the winding streets and past old houses on the way to Otto's vacation cottage which was more of a studio overlooking one of the canyons which fork into the wider geological scar into which the main part of town is nestled. A rock retaining wall with a green picket fence on top was pierced by an arched opening which immediately rose by high steps to an enclosed deck surrounded on the outside by a parapet or half-wall made of masonry.

The house was board-and-batten with a gabled tin roof and a porch extending on three sides to protect the walls from the sun in the days before airconditioning. The restored windows retained their original glass panes, identifiable by their wavy surfaces and bubbles.

Above the charming entry door with its oval window was the framed mosaic of leaded glass whose colors were pulled out by the light and laid in shimmering patterns upon the surfaces within.

Opening upon the deck and occupying half the house was the history professor's study, ringed with shelves of books and souvenirs of his life and travels. A large, oak desk sat in the middle of the room, covered by a computer, notes and books, and faced outward toward the deck and the skyline beyond.

Outside the deck wall was a rock garden with a variety of desert plants, which Otto tended well, and towering over it like a patriarch stood a giant saguaro upon whose aged arms were clustered the fragile spring blossoms which gave birth in an ancient recurrence to the young of the species.

Fo and Letty knew the place, and had visited it many times.

What follows is a general account of the conversation that took place at Otto's house between two friends on that spring afternoon soon after the century turned, and with it a new millennium.

*　　*　　*

WHETHER OR NOT the dramatic events of that year had something to do with these milestones in the western calendar two thousand years after the legendary birth of a prophet, or were simply coincidental with mythologies which have long spoken of a great revelation and renewal is anyone's guess, and even renowned historians like our host could only propose conjectures largely influenced by their own cultural and temporal perspectives, in the conundrum of history interpreted by the individual mind.

Letty and I sat out on the deck under the tin roof on this pleasant afternoon, drinking iced tea brewed by the sun in a gallon jar, a small table between us.

Her husband and his old friend walked about, or stood in different places talking, the intense train of their conversation continuing even as Otto pointed out his desert plants, naming each one and its family, its role in nature and its life cycle, with the astrophysicist digressing from his concerns to ask questions in sincere interest, just as he had done about mangoes.

"You know," I mentioned to Letty, "when I first heard about the famous Dr. Fo and his class, I somehow assumed the professor to be of Asian descent."

"Because of the name, Fo?" Letty smiled.

"I suppose so. 'Fo' sounded oriental to me, although I never really gave it much thought, other than being curious about the teacher and his ideas."

"Well, you're partly right," Letty spoke in a low voice, as the two gentlemen stood not a dozen yards away. Otto had pulled some leaves from a creosote bush and offered them to Fo to smell.

Then she told a surprising story about her husband's life.

"Fo's grandmother, a beautiful woman who was of Japanese descent, married an English immigrant to America named, Foglesby, who died in the influenza epidemic at the end of the First World War, only a few years after Fo's father was born.

"Fo's father was brought up by his widowed mother and eventually married a girl from San Francisco who was, herself, half Oriental, and who died in childbirth when her only baby was born. The boy was named after his grandfather, Lloyd, and I have never known how the name Man was given, but the pronunciation may have an oriental meaning.

"During World War Two my husband's father, who was a successful merchant back east, returned to the West Coast to find that his mother (Fo's grandmother) had been placed in internment with other members of the family in one of the holding camps set up for people of Japanese descent. He traveled to the camp to plead the cases of his mother and other relatives and while he was there was himself investigated and detained.

"So it happened that my husband as a child, with his father, grandmother, and other family, spent the years of the war in an internment camp in Wyoming, even though all but his grandmother had been born in the United States. Ironically, while these members of the family were interned, Fo had two uncles who died fighting the war in Italy- on the American side, of course.

"Fo's mother's name was Amagumo..."

THE TWO men had made their way back to the shade of the porch and were at the far end from where Letty and I sat. The elder man sat on a bench there as Fo stood leaning against the deck wall facing him.

Letty fell silent. I hoped I had not set her to thinking about family, as I already knew about the daughter they had lost.

We sat sipping the tea and talking while the voices at the end of the porch continued the earnest dialogue that had begun in the lobby of the hotel. It was the first time Fo had spoken with his old friend in some months as Otto had been abroad, so that the matter at hand and its complications were new to Otto, who was trying to absorb and analyze them at once.

The analysis of history in the making lacked the secure element that is both the friend and adversary to historians, and that is the perspective of time within which history both conceals and reveals her secrets.

The colleague and friend through whom nature may have revealed her greatest secret to humanity was now caught in the most mundane of nature's social manifestations, and it seemed inconceivable to Otto that the same mind which roamed across the cosmic expanse of spacetime could be trapped in the leaden maze of a witless bureaucracy.

What use the evolution of the species may have had for bureaucratic mediocrity and its malevolence was ever a mystery to the historian who had studied and observed in retrospect the immense mischief wrought through history by those who anoint themselves to rule over others. In whatever form of government, he noted, this tendency exerted itself and behaved similarly: It is immensely self-interested and lobbies for more power and more control under the guise of public good, or public need, or national security as defined by the same bureaucracy in a justification for its increased authority over the personal lives of the majority it purports to serve.

The difference in government's behavior in totalitarian, or in democratic systems, the professor had argued, was a matter of degree: Communism as a form of government was simply more efficient. It had every third citizen watching the other two in a regime of force which corrupted and demoralized both the watcher and the watched, foretelling a state of war within the individual and her society.

The ultimate aim of such a state, the historian had offered, was to control thought, as this is the most intimate possession a man or woman or child can have, so that the gross perversion of authoritarian control over a human life is its intimacy. Steal a man's freedom, and you have stricken his soul. Strike his soul and your power has a Promethean completeness, even more effective when the subject is aware of the freedom he has lost. Why this condition asserts itself generation after generation and century after century, wherein a fraction of the species is able to gain the upper hand over the majority, and dictate the latitudes of its freedom was for Otto the central question of his life's study.

Fo stood quietly now, his face illuminated by the golden light of the declining sun. His thoughts were far away in space and time, among galaxies and suns which somewhere in the chronicles of time may have harbored worlds like ours, and beings to whom were given the secrets of knowledge, the cup of understanding.

Did it save them? Did that knowledge save them? Did it make them better, show them the way to love? Did it end the solemn rituals of their goodbyes?

Fo held a smile which lengthened the straight line of his lips and deepened the little creases which lay at the edges of his black eyes. Anyone who has seen the brightness knows the answer with an unexplainable certainty.

A FAMILIAR sound from far away, like waves washing upon a distant beach, pushed against the silence of Fo's thoughts. He turned to see his old friend speaking to him in a low voice, almost fatherly.

"Have you decided how you're going to manage it?" Otto was asking cautiously.

"I haven't signed their order yet," Fo mumbled. "They gave me until three days ago, so I guess I'm overdue."

"You've been ordered to sign an order ordering you to sign?"

Fo's mouth opened and his black eyes twinkled in silent laughter. "What is it you would be signing?" Otto continued.

"A relinquishment of the discovery.., temporary, of course. An acknowledgment of the matter of national security... An agreement not to disseminate the text without proper authorization, et cetera... An agreement not to talk to old historians about the subject would be included, of course," Fo added.

"Well, it's a relief to know you haven't violated a signed agreement," Otto breathed, looking down at the deck of the terrace. "And a joy to know that now I'm a party to your intrigue."

"I thought you wouldn't mind," Fo answered wryly.

"Mind?" assured his old friend, "I've been out of the loop too long... I wouldn't miss it for the world... Of course they'll get nothing factual out of me even if they pull out my fingernails, since you've only told me what you haven't told me."

"That alone is too much, according to the order I haven't signed."

"So you are in a bit of a dilemma," Otto concluded. "This is why we're talking."

"Yep. That's what friends are for, to walk with you to the gallows," Fo smiled.

There were some moments of silence as both men stood looking into the distance. Otto, as in an afterthought, turned to the gallon jar in which tea was brewing in the afternoon sun. He filled a large glass with ice from the tumbler, poured the tea into it, and handed it to his friend.

"I was wondering if you could tell me what I might expect if I don't comply," Fo asked after taking a long drink of the cold tea. He could have asked a lawyer, but had always tried to avoid lawyers.

"Well, I can tell you in general what to expect," Otto began. "They'll try to pressure you. They'll bring out the dead souls to watch and listen. They may try to get you through your family and friends. To threaten the things you love and are loyal to. And depending upon how serious they are about your case, they'll bring all their resources to bear against you...

"They'll try to keep their business quiet, to stay in the shadows, but when the matter becomes public, then they'll have to declare you an enemy of the state. If you don't obey their order to stop, they'll shoot."

"Metaphorically speaking, I hope."

"Oh, not necessarily," Otto answered, unsmiling.

He had studied authoritarianism and its institutions for many years, their self-protective nature and capacity for the extreme, and although he did not at this moment foresee such a scenario for his friend, he thought it best not to mince his words. The NSA had had its share of misguided fools in the past.

One advantage of a secretive agency is that one cannot predict which way or how far it went. In a regime of secrecy the kooks are indemnified in their mischief. It was endlessly fascinating to the man of history.

"They're going to try to determine your reality so that they can control you," Otto offered his friend a bottom line.

"It's called the authority of law," Fo reacted.

"The rule of law; the authority of persons, and it's intensely flawed... It's a system wherein blind mediocrity can wear the badge and gun."

Fo looked amused at Otto's spirited mannerisms. He was glad to see that the fires of passion had not abandoned the aging intellect, though he was not surprised. Otto had managed consistently over the years to take sides on strong issues, which had landed him more than once in what he called, "honorable detention", in causes ranging from civil rights through Vietnam, nuclear proliferation, ecology, species preservation, population growth, and latest, the war in Iraq and criminal government. He served on numerous advisory boards and used his considerable influence to lobby for causes he believed in. Otto was never neutral in matters he considered important.

"Fear thee not, Otto. I have no inclination to become an agent of the state, or its enemy."

"I know that, if I know anything, Fo," Otto responded, grasping the tone of his friend's utterance. Then, with a wayward smile, he proceeded:

"Then for what reward offered would you become an agent of the state?"

Fo recognized the bait.

"For what level of punishment withheld?... That would be the ultimate punishment, now wouldn't it?"

"You're a nonconformist, Fo, albeit a kind and gentle one."

Fo thought a moment.

"I don't see myself as nonconformist... It's just that I've never given conformity much thought."

Otto laughed heartily.

AS LETTY and I continued to visit quietly, some dozen steps from where the two men were talking, the herd of pink elephants stood just over there among the trees, sometimes raising their trunks as if to trumpet loudly.

Letty once looked at me as they talked, holding her glance just long enough that I felt that she may have been passing me a message- that we were to be witnesses to an interchange between two great intellects regarding a crucial matter, perhaps for unforeseen contingencies. I now believe that she sensed a danger that her husband was not disposed to appreciate.

What less obvious vessel, I vaingloriously mused, than a merchant of fruits and vegetables could there be in which to deposit a priceless oil, though I feel certain now that the occasion could not have come to pass without the singular appointment of the stranger on the bridge and his connections with the events unfolding on this day.

"Well, look at it this way," Otto was proposing: "Let's say most folks are like a thread.. You're like a cloth. You've got many threads going this way and that, woven together in a way that makes sense to you and produces a pattern which for you is flexible and interpretable. Some single-thread folks- lets say your friends in government, in this case- don't know how to interpret or appreciate a cloth. They prefer to keep everything in threads, where they can be tallied and counted... Do you see what I'm saying?"

"Well, can't say as I do," Fo's eyebrows canted upwards curiously. "Look, I think you're saying that a cloth cannot be returned to a thread without unraveling, right?.. Meanwhile, I have a growing problem with the Federal Government."

Fo was humoring his friend as a way of lightening the situation. Both men knew that in matters of intellectual honesty there were really no alternatives.

"Because of a historical abdication of reason and intelligence, mediocrity rules the world," Otto lamented jokingly, repeating a common observation. "Mediocrity, and outright corruption."

"Not my world," Fo answered, smiling.

"Well, that's the important answer," was the reply. "So you won't be signing the stuff."

"No."

"Okay, okay."

There followed a lot of questions and answers, back and forth, as the two formidable minds considered the painful practicalities of this kind of refusal. Fo would forego the politics. He would not know how to play to the publicity, would not answer charges, or make charges, of course. He would neutralize himself as a player in a game that wasn't in his nature. He would conduct himself as a scientist and a human being.

All this was easy enough because it was what would come naturally to the man to whom had been passed the greatest secret of the universe.

*　　*　　*

IF WE TRY to understand in some way the great contrast in dynamic forces which must have been at work within and upon the scientist and teacher at this moment in his life, on one side arising out of the pettiness and even meanness of man's doing- out of his forgetfulness, as Colin Wilson called it nobly, in view of the grandness of human possibility- and on the other side, descending to this moment in time from the infinite resources of being which Lloyd Man Foglesby deemed to be man's destiny, whose themes he had taught to legions of college students eager for a greater vision of life's meaning, we can see that there was really no contest. The dimness of one does not compare with the brightness of the other.

One supposes, in that curious way that humans have of explaining past events, that destiny groomed Lloyd Man, billowing his sails with early adversity framed historically in remarkable circumstance, while generously recognizing and providing the gifts of love and intelligence which would serve to anchor his soul to reality. Fo would never forget throughout his years the symbology of a boundary, a fence, prescribed and laid out by another upon his life.

It had been the experience of the war years spent in confinement with his proud father and his family with no explanation adequate to suit their humanity which most sculpted Fo's early character and infused his soul with a passion for freedom. The pursuit of learning was to the impressionable child an escape from confinement, and when he became a man the broad vistas of knowledge were fields of freedom and discovery, the more beautiful when it seemed no human had stepped upon them since creation.

Mathematics, the language of light in which creation spoke its presence to intelligence, was to the young Lloyd Man like the lantern which shined through an opening in the wall and revealed in the clearing of dust the treasures of King Tut.

The pure delight of a first learning remained Fo's greatest thrill, when history rejoiced as well in the fruition of labors begun by others long ago, and realized in the moment of discovery. There would be plenty of freedom to pursue now, that was for sure, for the boy who once stood inside the perimeter of a guarded fence, and looked upward at the unbounded stars.

"When you are at the lowest point in your life," he remembered his father's counsel out of that experience, and would offer it to his students, "is when you may have your most extravagant dreams."

They were the dreams, born through an extraordinary experience and nurtured by a steadfast and noble family, which fueled the vision of greater things and of a freedom that knew no boundaries and was more than enough to fill the mind and heart, which lay at the center of Fo's life. And the wonderful silence to which he constantly listened, of things infinite.

Letty's husband had always sought out the quiet places, to think and to teach, and when he could not find them he had made them within himself.

She knew his discomfort with publicity, which was to him a reminder of confinement, and she worried for him although he did not for himself.

Perhaps it was just a flicker of concern, quickly passing, which prompted Fo, his mood reflective as he looked out at the skyline, to remark to Otto that he sometimes dreamed of a place far away, "a stone house with a veranda overlooking the sea."

It was the quiet he was thinking of, and would miss in the months to come.

The two friends turned their attention in the time remaining to matters concerning the discovery, and Foglesby spoke animatedly about the veritable flood of revelations which the key had opened to every field of study.

Otto seemed dumbfounded as Fo spoke in his steady voice about the most astounding aspect of his discovery:

"It seems the answer was within us all along."

"What do you mean.., inherent in consciousness?"

"Within us..."

"It seems the mathematical code is replicated within the code of life, and has been since the beginning of life on this planet- we don't know about any other worlds- within the DNA itself, within every cell of our bodies and brains. It was written inside us from the first. We were the holders of the key all along." He tapped a finger on his chest, and continued.

"As knowledge grew clearer, like a reflection on a lake, and the rippling waters settled infinitely smooth, it was our own image that we saw reflected, the image that looked back at us in knowledge.

"We *recognize* knowledge. It is 'familiar' to us, because it is of us, our family and home."

Otto was speechless, his eyes studying his friend's face as if looking into a rare innocence.

"If you take the whole code, mathematically transcribed," Fo continued, "the forces which control and define the universe as we know it- *as we know it*- when unified in a mathematical structure, *look like us*. They are symbols of the double helix, the blueprint of life itself, of the expression of thought. Life, in its knowing, *is* the unifying force!"

Some moments elapsed as Otto remained silent. He suddenly seemed agitated by something.

"So this is what the NSA is sitting on!" he exclaimed. "No wonder!"

"Oh, they don't know this," Fo quickly assured him. Anticipating Otto's response, he continued:

"They have the full code, laid out neatly and bound in a volume with a blue cover, and they have the key equations.., but they won't be able to automatically recognize what I've just told you.

"You might say there is an outer key and an inner key, and you have to have them both to turn the final tumbler on the cosmic lock."

"Insight" Otto could not resist the irony of the pun, "Beautiful!"

He sat again on the old bench near the wall of his house, and seemed to be resting, while deeply in thought. Fo stood across the terrace, leaning upon the half-wall, as he looked out at the desert landscape in the lengthening shadows.

A wren caught his notice as it flitted among the spiny arms of the saguaro, and as he watched she suddenly vanished from sight, simply disappearing into the arm of the great plant.

She had entered her nest, a pocket hollowed out of the high trunk, perhaps centuries ago, by ancestors of her species. The abode had started small, a modest pocket set in the cool, pithy interior, and guarded by phalanxes of spines. But as the host grew stately, inching upward through the decades, the small pocket stretched upward and over, molded by time into a scar as the plant grew in height and girth until the hollow scar was shaped like the interior of a shoe, perhaps half a meter in length, a vintage cottage with a high ceiling and leathery walls, insulated from the elements outside and protected against the ever present threat of predators who would opportunely feast upon the bird's misfortune.

For some moments Fo stood looking at the silhouette of the great cactus around which the bird had lightly slipped from view. His hands were opened, fingertips bearing his weight against the cap of the masonry wall, as he leaned forward, deeply attentive.

A car eased past on the narrow street below, its engine idling quietly with the same sound Letty had heard in the times she had counted through the afternoon. Only the white of its door panels could be seen moving across the narrow slit of the gate opening at the bottom of the flight of steps.

Not seeing the wren reappear, Fo suddenly made a light springing motion with his hands, stood upward and turned his head toward his wife, eyes sparkling. He had just witnessed an ancient ritual, much older than the human species, and its replay enlivened him with a sense of the long history which the creature expressed. The long history, and the long future which lies outward in the direction we signal with our outstretched hands, with the courage of our thoughts.

A mischievous smile widened his lips, his eyebrows lifted and the little creases of laughter appeared at the corners of his black eyes. He fixed his hat as if ready to leave.

LETTY AND I made our way to the end of the porch and stepped down to the level of the entry walk as her husband and his friend spoke their goodbye. The two shook hands and Otto reached around and gave Fo two strong slaps on his back. Then he spoke something without elaboration which seemed reflective, and admiring of their friendship:

"I feel my life has been a protest, and yours, an affirmation."

Fo hesitated a second, and then said, "Protest *is* affirmation, isn't it?" Otto smiled.

"You'll keep in touch, won't you?" he asked.

"Oh, I don't know," Fo hesitated. "I don't want to make you an accessory."

"An accessory to history?" Otto responded. "I should count myself so lucky!... I know your teaching, Fo. Would this be what you've called the threshold of history?"

"More than a threshold, my friend," Fo's face was serious as he spoke. Only the black eyes smiled. "We're standing in the doorway to Destiny."

He seemed to be repeating a favorite line, carefully enunciated, as he clasped the shoulder of his old colleague.

"These are the times of which the prophets spoke..."

Letty stepped forward to embrace the old friend. Otto then shook my hand in a way which made me feel he had no question of my presence, and we turned to descend the concrete stairway to the street.

Just as Fo took the first steps down, Otto's voice called out to him.

"Oh, young man... You know that legend has it that whoever finds the Grail will not claim it for himself, and that whoever tries to claim it will not be able to use its power.."

Foglesby had stopped and half-turned, his face illuminated in the rose light of the setting sun, the brim of his hat cutting a shadow across the contours of his face. His dark eyes smiled.

"...But that's just the mythology of King Arthur," Otto added as his friend turned to descend the steps.

I rode with Fo and Letty back to Tombstone, where I had left my car. On the way I spoke to them about the stranger on the bridge. We said goodbye and I thanked them for the privilege of the day.

That was the second to last time I would see them together.

*   *   *

CHAPTER *SEVEN*

FREEDOM AND REMEMBRANCE.
THE INVITATION

*THE UNIVERSE 'out there' is, in reality, within you. All of nature
and history speaks in your living moment, not from without, but
from the center of your soul and being. You are the womb of reality.*
-notebook "8", red cover, p57.

EACH ERA IN the course of history blends into that which follows,
merges with it, gives birth to it as a parent to a child, inspires and imbues
it with heritage, and tints it in reminiscence with its emotion. Emotion
carries history and writes its choreography. Emotion makes its myth and
music, elicits its remembrance, the lingering fragments of its thought, and
gives it substance and meaning.

All this is commonly known and appreciated, and so I was to be struck
by their comment-I should say, by their reference to a time near to our own,
when an era of history left its successor orphaned for a rueful period until
history gathered its resources and restored itself in a new beginning.

What can happen to stop the progression of eras, one dissolving into
another; what circumstances or concatenation thereof; what shock or
cataclysm or capitulation can affect the will of a culture and a people to
build upon the strengths of their past, I am perplexed to determine still,
as I reflect on Otto's counsel to Foglesby on that sunlit afternoon of a
Spring near the millennium's turn, although I wonder now if this counsel

does not hold a clue to what may happen in the scenario which this book describes.

How much did history turn upon the wheel of freedom and remembrance which carries human experience to its heights of meaning and beauty?...

That is the question.

"For a time, it seems, the poetry almost stopped," is how one of the beings, in a low and measured voice, answered my question on that future day, alluding to the tribulation which is to follow.

How can the poetry stop except that we are not listening to it?.. The poetry *is!*

It would have to come after a loss of reason, a loss of faith, or a deception, or a loss of understanding, a forgetfulness. The living species values its survival.

How else can you explain that great numbers of the most defenseless of humanity died off, and the void of them was left to haunt the rest, whose priority was not to save them? That the earth was overwhelmed and laid waste, while the powerful fought over the last spoils?

But these are questions of this moment, about matters which are surely not fixed upon history, unlike the planets and moons, is this not so?

The drive back home that night was compressed into the intensity of the day, and seemed not to occupy time at all, although the flow of thoughts which filled my brain arrived in sequence and so were measured against the miles it took to return. The drama I had witnessed, in which a range of realities I had never imagined literally burst open in a matter of words between two individuals I had not met before that day, was to play itself constantly within my thoughts in the weeks ahead.

I had no way at all, or reason to anticipate what would transpire soon, and it seems to this moment unlikely as I myself have met, and know of many others more qualified than I to receive the experience of which I find myself writing now. I think I owe it to an event which occurred on that morning when someone I am still learning to know, whose love must have equaled mine, I can see now, passed that infinite moment which separates life from the eternity around it, and left me with a radiance, a brightness I am trying now to explain.

One is tempted to conjure symbolisms in retrospect, and move them about on a chessboard, and wonder about the dynamics which bring into play such contrasts when a good and noble thing appears, as if an

Authority were disinterested until awakened by a sensation of movement or light, whereupon it instinctively springs into action: No, this is different! I wasn't consulted. What are the rules?... The creative, and its antithetical opposite.

Fo didn't care about such things, not that he considered them trivial. There was simply no room left over in the universe of his thought for convention. The explorer happily found his way across steppingstones of the revolutionary, in which journey the different and even radical are the norm, and all expectations are set aside.

The professor of history, on the other hand, was more in touch with the forces of and by which history is made. This was his business, even as the business in theoretical physics is to look forward in space and time to where Nature hides her secrets in knowledge yet to be known.

A GENTLE intrusion upon my train of thought came out of the car speakers, inducing a sense of great tranquility and smoothing out the residue of questions from the day. The effect, like that of the day itself, was exalting and provoked a kind of gesture from which there was no turning back: Keys and locks and noble thoughts do not coexist well, someone has noted, and I had been introduced to a world 'without walls,' and then to individuals with such an expansive sense of freedom that I too was inspired with that sense.

While a concerto composed a quarter-millennium ago played at KUAT 91.7 on the car radio as I drove down the empty highway under a resplendent moon of midnight, I loosened the key ring tethered to my belt and began to strip away the keys I no longer recognized but kept by habit as if the locks they once opened were a symbolic access to valued things and places.

I heard their metallic clinks against the asphalt behind as one by one I let them fall to become embedded among the gravel on the black road. Only five remained upon the ring, which seemed the most essential because they were familiar from recent use- home, office, warehouse, mail, and the safe wherein I kept the notebooks when not reviewing them.

Although the relinquished keys weighed less than an ounce I felt lighter and freer for letting them go. Something in my life smiled at that moment, and a sense of clarity lifted and spread across my thoughts in moving photographs of the music itself, transposed into deep dimensions by messages and visions I fancied at that moment to be direct from the composer himself, sent outward across time from his creative act.

I was liberated at that moment from having too much.

In the days and weeks ahead I read voraciously, and was amazed at how answers or explanations seemed to fall into place, and how things learned were intimately connected. I referred often to an entry in the notebooks describing knowledge as a recognition- a re-cognition- as if somehow we know these things innately, and through learning they are made familiar, "of family," the family of the known, of course, which embraces us in reality.

'To learn is an act of creation, in which the universe takes form within the mind, and spirit is born...'

*   *   *

THE BRIDGE APPEARED around the bend, as it had on days through the order of seasons upon this earth as I moved back and forth from work to home and home to work. Except that now everything had changed. Even the mundane of physical things, a bridge totally unremarkable, utilitarian and ordinary, took on an aura of presence, even of *being,* which seems strange perhaps only because the mind blinks twice and declares it so.

On more than one occasion I had thought I saw from the distance as the railing came into view a form standing there suspended in the light, only to find as the branches of the cottonwoods passed across it that the perception would disappear as in one of those mirages of childhood.

Finally a day came when in the evening I thought I caught a glimpse more physical than before, and even though it did not materialize I felt an energy as I passed, and, a few days later, again, an image, then an invisible presence, almost a scintillation within the brilliant light cast by the setting sun.

I had begun to imagine that the possibility of again meeting the man on the bridge was related to my studies, and to the desire I felt for understanding to the best of my ability the new reality, though the insights themselves were sufficient payment and suggested nothing more, and I dreaded, as humans do, the thought of losing them.

At last one vivid evening the leafy branches of the great cottonwoods which obscured the bridge slid sideward like a curtain as I rounded the curve, and exposed the figure I had imagined seeing again.

He was just standing there, by the railing, relaxed and looking westward into the colors of evening, but as he noticed my arrival he turned to face me, his white teeth showing in a smile, and drew a hand from the pocket of his loose trousers. He raised it to me, rotating it once or twice in a casual wave as if this meeting had been entirely expected.

I felt my heart accelerate and I pulled to the side of the road just short of the bridge and walked over to where he stood, holding him in my view. I felt a calming, and a loss of the contingency which occupies our normal lives, as if in his presence the world was held in repose.

He reached out to grip my hand, at once laying his other hand upon my shoulder, and his grasp lasted that fraction of a second longer in which is conveyed the assurance of a special greeting.

Throughout the visit which followed I did not ask him who he was, or why I had found myself in his presence. It is curious how we lose our vanity in momentous occasions, in whose greater measure the ego happily concedes its place.

We talked, rather, of those deeper things which interest the soul, and which call our attention in uncommon passages of emotion. He listened as I freely expressed questions about mortality and existence, and he obviously understood the full context of thoughts and the mediums of experience and conditioning from which they are translated. I spoke of the loss of years with my father, and of the wonderful redemption of them, and of how I had come to believe that love in some mysterious way is the answer to everything.

He smiled, and stood against the railing looking down at the slow moving river, within that "compassionate, joyful stillness," of which Paul Davies spoke. After a time of silence brushed gently upon by waters, he thoughtfully spoke:

"You give a name to a river, and what is it?... It is everything that it is, that causes it to be, and that it causes to be. Its length and breadth unseen, to that slice of it within your view, to the ripple caused when you place your finger into its waters. Not only that part you see and feel is the river, where it appears and disappears around the bends of space and time: The river is a flowing, as real and as imaginary as is life."

He waited a moment to continue, slowly, in a low voice:

"The river is its history, flowing within the banks cut by prior flowing. The river is an expression of the sum of its past, as is everything. All of its history is written in its character, if one could read it. But something infinitely more than the events of history, it is the sum of history which flickers into existence with this moment, with this view and this thought, reborn forever in the present."

He extended his hands outward as if to frame within them not just the humble, seasonal river before him but the family of rivers to the mightiest of Earth, or, for that matter, the streams which flow invisible across space from galaxy to galaxy within the channels of time.

"Nothing is separate. All of reality flows with the river of consciousness, beyond what we see or touch or know, beyond this moment, and across time."

NIGHT HAD SETTLED over the valley and hills around, and from behind the ridge of mountains to the south the moon, lifted effortlessly into the starry sky, cast its enchanting glow like a velvet sheath upon the nightscape. A bank of clouds lay off in the distance above the ridge, its top illuminated by moonlight while flashes of lightning alternated within, too far away to hear. Curtains of light rain streamed downward in a silhouette against the backdrop of darkness on the mountain slopes, and the fresh scent of ozone drifted upon the cool atmosphere. The summer monsoons had arrived.

I thought of the unusual characterization of "magnificence" made by the visitor at the end of our first meeting, attended so auspiciously by the black cat, and how he had attributed the term to the human, saying that man's greatest failing was in not realizing this aspect of his own nature. In the grandeur of this splendid evening, as Nature put on her diffuse light show within the shadow of night, I began to sense the meaning of his declaration: *that if we could but understand our moment and our miracle we would no longer be strangers in paradise.*

When we feel magic, we hear the song that is being played for us, and we know our own magnificence as a part of that magnificence which surrounds and includes us in reality.

Before we parted I lingered for just a moment, wishing not to let go of the connection his presence implied, perhaps wanting, as all of us want, to hear an answer, some wisdom of the ages offered in a sentence.

He must have read my hesitation, as he offered this turn on words, which remains still in my brain, as I try to unfold layer by layer its meanings: "Know this thought," he said. "To know one thought is to be awakened forever."

I had turned, after the strong grip of his hand holding mine, his other hand clasping my shoulder, and taken perhaps half a dozen steps toward my car, when he called to me, smiling as he spoke.

"Would you like to know?" he asked. "To go to that place of knowledge?"

"Oh yes I would," I answered without hesitation.

"Well then..," he seemed pleased. "Meet me in the morning at daylight. A car will come to pick you up."

*   *   *

THE SLIGHTEST rustle, barely a sound, called my attention the next morning to the street outside the window of my study, opened to let in the freshness of the pre-dawn air. A short serenade of coyotes off in the distance had just ended and I was listening intently to the ensuing quiet as I sipped a cup of coffee. I had awakened an hour earlier, and prepared myself for this mysterious trip "to that place of knowledge," putting on the best of my everyday wear and giving my boots an extra polish.

I sat contemplating the prospect of such a place. What could it be?

A library, perhaps? Or a museum?... Maybe a place of great historical moment, where profound sacrifices were made by heroes of humanity for the benefit of others?

How many of these places there surely are, scattered over the hallowed Earth!

Could it be the Oracle? A circle of Magi? A mountaintop?... I thought of my life as a mango salesman, and smiled.

The recurring sound caught my attention as it carried across the cool morning air.. I recognized it as the approach of a vehicle from down near the river, sending out its signature of sound as it rounded the curves leading up to the village. Within a minute or so I could hear it slow, then turn and come to rest at the driveway, its motor silent. As I closed the door and walked towards it I could see that its interior was dimly lit and there was only the driver inside.

Only then did I notice the extraordinary appearance of the car: Its wheels were tall, perhaps four feet, and thin. The body was domed and seamless and extremely modern and it occurred to me momentarily that it was perhaps one of those new designs that Chrysler produces from time to time.

I noticed the young driver looking at me, smiling. He raised his hand in a wave just as an opening appeared in the side of the car. I heard a cheery "Good Morning!" as I stepped upon a sideboard and was lifted silently into the interior, which had a center aisle and exceedingly comfortable seats along the sides and back, and around to the front on the passenger side. The driver's seat had swung around so that he was facing me, thus integrating his own seat with those of the car. He was handsome and intelligent looking, with bright eyes and wavy brown hair and that enviable enthusiasm of youth.

"Ready, my friend?" he asked, opening his hands and offering no further explanation.

"Ready!" I answered as I sank into one of the comfortable seats. And without any noticeable sound of an engine, the van eased away from the curb and turned upon the road leading to the river and across the bridge. The driver's seat had swiveled so that he sat facing the road ahead, illuminated into the distance by the headlights. He did not seem to actively guide the car, but nonetheless watched its progress as we moved briskly forward. Behind the dark ridge of mountains back of us the first signal of dawn painted a craggy silhouette against a faint backdrop of blush. My heart began to race with excitement and a tingle rose up my spine. "What a day!" I repeated to myself.

The driver did not speak again until we had pulled up to the fence in the parking area of the airport. It had not occurred to me to bring a change of clothes! I looked quickly around but saw no plane at the terminal, and so assumed that we would be waiting for its arrival, when the opening appeared and I felt the cool morning air.

"It's been a pleasure, my friend," the pleasant voice announced, as the eyes in the rear view mirror smiled. The young man then turned and looked for a moment at my face, a deeper look than one would expect, and I noted its kindness.

"Your plane is waiting there," he spoke, pointing over into the darkness away from the lighted area of the terminal. He smiled and wished me a pleasant experience.

I stepped out and looked in the direction he had signaled and it was then that I did see the outline of an aircraft which was parked some distance from the others on the ramp. As I walked towards it I could see that it was, of all things, a rare vintage model called the DC-3, known to every air traveler some generations ago, but now seldom seen. This one was immaculately kept, its stainless steel skin emitting an almost ghostly reflection in the dim light. A ramp of some few steps swung before the open door near its tail. The three silvery blades of each of its two propellers, though dead still, seemed eerily poised for motion. A faint glow lighted the doorway as I approached, and I could make out the outline of a figure through a window of the cabin, high in the elevated nose.

I hesitated for a moment at the steps, expecting to see an attendant, but seeing no one I entered the door and glanced back at the galley, then forward the length of the cabin to see that no one else was aboard, save for the pilot I had seen sitting in the cockpit.

I stood for a moment in the doorway, and hearing no invitation to enter I then moved forward leisurely and took a seat on the plane's right side, just forward of the wing. Mixed with the freshness of the interior was a slight odor of aviation which the modern jets do not have, and it brought back pleasant memories of a youthful experience. They say that the memory of odors is the most indelible of memories, so that a singular smell can be retained across the span of a lifetime and recalled precisely as familiar when awakened by a likeness decades later.

More than once, as I sat relaxed and increasingly reflective, I caught a sense that other passengers had boarded, but looking back saw only empty seats. Perhaps it was the ghost of history that accompanied this living relic of an era past, a kind of memory by the machine itself of its human adventure.

I detected a slight motion in the cockpit, and thought I heard the movement of switches, just as two distinct sounds came from behind, which I recognized as the lifting of the low ramp and then the closing and securing of the door. Looking through one of the windows back of where I sat I saw the young man who had driven me as he stepped away from the fuselage and then walked under the wing and out some ways to the front. In the darkness I could see him look upwards to the pilot's cabin and raise his arm in a circle. I thought he looked my way and smiled, as the first whir of movement came from the right engine.

Thus was to begin the journey to that place of knowledge, though all journeys of the human really began long, long ago, at the first dawning which awakened thought.

We have always known the destination, sensed it in the residue of certainty left over from the miracle of our birth, visited it in dreams and visions and intimations, embraced it in faith through times of difficulty, and enveloped it through the ages in myth and legend, as our own true story.

*   *   *

CHAPTER EIGHT

RIVERS OF LIFE.
THE JOURNEY

Somehow, in a way and for a reason unexplainable, the apparitions of time come to life, more real than reality, expressing time as a presence.
-notebook "2", tan cover, p23.

THE STARTERS strained against the lifeless compression of the radial cylinders. The creature coughed, sputtered, then flowed with its melody, weaving the song of one engine with the other in a cadence sensually pleasing to the race who designed it a human lifetime ago.

Although the machine was aged in human years, it vibrated with a rejuvenated energy, the two noisy hearts fixed to its outer wings pumping an exhilaration of air across the blades of its whirling propellers, pulling against the ocean of invisible blood which bathes our planet and passing it across the tissues of its wings to exert lift, the two simple processes wedded into its celebration of flight.

Here in its elegant function was the form and being of man's ancient dream of escaping the bonds of gravity. In her singular expression, equal to that of the sleekest of craft which had succeeded her, there spoke true royalty, for in her humble cabin, just as proudly as in any other, sat the goddess of flight.

The old plane shuddered as the pilot revved the engines. His left arm was resting on the open side window, his head turned backward to register the movement of the wing against the dark apron below it. Then, as if unsticking itself, it began to roll against the inertia of rest, the weight of its tires pressing against the tarmac as it engaged the curve of its heavy wheels.

From where I was seated at the declined aisle just back of the cabin I could see the silhouette of the pilot against the red glow of his instrument panel with its myriad gauges and dials and switches, each known in a glance of the veteran driver. A predawn light suffused the air outside and pressed against the rounded windows of the fuselage, within which were trapped for some moments longer the reluctant shadows of night. Within minutes the sun, though not yet visible behind the dark images of the mountain ridges some miles across the Santa Cruz basin, would awaken a dream of color to rise and spread across the further horizon.

As the craft idled up the taxi way toward the runway's end, I considered the extraordinary aspect of this experience. This personage, who had first appeared on the bridge on that phenomenal occasion which saw the visit of the black feline, conveyed a genuineness which left me no doubt as to his character or motives. Strangely, I had asked no questions about this trip or its destination, and yet, although I made a conscious search for misgivings, I could find none at all. It seemed perfectly natural to be here at this moment, the only passenger in an aged aircraft piloted by a mysterious stranger to an unknown destination.

THE ENGINES loped with the sound of their idling gait as we moved steadily on in the predawn light. The red lights on the wingtips flashed back and forth, alternately casting a glow upon the black asphalt moving backward beneath the wings. A slight rumble issued from the rolling gear beneath my seat, and the lesser tail wheel rattled steadily from behind.

The sensations relating to this vintage machine came forward in just that moment, as if time had regressed and the figure up front shimmered out of a kind of mythological drama from scenes of yesteryear, as though he were piloting every flight this craft and her myriad sisters had ever flown, invisibly accompanying every crew who had flown them the world over, through peacetime and the tumultuous times of war, in which these old machines had given so much of themselves, taking their men and women to their destinations at the ends of Earth, and when they did not return, carrying their spirits away into destiny, borne by the enigmatic bond between them.

I felt the brakes engage as the plane reached the end of the taxi way and turned to position itself for "run-up," before committing for takeoff. Holding his brakes, the pilot revved up one engine, and then the other, checking his instruments for the normal readings which indicated the readiness of fuel and electrical and other systems. He rotated his yoke to test the controls, then spoke some words into the microphone as he eased the plane up onto the take-off ramp. Without fully stopping, he pushed the two throttles forward and the engines roared powerfully as the thrust of three-thousand horsepower bit the propellers into the still dawn air, pulling the heavy machine into its own wind which shortly lifted the tail and cabin horizontally as the vehicle gathered speed for flight.

More and more with increased velocity the air beneath the wings lifted upward against the bottom surfaces, until the rolling tires began to skip and float upon the pavement, carrying a diminishing weight until the last ounce had taken flight and the old machine was airborne once again, in a voyage unlike- perhaps unlike- any she had ever made before.

As the nose lifted in a climb, I studied the pilot, who was engrossed in his work at this critical stage of flight, even though he seemed totally relaxed. His head would move, over and to his right, as he calmly reviewed his instruments. His ear was tuned to the precise vibrations of the craft and her engines, his senses to the subtle whistles of the wind. It was, for him, like a symphony conducted by history in which the musicians were each and every soul whose life had been touched by the concepts and shapes and services of this instrument of flight.

His right hand, remaining over the two throttles since takeoff, now pulled gently back to ease the stress of initial climbout. Simultaneously, the engines lowered their whine into a smoother intertwining tone as the nose dropped some degrees to adjust the angle of climb to the power output of the motors. The balance would assure a steady ascent until the level of flight was achieved.

A shiver of excitement interrupted my attentiveness to the process of this unusual flight as I recalled the only other time I had flown in a DC-3. It was while crossing the Yucatan Peninsula on the way to British Honduras on a day which happened to be my nineteenth birthday. I smiled to recall that I was the only passenger who boarded that flight as well, and that I had sat in about the same place in the cabin on that youthful adventure, as we droned over the green jungle studded here and there with small villages and with the grey stone relics of structures abandoned by a civilization a thousand or more years ago, when the reasons for their being no longer served, or resources depleted.

For a moment in my memory that world of the young first-time traveler seemed within the touch of a finger, although some forty years had passed, and worlds unimaginable in that time had turned over. The first visit to the tropics by a young person is an immersion into a world of the senses, where the romantic pulses of first things saturate the brain and, years later, imbue recovered memories with a freshness of sights and sounds and smells, and renew a thrill of discovery.

The subtle whisper of the sea breeze, whooshing through palm fronds behind which emerges a refulgent moon; the smell of the sea, captured into memory for the first time; the lilt of strange music and languages unheard before; that look into the eyes of fellow humans in which the great, long lineages of different cultures finally converge in a recognition between souls of the same family.

There is a saying that once a young person visits the tropics, that person never fully leaves. It is true in general, of course, in that we carry our experiences with us through life, especially those first fusings of them with our unfolding identity. In my own case, the adventure of those weeks has remained as a point of reference throughout the decades since, of a place elevated and romanticized in a pleasant mix of memory and forgetfulness.

Even now, I mused, whenever I enter the cool warehouse with its store of fresh mangoes, the smell of them awakens a sensual bouquet of imageries drawn from that first experience, inducing pleasure in the brain. The earthy, crisp freshness of the jicama is reminiscent of the tropic soil, and the citrus is redolent with the vision of a low valley awakened by the sun from its misty bed, and attended to by the hum of a million winged creatures sipping from the blossoms.

Perhaps it is that connection, a kind of bridge over from youthful impressions of the tropics, which drew me some decades later into the line of work which returns me to some aspect of the tropic world, as its products are unloaded at my door, ripe with their sensual essence.

In any case, the astounding events of the last weeks and months, as if upon a great axis, had turned me toward a new calling which I did not yet comprehend, but which I was sure would take me from my carved niche in the busy, two-dimensional world which had occupied my life.

MY TRAIN of thoughts was intruded upon by an awakening sense of the present moment as I became aware that the plane had leveled off high above the white pillows of clouds lighted by the morning sun. A shaft of sunlight twirled in lazy spirals through the rounded window beside me, and across the narrow cabin, where it began to creep up the sidewall in a steady movement which told me that the plane was banking gently to its right, perhaps pointed by its pilot into the direction of our destination. What this might be, and the time of our arrival seemed matters of little concern, as the steady, interweaving drone of the two engines, and the low vibrations passed by them into the metal fuselage lulled me gently into a pleasant drowsiness.

I caught the view of the mysterious pilot, his upright form illuminated by the morning sun, his wavy hair glistening, a relaxed hand placed upon the yoke, as he looked forward into the open and unending sky.

I thought I heard the hum of a voice, a song different from that of the machine itself, whose low, rich tones rose free and joyous from the creations of man- and to the dreamy sense of this superb melody my eyelids grew heavier as I sank into a quiet sleep.

*　　*　　*

WHAT FOLLOWS NOW is an attempt to portray in ordinary words the experience of another reality.

How much time may have elapsed in my deep and peaceful slumber, I have no way of knowing, for time is measured into intervals which call our notice- hours divided into minutes and divided again, down to their discreet limits and beyond, depending upon what it is we are waiting for, or what it is that absorbs us and stills the rocking pendulum within. An afternoon spent in an esteemed lover's embrace flies as the moment, and the moment passed in tense expectation crawls interminably. And by this simple, arbitrary calendar of time, we measure and predict our lives, and lament, or celebrate their passing.

Since the dawn of self-knowing, time has been the wingsmen at our shoulders, inexorably marking our passage through this mortal experience, through moments which come once in a lifetime, and days which will never come again, and events infinitely unique and exceptional.

And so it is natural and befitting that knowledge, so as not to be naked and alone, is enveloped in spirit and in her robes enjoys the timelessness of truth and meaning. What it is we knew in this life is thus forever known, what we felt and loved, sent undiminished to precede us through time, and to meet us with open and welcoming arms, in destiny.

My first recollections of awakening are of a sense of gravity, as in a turning, or decelerating. A light suffused my waking sleep and filled me with a sense of warmth and well-being. It was almost as if I were being carried by the light, as a child, bundled and secure in the whitest of soft blankets, is carried by its mother.

I thought I had opened my eyes, but could see only this perfusion of glorious light, filling and supplanting space within and without. I felt it inside me, as an energy, imbuing and awakening my body, cell by cell, and organ by organ, as in a re-creation in whose process all things remembered were gilded in understanding and in a supreme meaning.

I remember thinking that if this was death, then it was not sad, but pure and joyful beyond measure. I recognized in a new language that the essence of this glorious and transparent light was love, but a love infinitely greater than human understanding had painted with its finite colors. I saw that the portrait of love was done by a divine hand, but upon the priceless parchment of mortality, and that it had to be that way, so that the immortal could remember, and remain human.

The luminescence slowly took form, as I tried to see what it was that enveloped me. Because the human looks for shapes and forms to distinguish his surroundings, translating out of pure energies the inner creation of sight and recognition, it was this resolution I sought in a manner most natural to my experience. I thought I could finally make out some dimensions, through some differences within the bathing light, as if looking into the bright mist of a cloud and seeing some faint shadow, or subtle difference in density through the faintest appearance of a color.

The light-filled space seemed to curve upwards, and perhaps around, as I thought I could distinguish formations within it. And when I looked forward I saw a gathering of light which, as I focused on it, took a shape that was nearly distinguishable, which in scintillations of energy varying from the light-space around resolved itself into an image seated in the midst of the revolving light, as if central to, or guiding the radiant manifestations around and within.

The radiance of this shimmering image projected an ineffable sense of quietness, and of a seemingly eternal power, held entirely in restraint by the benevolence of love, and oneness with all creation. Although I had no way of comprehending how, I knew it to be the pilot, whom I last saw in his mortal form, seated in the deck of the old craft as he guided her flight, singing his song to the victorious cadence of the motors, and looking forward into the distance of space and time, as I drifted away into the depths of sleep.

Again, I felt the nudge of weight upon my body, of a changing inertia which appeared as a sensation of heaviness below me. The drone of the noisy engines was gone, though for the first time I noted another sound, barely sensed, of a whirring, or a whisper, steady and low, coming from within this chamber of moving light which turned and moved as if within a guidance which held me, also, under its benign control, as streams of incandescence spiraled outward like the pinwheel of a distant galaxy held centered within a timeless portrait of its own gravity.

I felt a sense of dropping through space, of passing through a distance, as if I, still held within it, were receding from its center, being pressed by gentle, rhythmic contractions of light, as in the imaginings of birth.

All movements ceased, and all sensations were suspended in a weightless energy in which the mind itself floated free of space or time, traversing the eons between atoms in a vacuum which held in its shimmering nothingness the wombs of infinite universes to be born, and the innate memory of all those who were.

As I continued my gentle descent I felt a weight pushing against my back, and beneath my legs and arms, and began to notice the sweetest fragrances, which evoked remembrances of a high forest, of damp earth, and lush, green grass, and dewy clover in bloom. There was the distinct scent of pine, which elevates the mood and opens awareness, and the intricate music of water rippling and gurgling through a streambed, and the bracing sense of cool shade hanging within the still air.

What at first seemed like a sparkling sensation within the brain, a residual energy from the brilliance of the swirling light which had lowered me from its midst, became apparent as I adjusted my eyes to its patterns as that exceedingly lovely and spectacular behavior of sunlight as it streams through openings in a forest canopy, sending shafts of light in straight wedges to bathe and saturate in photons a spot laid out as the photograph revealed by those photons interrupted in time and their flight from our mother star. For a moving moment in this ethereal reality the living details of nature shimmered in their intricate glory, infused by the energy of creation from that first day, without which there would be no animation, and no witness through the lenses of sight to the magical essence rendered by the mirrored chambers of thought into a beauty which cannot know itself, but must be known.

A slender green leaf, glistening with its gems of beaded dew and their myriad kin set out upon a carpet of cool fragrance recalled in an ancient memory inherited by each generation's child; a bed of flowers singing their colors in an answer to a distant star wherever there is a rapt audience of even one; the tall and stately pines whose growth-launched flight streams upward atop their solid plumes adorned by outstretched arms whose fingers hold great long-needled clusters of green nurseries whose birthing cells are instructed by light... A world seen in the miraculous.

I raised myself, braced by my elbows, and looked around to one side, from where I heard a sound. A deer who had been grazing on clover not a dozen feet away raised her head suddenly in response to my movement, ceased her chewing, and looked directly at me without the slightest alarm. Her twin fawn sensed their mother's alertness and stood perfectly still, awaiting a signal from her to flee. The doe hesitated, then flicked her white tail and resumed her grazing as the fawn romped in a circle of play, their dappled coats, designed by nature to hide them, serving to enhance the notice of the human who observed them as the beautiful and endearing children of a kindred species. Birds flitted overhead, their browns and blues and bright reds silhouetting them against the green cast of the foliage, the taller of it thinly veiled in a light mist or fog which lent an ethereal loveliness to this enchanting glade.

My senses awoke at once with an energy and a thrill, and I sat upright, and then sprang to my feet as if I were a child of ten. The nature of my arrival at this place could not be understood, although I quickly reviewed the clear recollections of the first of the journey and the events which preceded it and found an accordance with my being here, through the strange and wondrous intercession of the lighted presence whose immortal grandness seemed folded within nature herself in an eternal union, although I could not fathom how.

Without forethought I began to walk across the lush bed of grass and clover toward the familiar sound of water, so written in the lexicon of human memory that its voices are inseparable from the blood which flows and swishes through our veins in the internal coursing of life itself, the greatest part of it being the identical substance which covers the earth in liquid seas, and lays for ages within its crust. Streams and rivers to the land-bound soul are pathways which lead somewhere to a place, to a heart, and so we may safely follow them, as have our ancestors throughout time, and draw nourishment from their familiar source.

As I stepped over a grassy hillock and down the slope beyond, the rippling, flowing sound grew more distinct and the air took on a humidity, and the fresh smell caught by the senses heightened in this natural place, even as the brisk stream appeared from within its low banks just yards away from the grove of white birch through which I had crossed. I stood for a moment in pure enjoyment as I recalled similar streams from days of my childhood, high in the New Mexico wilderness to where our parents would take us for weekends of camping in those fleeting summers when we were all together.

I approached the stream and knelt upon a large, flat stone which extended from the bank down into the streambed. 1 leaned forward, hands placed upon the rock, and put my face against the surface of the cold, crystal waters, to feel the tingling vibrations of their flowing. And then I drank, deeply and enjoyably, from the pure liquid, drawing the stream into me until I was full.

Along the stream banks just down from where I began to wander leisurely, patches of yellow, white, and blue flowers spread themselves over the gentle slopes which led to the water's edges on both sides of the vigorous stream, roughly corresponding to the sunlight which fell brightly upon them in splashes, and across the water, rendering it almost wholly transparent beneath the refraction of its rippling surface. Near the water, where the grassy slopes steepened into banks, varieties of fern abounded, cascading in feathery shades of green and yielding from themselves a moist, almost womanly fragrance which was lovely, and fully delightful. Tiny, exquisite flowers which first appeared as minute points of color revealed themselves upon examination to be complete miniature specimen, with the daintiest of petals circling their sweet centers to allure and attract the notice of equally tiny insects in whose incidence of feeding nature arranged the intimate coincidence of seduction.

As I continued my unhurried descent from the high, alpine meadow which first caught me upon its breast, I simply made my way along the winding stream, choosing the path arranged by time in a compromise of infinitesimal degrees as the flowing waters responded to irrepressible undulations of the mountain massif over eons of time. Sometimes a grassy flat stretched out along the stream, over which I stepped easily, and at times the water cut through ridges between steep banks, which left little room for passage other than within the stream itself, and so I would spring from stone to stone as I could, until an accommodating space appeared along the bank.

At one point I noticed a faint trail, more of a shadow pressed into the grassy floor, which appeared upon a slope just adjacent to where I was making my way. It dipped down for some meters as it followed the easiest path over the terrain, just as did the flowing stream upon the path it had made. Then the trail veered back up the slope, and out of sight in the vegetation.

And so I began to follow this borrowed pathway, though I could not tell by what footsteps it had been marked, whether animal or human, or both, though it did not seem to matter, as its use could be recognized by either. In any case, the path is shared, and one cannot walk upon it without being accompanied by those who left, or will leave, in their passing, the shadow of their footsteps, and some essence about themselves and the places between which they made their way.

The trail led generally along the course of the flowing stream, descending as the running waters did, though with the freedom to turn and climb where a slope presented a more direct, though inclined route which led to a smoother way beyond. The descent was perceptible, from the ease of walking, of course, but also from the changes in flora which appear at descending altitudes: the forests of immensely tall pine thinning and giving way to deciduous growth- birch, a variety of large oak, sycamore, and communities of trees whose species I did not recognize, within whose foliage flitted and sang birds of every description and color.

The trail grew more distinct as it descended from the highland, following the natural contour of least resistance- along this ridge, over this hill, sometimes continuing along the bank of the stream, which like the trail itself had become increased from the confluence of other streams and rivulets which drained the adjacent watersheds, and now flowed more sedately so as to almost be called a river.

Here and there, as well, faint lesser trails had converged with the pathway I was walking, in a kind of ghostly confluence whose evidence could be seen in a greater wear upon the pathway. And so I made my way along, guided within this vibrant setting and lightened by the vivid energies which scintillated upon the landscape and its lifeforms, and resonated from the space here about, and from the infinite days before this one, which, added one by one, in nature's subtlest confluences, to the flow of time and the imprint of experience which, like the swelling stream and the deepening pathway, compose a flowing, visible and invisible, across the landscape of history.

After a gentle ascent up a shaded slope, and across a streamlet fed by springs bubbling from within an outcropping of sandstone, the trail led onto a sunlit plateau which flooded the eye with a regaling abundance of flowers such as I had not seen before, laid out before the view as if in overlapping waves of colors, reminiscent of the Texas hill country. I stopped suddenly in delightful surprise at the visual feast. Legions of golden flowers spread outward into a sea from which islands of bright purple and blue rose up and merged with peninsulas of red and pink. Patches of violet floated here and there upon the sea of gold- color, floating like sailing ships upon color in the splendid leitmotif of brightness.

Off in the distance where the surface of brilliance met the horizon, a coronet of white clouds lay luminescent upon the brow of color, as if painted in by the finishing brushstrokes of genius upon perfection.

I felt pangs of yearning, as I had often along this lovely pilgrimage on an exquisite day, inexpressible except in the names of those I loved, uttered in exclamations of the heart by one to whom the only greater meaning would come if they could also know these moments, if even in my place, to magnify them in the knowledge of another.

After I stood for some undeterminable time, drawn into captivity by the living marvel spread out before me, I bounded forward into the flowery sea, realizing as I did that the trail had diffused itself in the diverging footsteps of those who, before me, had obeyed the impulse of freedom which the beauty inspired to wander afield in its midst, against the conventions of a marked passage. I stepped through the exuberant sea of colors with a delight, innocent and spontaneous, and a sense of lightness as if I were equipped with wings to alight upon and circle within the bright corolla of beauty, and touch, with intimate feeding, my tongue within the sweetness of its heart.

Oblivious to the distance I had traversed or to the time convened in my spirited passage, I found myself upon the rim of the plateau upon whose horizon had sat the billowy clouds across the florid sea. As I approached the vantaged edge, a view rose into sight in a breathtaking panorama, in the sweep of distance and an awesome explanation, to tell me where I was, and what had lain beyond the preternatural mystery of my journey from the humble bridge of my homeland.

Far below, cutting through the greenness and winding around the descending hills and tumbling down the steep slopes in a frothy silence which sent upward rainbows of mist, the river from whose childhood I had drunk my fill reached at last a broad valley through which its silvery ribbon stretched in languid curves and bends into the distance beyond my view. I could make out along the river's banks patches of square and rectangular shape, uncommon to nature, which indicated small farms and settlements sustained by the water's source. And farther, where the horizon met the sky, the billowy clouds which I had seen set upon the horizon of flowers lay over the blue, blue distance of the sea.

I sank down upon the bed of color, sitting with my arms wrapped around my knees, and gazed out upon this ethereal world of loveliness, marveling at the sense that this vision and I were somehow one, that I was not separated from the beauty, but that we were the same passion, mirrored in one another. I had never in my life experienced such an overwhelming sense of belonging.

As I rested in the stillness of reflection, out of the long ago in faint resonances welling up within the depths of memory and growing clearer as I listened to them, the sounds of voices in a distant singing drifted across time and brought with them a vivid moment of my childhood, long buried in the clutter of busy things. I am seated on a wooden bench in the company of my family: my mother and father, and beside them in a line, the five of their children.

It is in that little country church made over from a house whose interior walls were removed to make room for the sanctuary. My father would come early on winter mornings to rouse the fire in a gas stove set in the corner, and dust the pews and window sills. He also served as deacon, and when Sabbath School was finally dismissed and the church service began, he would sit up front and generally assist the minister in his duties, sometimes saying a prayer, and often leading the singing in his fine, tenor voice.

And because the pastor served more than one of the small rural congregations and was not always present in his rounds, my father would sometimes fill in and offer the "study", movingly rendered, which often dwelt on goodness, and the uncertainties of life, and the soon-coming of the Lord and Creator to redeem his own. I remember seriously doubting that I would reach the age of my older brother, who was sixteen, before the end came and the world was swept away. And because we were all poised in those years upon that wielded and unsteady knife edge of the Cold War, it must have seemed to our parents that the Lord had better time his coming well, if any of us were to be rescued.

That he would was held sure to them in the faith they kept sustained through all those years.

The old, worn hymnals are open.

I am sitting next to my mother, and we are sharing ours, as people did, even though the words were known by heart. Her slender fingers press the page, to keep it from turning. My smaller hand is placed below the faded green cover, touching hers. The voices around and back of us merge with our own in the melody of words we children could not have understood because we had not yet felt the pain of loss that deepens the well of emotions, the well of memories.

I can see and feel my mother's green-plaid wool coat, and smell her clean, motherly scent, and sense the emotion in her voice. I can hear the harmony of my young father's clear voice, earnestly speaking the sentiments of the old hymn written near the close of the Civil War and handed down in childhood through generations laid to rest until this moment when its profound essence is reawakened in living voices undiminished by the passage of time, because it is so written, also, within the soul of human life.

Below, spread out in wistful loveliness, as I sit upon the bed of living color and clutch its fragrance in my hands, is the vision of an aspired creation, of a world whose perfection is measured against the heroic sacrifices of mortal existence, filtered and purified through passages enabled and engrandeured by unselfish love, in an uncommon and imperfect record.

Perfection is not born in any world, but grows into being in a wisdom of meaning and sympathy and reprieve, etched forever into beauty by the memories of loss.

The gentle river, far below, winds placid through the ancient arrangement of its waterway with the valley floor, and upon its banks reside, in little compounds carved into geometric messages, in lives of emotion, neighbors and friends and families, bonded within the unique music of life.

This river, cascading through the rapids of its mid-life in mist and spray, into whose sweet, pure waters of childhood I put my face, and drank of its cool fountain, smoothes out in maturity seen from my privileged view into a tranquil flowing narrowing to a thread in the distance where it meets the sea.

Man has always been drawn to the rivers, flowing as they do within his veins in the internal coursing of life itself. They are symbols in their eternal moving of his wish for a never-ending of what it was he knew and loved- a wish more for that than for himself.

The voices echo in their song, in a ghostly recording etched by vibrations into walls of a building that is no more, into a place once dedicated as a sanctuary of spirit, which is not a place, therefore, but a moving presence flowing across time beyond the poignant boundaries of mortality. Its music, in a timeless longing, reawakens into thought and emotion as a resurrection whose lovely sentiment grips and consoles the heart.

The childhood, just back aways, into which we plunged our face and from which we drank, flows still within the memory's view, and maturity's turbulence sends up its quiet mist from the distance below. And off toward the horizon, down the peaceful valley's length, winds the silver ribbon which narrows to a thread where the river meets the sea.

> *"Where the charming roses bloom forever,*
> *And where separations come no more,*
> *If we never meet again this side of Heaven,*
> *I will meet you on that beautiful shore.."*

*   *   *

CHAPTER NINE

TO A MEETING WITH FRIENDS. THE WAY OF STONE

The future is born out of intuition, and inhabits it.
-notebook "3", blue cover, p7.

THOUGHT is recognized by thought, and emotion by emotion, from age to age, In this is immortality.
-small brown notebook "32", p57.

SOMEWHERE, they say, within the circumference of directions which surrounds us, is the way in which we will travel, the way which points out our destiny. And it may be shown to us unexpectedly and in a surprising form, or it may draw us subtly, in steps mostly unnoticed. And it may be in opposition to the way we have envisioned for ourselves, or to the way into which we have simply fallen in the pattern of habits and acquiescence in our lives. However it may be, and whatever leads up to that moment of direction, there must be a point at which we choose to embrace the greater vision of life and our role in it. To answer the bolder voices of our inner nature.

These thoughts occupied my mind as I descended from the high plateau of flowers on the recovered trail which had deepened with use and broadened into a walkway, splitting at times into lesser trails, then converging at some place beyond. At various places, though I did not count them, the trail presented itself upon a promontory, silently recording, as it did so, by their footmarks, the presence of the many others who must also have exclaimed at the sheer panorama before them, noting with each ensuing view the approach of the valley and its detail, drawn nearer and lifted by the passing steps in closer revelations of its charm. Perhaps they also would feel a long sigh emerge from their chests, and a joy beyond expression flow into, and fill the place from where it came.

I felt an anticipation, and a longing to walk forward into that distant valley and to know what it had in store for me. Before I knew it I was bounding down the pathway, stirring the morning air into coolness by my fleeting passage. I walked at last along a hillside parallel to the river which had stretched forward in a silvery band when seen from the heights behind me. Breathless from its vigorous descent, it now lay smooth within its flowing bed, only occasionally rippling over and around rocks washed clean and polished within its clear shallows. As I stopped to listen, only a faint rustle could be heard across the hundred or so meters from where I stood. Below the wavelength of human hearing I could imagine the lower frequencies of the river's voice, felt within the ground at my feet and through the skin in an ancient resonance within the flowing blood which swishes through our veins in the internal coursing of life itself.

There is something calming and familiar about the river's flow, reminding us, as it does, of our elemental kinship through nature's design, which connects its inner distances in time and space with a flowing through whose light and musical voices one part knows another in a cosmic unity.

In those moments of deep attention through which I was listening, more than anything, to the quietness between my busy thoughts which in themselves, like the river, had arrived breathless to this languorous place, I had not noticed through the branches of a tree just below and to the right of where I stood the arching lines of a little bridge- not wide enough for most vehicles, more like a footbridge, I thought- which crossed over the river at a slight narrowing of its banks. Stepping only a few paces further, clear of the tree's foliage, I was most surprised to see people gathered near an orchard's edge, not far from where the bridge rested upon the far bank.

There appeared to be a table before them with baskets upon it, and they were engaged in some activity, four adults seated about the table, and three standing, of whom two were men. The women wore hats or bonnets, except for one, and those I could see were clothed in long dresses, brightly colored.

There were children at play nearby, who were tended by two older children as they ran in circles amid squeals of delight. I could almost hear the adults as they talked together, and I did hear ripplings of laughter which lifted across the still morning air.

Suddenly one of the children spotted me, a little girl with a white hat who raised her arm and pointed in my direction, turning her head toward the women seated at the table. Their heads turned, and they just looked for a moment, as did the others, toward the stranger who stood upon the trail's edge, beside the crown of the tree. Then they began to wave, and the women at the table stood up and turned towards me, one walking forward a step or two, as they all waved, some with arms held high as their hands moved back and forth in arcs, in the manner of someone welcoming a dear friend or relative after a long absence.

I suddenly felt their joy and familiarity, and I began to wave back as if this were a homecoming, my hand raised high and moving vigorously in a salute.

Two of the children, a little boy and girl, suddenly dashed out from the others, the little girl's bonnet flying back, suspended by the string as it bounded against her back, the little boy racing just ahead as they neared the footbridge. Suddenly he stopped and raced back over to the women near the table, retrieving something handed him by one of them. Then he returned to where the girl had stopped, and they both hurried across the bridge and began to climb the gentle slope which raised itself to where the trail crossed horizontal to the river.

As she pranced along, the little girl stopped and bent down, reaching her hand among some flowers which bloomed in bouquets of variegated colors upon the grassy slope. She pulled at them, and her hand emerged holding a little bundle of color to which she added in a couple more pauses in her approach. Her companion stopped with her, and watched as she selected the kinds and colors which added to her bouquet. Then they approached to where I stood, the both of them smiling happily. I'm sure I said hello, but don't remember what they answered back.

The boy, having stopped a few feet short of where I was, then came forward and handed me a little straw basket in which there were a beautiful fresh peach and a large blue plum, placed within a white cloth, for which I complemented, and thanked him profusely. The little girl moved forward lightly, and with a manner full of grace, and a smile which was the memory of my own daughter, held out to me her gift of lovely flowers. As she did she smiled brightly, and then stepped slightly back and bowed, making a curtsy. She smiled again, looking at my face, and then reached back to fix her hat over her golden hair, as they both prepared to return.

Once more they nodded to me in a happy recognition, and as they turned to go, I said, Thank You, and Goodbye.

"Hello," they answered, faces glowing, and then they skipped away across the grass and flower bouquets, racing across the little bridge to where the others waited.

I was delighted at the gestures these people offered me, and at the dear, lightfooted children who had come with their simple and true gifts of refreshment. And yet somehow I knew, as did they, that I was passing by on my way to another place. I reflected after they had disappeared from view behind me that I had not seen a trail veer off to meet the landing of the bridge, but did not consider it further.

I TASTED first the peach, as I continued along, having squeezed it carefully into halves along the septum of its flesh, and watched as its nectar beaded up in little domes upon the shiny surfaces of its wound. It was cool and sweet, and rich with a flavor really tasted, I felt, for the first time in my experience.

When I was finished with the peach, while still maintaining my pace, I placed the ripe, full plum within my lips and bit into its sweetness, sucking away the savory juices and noting its subtle array of flavors, perhaps more sugary than the peach, for which I would consider it a dessert of my delightful repast.

In partaking of this fruit, commonly tasted before in my experience, I entered a dreamlike quality beyond taste and the visual sense, encompassing a greater reality which in our busy lives we delay to discover, if at all. By eating the fruit the children brought me- beyond the sensual taste and nourishment- I was at last eating all before, recalling every sense from years of my life, out of history and prehistory, to consume the fullness of reality from the first eye of matter awakened into life, and the first thought awakened into mind, to see, and then to watch itself in sight, the taste sense of the first responded forward in a touch upon the last, to taste itself eternally. This is the only way to explain such transcendent things in common language, though we can see from the closing vision that the transcendent was around us everywhere, the most in simple things.

I was thankful to Mother Nature for providing her delicious fruit, and for the nutrition it offered as well, and for the memorable pleasure of the feast. And for the delightful children and their folk, from whose offering of the fruit and flowers I rather considered this experience a sacrament, to be distinguished amid the exquisite unfolding of this supernal day.

As I strolled upon the path, climbing the second rise from where the children had bade me their sweet hello as they departed, and caught within a joyful reflection, I had not noticed the two heads rise into view with my advancing steps. And just seconds later they appeared as a couple, sitting upon a stone bench just down past the crest of the hill which had brought into view, for the first time since I sat upon the high plateau and viewed it in the distance, the majestic image of the ocean, lying still some distance ahead, beyond the green hills through which, in lazy, artful bends, the tranquil river moved.

I observed the couple in a glance before they noticed my approach. They sat turned toward one another, their knees almost touching, and they were visiting quietly and intently in the manner, one imagines, of people who are in love. A kind of aura surrounds such people- and they are famous for it- which is enchanting to others, old and young, because they remember, and because they dream of, in the happiness revealed in others, the magic of their own.

THE SOUND of my footsteps caught their notice, and their heads turned to me, the young man leaning forward to see me, as he took his friend's hand, and rose to stand. It was apparent that they had been waiting for me, though I did not know why, or for what occasion. For just a moment I felt that I knew them, or had seen them before.

They both seemed happy to see me, smiling and stepping down upon the trail to await my approach. The young woman was exquisitely beautiful, with lovely ebony skin, black hair, and dark smiling eyes. She was dressed in an airy purple dress with small, white markings, a narrow, rose-colored cloth belt around her waist, and low-heeled sandals which matched her belt.

The young man was sandy-haired and tall, and stood with his arm around the girl's shoulder, his face set in a relaxed smile, his eyes sparkling. As he stepped forward to greet me he reached out his hand and clasped mine vigorously, saying, "We're glad you came. It's very good to see you here."

He said his name was Boris, and had begun to introduce his friend, when she extended both her arms and caught my wrists, squeezing them, and saying, "It's wonderful to finally meet you! How was your journey?"

I hesitated for a moment and then answered, "Well, phenomenal.., and marvelous! Thank you."

"Marvelous," she repeated, looking up at her companion, who smiled an affirmation. "Yes... And, by the way, my name is Monami." And then she reached her hand out and placed a palm over my forehead, holding it there lightly for a moment in what seemed, to me, an intimate gesture.

"Hello," I responded, and introduced myself, to which they nodded, and smiled.

"Yes," the girl confirmed with a delightful smile. "We know your name."

"We've come to take you to meet some friends of yours." Boris answered the question in my mind. "Are you ready to walk a ways further?"

"Sure, certainly," I assured them, noting just then that I felt no wear at all for the long hike down from the mountain meadow. I felt rested and energetic, my legs strong, feet cool and comfortable within the boots I had pulled on before the dawn of that morning, as if I had not walked at all. Neither did my hosts inquire directly about my comfort.

I thought of that old verse, now indistinct through unstudied years, something about, "They shall walk, and not be weary.."- or maybe it was, "work, and not be weary"... In either case, the clearness and vitality of this day and its sheer, unencumbered joy were senses long in the waiting.

Often in my life I had recalled an occasion of my youth, when I was perhaps fourteen or so, which happened while we still lived on the farm: My father and I were on the tractor at the far west fence line of the home place, a full mile from the house. The John Deere tractor stalled, and it must have been that we ran out of fuel, as John Deeres of that day were very unlikely to suffer mechanical failure.

I offered to run the mile down the listed rows to retrieve what it was we lacked, and my father thanked me. It seemed a fuse had been lit, and I simply glided down the long row, hearing the steady thumping of my feet through the sod, as if it were someone else's, and not my own, as the energy rushed to my legs, pushing them even faster in an effortless pace.

I recovered what it was my father needed, drank water from the well pipe, and proceeded to run back up the mile rows to where Dad waited. I remember that he was smiling, and how he complimented me on my phenomenal dispatch. It was a personal moment with this man who was so central to my existence, and I have retained it in clearest detail throughout the years, for the sheer, unencumbered joy of that day.

Such days of joy are kept and guarded in memory, encouraging and persistently reminding us that in them is life's true meaning and grace.

1 am hearing again the soft rhythm of my footsteps, and I see the easy steps of my new friends on either side. I feel strangely and totally secure in this moment, that everything is as it should be, and so I let time pass by in my enjoyment, without questioning or speaking. It seemed natural to me to be with two friends in this circumstance, walking along, immersed in the perfection of the day, like swimmers in an ocean of reality which bathed and sustained us in an ancient presence, of which we were simply a part.

I hear the song of a mockingbird, its lilting melody wafted upon the waves of memory from another time, when sons ran blithely from their fathers, and blithely returned, to reap the smile's reward.

As the pure modulations of the lone birdsong echo within the deep stillness of my reflection, in unique notes heard never the same twice in any world because each hearing comes imbued with the experience before it, and produces within the brain in ever grander scales of appreciation the mind-perched soloist within a symphony of memories and their emotions, no creature thus sings alone, whose song is heard and listened to.

As the melody faded within the silence of my thoughts, another appeared, lovely and pure as well, which floated out of the stillness in tones of the human, to a joyful pulsing rhythm of life. The girl beside me was humming as we walked, shaping in her light breaths a soft music to which I thrilled, for its vibrant happiness and freedom, and for the excellence and beauty of the spirit which formed it.

It seems we conversed little during the time of our walk together to where, I was told, friends waited. The passage was more like a communion among souls, and I was satisfied with what was revealed wordlessly in a magical and expanding reality. We strolled across and over the hills above the sparkling river, through islands of sunlight, and through the drifting, amphibious shadows of billowy-white clouds freighting their loads of mist inland from the wide sea.

Beyond a turn, around the gentle contour of the last hill, a valley suddenly appeared, framed within a magnificent enfilade. Great aged and arching trees with massive boughs suspended by the sky reached out to create below their canopies of foliage acres of shade into whose cool doorway disappeared the trail before us.

Off to one side wild animals grazed upon the green meadow above which a flock of seagulls circled in lively pirouettes amid the white flashes of their wings. The river in whose company I had descended from the forested heights came once more into view around its final bend, from where it entered the valley's plain, and slipped leisurely across the grassy distance to its quiet reunion within the blue sea's embrace.

*   *   *

WE HAD JUST entered the cool fragrance of shadows beneath the great trees when the path widened into a lovely lane which had been paved long, long ago, it would seem, from the wear upon the surfaces of the large, flat stones, some of which were two or more meters in size and completely solid to the step, as if they were of considerable thickness. As we walked I noted in the shaded light that these stones were not laid approximately and then filled in with smaller stones and wide mortar joints, as may be the style with common flagstone. It was more as if they had been hewn before laying, to join with their neighboring stones with an extraordinary precision which did not require the use of mortar.

Along the lane on both sides were what I first thought to be curbstones, extending upward and then out about a meter, but on closer inspection I saw that these were not curbstones, but hewn extensions of the paver stones, which had been cut to curve upward and over, and that these had been mortised to join with a tenon in the adjoining stone, with stupendous precision. I began to realize the strength and mass of this structure when we came upon one of the enormous trees whose trunk had spread outward with time until it intruded upon the curbing of the lane, whereupon its great circumference merely spread over the curb to the base of the roadway.

Though it had exerted upon the stone, at the rate of a centimeter a year, the relentless force of a bulldozer, the stone was unheaved, and lay still perfectly true under the compliant girth of the wooden giant.

Just as I was about to comment upon the extraordinarily sculptured structure upon which we strolled, Monami touched my arm and said, "I believe these are your friends, coming to meet us."

Off in the distance ahead, obscured somewhat in the shadows and filtered light, were two figures approaching side by side. I could tell they were a man and a woman, but could not make out any features by which

I could recognize them until some more minutes had passed, when the woman raised her arm high, high, waving her hand as she moved her arm also, back and forth as she walked.

I instantly recognized the vivacious style, and was astounded to realize that these friends I had been brought to meet were none other than Letty and the professor, whom I had not seen since that day in old Tombstone, when I had met them at the Bird Cage Theatre and accompanied them to the summer house of their trusted friend.

I had not understood why I was made privy to the intense and personal conversations of that day. I had felt privileged, as one does when granted the confidence of private matters, and so I spoke to no one of them nor allowed myself to speculate, having been, as I felt it, placed in a trust accorded by my friendship with Letty, and by her vouching for my character in this matter.

My companions, Boris and Monami, with whom I had felt so at ease during the time we spent on the way down, enjoyed my delight at seeing Letty and Fo, and laughed happily at seeing Letty's enthusiastic wave. I walked a bit faster, watching the two figures approach, as my mind revolved rapidly in thoughts concerning the day, and how these friends of mine might figure in the strange otherworldliness of its events.

I had related Dr. Fo with the stranger on the bridge initially because Foglesby, though a scientist and mathematician, had spoken of and taught a phenomenology which I had been introduced to so coincidentally with the events on the bridge that I considered the matters connected, though without any direct evidence at the time, or real basis for thinking so. It was just a sense that came to me while turning the pages of his students' notebooks and seeing boldly noted the remarkable entries, underlined in recapitulations by the students, and surrounded and followed by notes and references which evidenced their inspired and intense processes of thought.

What their beloved teacher had passed over to them was the power of revelation, far beyond the mere acquisition of knowledge, and never to be forgotten by anyone who perceived it.

We were near enough now so that I could recognize their faces. Letty's infectious smile, which turned up the corners of her mouth, and showed the white of her teeth. The graceful, almost musical way of her walk. A bounce of her hair, which coincided with her light steps. And Fo's distinguished bearing and intense aspect, which remained a part of him despite his relaxed and casual way. A shank of his hair fell over his forehead, which he unconsciously plied backward through his fingers. His face bore a smile of anticipation.

I found myself thinking on two levels: One, the normal, on which I considered that I was now visiting my two friends at a place they maintained abroad, in a location lovelier and more picturesque than any that I had ever seen; and the other, not so normal, which reminded me of the manner of my arrival, and of the remarkable concatenation of experiences which had brought me to this place, finally, in the company of the young couple who I strangely sensed were my guardians.

It would be good to see Foglesby and Letty, the two individuals with whom I could speak about these most perplexing questions, who just happened to be walking towards me at this moment on a royal roadway shaded by ancient and grandiose boughs which defied the bounds of gravity and imagination.

"What better time?" I thought as my friends came closer. Letty was dressed in a grayish pantsuit which seemed liquid upon her, and Fo, in casual slacks, belted below a billowy shirt. They both looked rested, and immeasurably happy and free from care. They seemed vibrant, and even younger than when I had last seen them, but of course on the occasion of our last meeting they were experiencing stresses which could have not but weighed upon them in a difficult time, though they had seemed at ease to me, nonetheless.

Letty greeted me at first, with emotional hugs and a kiss upon my cheek, and then, holding both my hands in hers, turned toward Fo and said to me, smiling, "I think you've met my husband?"

Fo extended his hands in his characteristic two-hand shake, clasping my hand firmly in his. "I see you've finally accepted my invitation to visit our stone house with a veranda overlooking the sea," he offered, his face beaming. "This is good, really good!"

I did not recall such an invitation, although I remembered his reference to such a place during his conversations with his friend, Otto, at their meeting that day in Bisbee, saying with some wistfulness, while centered in the conflict arising from his discovery, that he dreamed of a place, a home, where he could simply do science and teach. Like most of his associates in his field, Foglesby was not an adept practitioner of politics, and had little patience for it.

"Thank you!" I responded. "It's good to be here, and to see you both!..., though I'm sure you assume I have questions about how I've arrived, and even why... To begin with, I've never seen a roadway like this... It looks like it was built for royalty!" I added, half in jest, as I tapped a foot upon the solid stone surface upon which we stood. The stones were so perfectly aligned that hardly a sprig of grass had intruded within the knife-thin cracks between them.

"Oh yes, perhaps it was," Fo conceded, "or for a god of some kind: We don't know yet. It was built long, long ago, before any historical record. It is definitely aboriginal."

"Aboriginal!" I repeated. "Where does it go?.. How long is it? It looks more durable than the Appian Way, maybe Incan? Why is it so straight?" I tried to add several questions into one.

We had begun to walk slowly back in the direction from which Fo and Letty had come. My companions, Monami and Boris, walked together some yards back, listening with enjoyment to our conversation.

"It goes nowhere, really," Letty explained. "This section is over two kilometers in length, beginning where you first stepped upon it, and ending in the sea floor, about six hundred meters out, where it is thirty-three meters below the surface of the sea."

"Really!" I exclaimed. "What happened, an earthquake?"

"No earthquake has affected it," Fo interjected. "We're certain that your 'Appian Way' here far predates the Roman era. It is in fact Pleistocene, as our dating techniques confirm."

"Older than the Romans?" The concept of Pleistocene momentarily escaped me.

"By about twenty-one millennia, 21,425 B.C., to be exact."

"Incredible! Wow!" was my reaction, although I accepted the great scientist's statement.

"Now you're going to ask, Why?" Letty anticipated correctly. "We don't know that fully, although there is no lack of conjecture to be heard around bonfires down at the coastline, where the road descends into the sea. It is a favorite gathering spot, and many make pilgrimages from far-away places to walk upon 'The Way', as it is called, and to sense its ancient resonances. They feel that this place holds great significance, and that merely standing upon it connects them with the powers of antiquity, and with the dreams that inspired its creation... And, of course, if it works for them, then they feel it is true.."

"Do you believe, Letty? Are you a believer?" I teased.

"Oh, I love a mystery," was her reply, as she made a light clicking sound with her mouth. "And do you want to hear a real mystery?" she continued. "Let Fo explain it..."

"Well," began the professor, "it's amazing...First of all, it's most certainly not a road at all- not as it was originally intended. Not a public roadway, at least... It may have served for ceremonial processions, and so forth, on certain days marking the solstice, or other events, though we don't think it was made for ordinary traffic.

"There is a story behind what we do know: An old mapping satellite was scanning with ground-penetrating radar and found an anomaly which didn't correspond with known surface features, and obviously wasn't geological, by virtue of its straight lines and other features. We had access to the satellite information, and our people were given authority to check it out, given the convenience that this site was located in our front yard, and that we had the experts who were qualified to conduct the investigation. So we began a careful excavation which expanded into a greater project which revealed the long structure, built with uncanny precision sometime in the remote past.

"Eventually we exposed the full structure as we know it, having at last a view of it.., less that part which remains submerged, of course. And it was then that we were given a further surprise: One of the many satellites placed in geocentric orbit, twenty-three thousand-plus miles out, was scanning in infrared, and picked up a parabolic 'slice', something obviously not geological, upon the earth's surface.

"That is to say, the eye of the satellite was the exact focus of a returning beam reflected from an object whose length was a precise mathematical proportion of its width- infinitesimally precise, in fact. The length of this object was curved with the precision of a telescope lens, ever so slightly, into a parabolic arc whose focal length intersected at the exact altitude of geocentric orbit."

I began to interrupt, when Fo held up his hand, continuing:

"But that's not all: The width of this 'Way', as we call it- just slightly more than four meters (or thirteen feet)- was also curved into a slight arc which must have had some significance, though its original precision is undeterminable because the surface is worn with time..

"The satellites, despite the inevitable degradation of the Way's surface over the millennia, were still able to pick up a distinct signal from the curvature of its length- a message, if you will, from an obviously intelligent and scientifically advanced civilization who focused its elaborate signal upon a precise place wherein sat, or would one day sit, a satellite transmitter and receiver, collaborating with the technology to intercept its data. Else, what would be the point, to use a pun.."

"So the surface of this 'Way' was highly polished, originally," I stated the obvious as a question.

"Yes, we think it was," Letty affirmed. "We think it was plated with some material, or substance, and highly polished, as the mere surface of the stone, especially regarding the curve of its width, would simply disperse the energies of incoming beams, That plating, or covering, was later removed, perhaps long after, when the purpose and significance of the creation was lost. We are still trying to determine who the builders were, how they achieved their level of technology, what their message was to us, and what became of them.

"But the most fascinating aspects of them are their connections to us... In the event of any archaeological discovery, or any learning, the reality of a past is bridged across time, and something of the past is reborn in presence. Thought, of course, is the eternal bridge."

WE WERE STILL walking along at a leisurely pace, the three of us alongside. And my young friends were following up some distance back. I was pondering the information shared about the antiquity we were walking on, which took on an added dimension by virtue of it. There is always more to something than we know about, or question. And yet, the truest antiquity is a forgotten one, remaining behind, while this instrument of scientific achievement, however ancient, with its resurrection into human knowledge, speaks again in the present tense, returning from the bottom of its long, unwritten page the flourish of its signature.

Its creators are sending their living message, not merely into space, but into time as well, connecting their thought with our own in the personal clasp of a handshake- intellectual, sure, but emotional as well, for as great minds have noted, there can be no thought without emotion... I felt, as would anyone in that circumstance, the shiver of a thrill.

Letty had made a reference to "this section" of the structure, and so I asked if this was the only artifact.

"Actually, no," she answered. "The old radar satellite discovered, perpendicular to the end of the Way that lies under the sea- that is to say, at a 90-degree angle to the terminus- a round, concave structure shaped like a bowl, about fifty meters in diameter. In our exploration we found that the exact center of this bowl has a spire, an obelisk, which is four-sided and rectangular, some ten meters tall, and flat on top. Buried within the base of the obelisk, at each corner, is a pin forged of a complex alloy which was not duplicated until the early 21st Century. The centers of these pins form the corners of a perfect rectangle whose width is two-thirds of its length. The investigators knew that this proportion of width to length had to carry a significance.."

We walked along slowly, stopping now and then under the shade of the magnificent old trees which lined the roadway. A fragrant moss hung down from the great branches and their stems which supported the cooling canopy of leaves. Lush grasses and clover lay low under the trees' shade, but grew thick and knee-high beyond where the shadows fell, and off across the meadow where the river ran.

"And now, to your question," Letty continued. "Once the image of the structure appeared from ground-penetrating radar it was excavated and studied exhaustively, of course. It was then that they discovered its geometric design, and its uncanny precision. The function of its parabolic curvature was immediately revealed when its signal was received by the geocentric satellite. But the reasons for, and the nature of its 'message' was yet to be learned... Perhaps Fo can further explain."

"Well, the clues to the mystery were written in such elementary math that, for a time, they escaped us. Our computer analysis began with the esoteric and worked down, until finally we discovered a simple scale which should have been obvious. The base of the rectangular obelisk, marked precisely by the four pins, represented a giant rectangle whose longer sides were in the same proportion to the structure we're standing on as this structure is to the length between the two pins on the long side of the obelisk. Simple math! X is to Y, as Y is to Z...

"By this same relative scale, of course, the lengths of the shorter sides were determined as well."

"Do you know what is the meaning of the concave bowl, in which the obelisk sits?" I had this question, and another obvious one, which the professor would answer without my having to ask.

"The bowl, whose concavity is also parabolic, simply represents the purpose of communicating information, we think, as does the presence of the obelisk. The information to be broadcast is contained with brilliant simplicity in the rectangular base of the obelisk."

At this point I was going to ask, "And did you find the other three corners of the larger rectangle?" but Fo continued.

"The dimensions of the greater rectangle are impressive: Two thousand kilometers by over thirteen-hundred- or about twelve-hundred miles, by some eight hundred.

"Of course the structure here represents one corner. Because the opposite corner of this side is twelve-hundred miles away, we could not identify its location precisely, although the line of the Way here points exactly to it. After the location was approximated, we were able to search for, and pinpoint it by the same satellite radar which originally revealed this one. It was also buried under some meters of earth, and when excavated it proved to be as suspected: the mirror image of the one we have here.

"It was easier to locate the third corner, as we had now measured by global positioning the exact length of the long side and we knew its proportion, so we made an arc out 800 miles at ninety degrees to where we are now, and were able to locate this corner, initially by deep-penetrating radar, as well, even though it was buried quite deep.

"When the last corner marker was imaged, part of it lay buried under a small town whose people had long ago built a park around a curious rectangular obelisk which protruded ten feet or so above ground. As the generations passed, no one could remember what purpose it had, and assumed it had been constructed by the town a long time before, as a monument of some kind. They had built a pretty plaza around it, with a fountain, shade trees, and benches for people to sit on..."

"Do you know what was delineated by the large rectangle, and its arc of twelve-hundred by eight-hundred miles, and why its position would be transmitted into space?" I asked, as a flurry of other questions came to mind. I wondered why a physical boundary would be so important that its corners, with half a continent's distance between them, would be set immutably in stone, and announced to a point in outer space where no one would be waiting for twenty millennia.

Here, Letty's husband chuckled lightly and paused, then offered his enigmatic commentary:

"Well, since history is what you make of it- both past and future histories- we can only assume that whatever foretelling lay within the structure the ancients marked with their sophisticated engineering and technology became, in a metaphorical way, self-fulfilling.

"When the first of us came here to establish research facilities, the government offered us a lease-in-perpetuity to a large territory which, most ironically, approximated the very area within the boundaries marked by the four corners of the Way, although the discovery wasn't to be made for some years thereafter. When it did work out to be so mysteriously coincidental, the irony was lost on no one, and so the strange reality came to be known as 'the Jerusalem factor,' referring, of course, to the legendary New Jerusalem, within whose great boundaries a new and peaceful order would emerge, to sweep across and change the world."

When I looked at Letty, to see her reaction, she was smiling as if she enjoyed Fo's telling of the story. I looked back at the professor, and raised my eyebrows, as if to ask, Is that all?, or Is there more?...

Fo shrugged his shoulders slightly, flashing a smile, and said, "That's the story."

I looked around to where Boris was standing, and Monami was sitting on the sculptured curbing, near his feet. He stood relaxed, one hand touching Monami's hair. Both were smiling delightedly, and watching to follow my reactions to the extraordinary tale.

As I stood half waiting for a punch line, I began to sense, given the evidence of things seen here before me- the strange fact of the stone monolith stretching outward in a dead-straight line behind and before us, and the fantastic nature of my arrival this morning, and the realness of its surreality- that I was on a journey of experiences I could no way explain.

WE BEGAN walking again, along the long, declined surface of "The Way", past the last few of the great trees and towards the open, sunlit meadow beyond, where the long, straight edges of the stone blade converged in the distance to where the sea had long ago risen around it. I had lost track of time, and was awakened from my reverie when Letty called my name. I had not noticed a series of stone steps which rose from a landing on the curbside, up and over a grassy embankment. Carved stone planters framing the stairway were filled with vivid, fragrant flowers, their velvety petals glistening in the warm sun.

An endearing white lamb stepped over from the grass and stood there on the curbing, looking, until Monami reached down and retrieved it, holding it in her arms.

"These steps lead to our front door," Letty announced, lifting her hand to show the way, her eyes sparkling. *Su casa,* she added, in the welcome given in the land of her parents.

I told her thank you and motioned for her to ascend with me. The professor was just behind, and my friends Monami and Boris had just stepped up on the landing behind us. Monami placed the lamb she had been holding upon the green grass and it made a soft bleat and hesitated for just a moment before it sprung happily away to find its mother. As we climbed the steps I commented on what I was thinking.

"What an entrance to your front door!" I exclaimed, referring to the massive and yet exquisite structure which stretched by in a straight and flawless line from the slope above, and down the meadow to the sea- which was not a roadway, or even a straight line, but an infinitesimally and invisibly curved lens made to focus energy to a precise point far outward into the twilight of time and planetary space.

By this creation of theirs, Letty had pointed out, those highly intelligent minds, whom she called, Pharaohs of Knowledge, traveled forward to us through time, to place their presence among us. By our notice we visit them also, there in the long past, where they have awaited our reply. In the regime of thought, time disappears.

A line from one of the notebooks came to me as I stood not four feet away from its author: *The purpose of thought is to escape the moment and join worlds of time, to exceed boundaries and find freedom.*

Something struck me just then, and I turned to the professor, who stood on the step below, his upper head framed by the blue of the ocean:

"What else did these ancient people leave?... I've never heard anything about this. You would think it is important enough for all the world to know," I asked thoughtfully.

It had suddenly seemed strange that such an astounding discovery, which could fill the soul of history with meaning, and change forever the way we humans view ourselves, could or should be kept secret. As a layman, I had subscribed to a number of publications, including *Discover, Archaeology, Smithsonian, The Week, Newsweek,* and others, and tried to follow the news, but had never heard of this antiquity. I was considering regretfully that perhaps my addiction to the routine of work may have actually blinded me to an event so crucially important to humanity, and how, beyond that, it must have affected the souls I love, including my own.

Fo stood looking back at me with that intense look in his eyes- eyes that took in everything easily, and yet only "proper knowledge", as he had called it, restraining his view into places into which his intelligence might not be invited.

His brilliant eyes seemed to blink politely, in the way that is subtly understood by people of the streets, by humble people who know how to measure other distinctions as fine as that which bends ever so discreetly, with infinitesimal trueness, the straightness of the megalith below into an invisible geometric form whose perfect note reverberates through time and space with the thrill of a mind who has discovered and then rediscovered an immortal thought.

It was Letty who answered, clasping my hand in hers.

"You didn't know because all this happened after your time," she said quietly.

"After my time?" I asked. "What do you mean?"

Some moments passed. Letty was emotional, and drew me into her arms, and Fo stepped up and reached his arms across his wife, and over my shoulders. Beautiful Monami and her friend stepped closer, and reached out to touch the little group. I sensed a premonition of the words to follow, and felt an inflowing of energies of love, both human and angelic, to strengthen and sustain me.

I heard Letty's beautiful, silken voice, her words swaying into a music made lovelier by the sweetest of memories from long ago, from a time inexpressibly precious for its passing, when children thrilled to the running, and plunged their faces into liquid life.

Her voice seemed to come from far away.

"Cowboy, you've come to us through time... This day, this moment, is in the Twenty-third Century."

JUST UPWARD FROM the ancient way of stone, cut and arranged in the form of a message through time- a vessel in stone to carry thought across the span of a thousand generations- the graceful stairway rose a few steps further to where a splendid courtyard lay under the shade of flowering trees whose blossoms were serenaded by the lively hum of a myriad darting wings. The bower of climbing roses breathed its fragrance into the mist of a fountain from whose hyacinthine tiers pure waters sang in their cool cascade, in voices of coolness added downward in the misty flow in a melody as ancient as stone itself and eternally soothing to the soul of life.

Beyond this ambrosial chamber, into which sunlight sprinkled softly through leafy shutters, casting in sparkles the music of flowing water in a timeless reassurance, and out to where the walkway made a bend, there appeared at once, set against a hillslope above the green valley, its graceful roof extending out on all sides to rest upon a shaded colonnade, a place known long ago, in the reality of dreams, as home.

I turned to see the smiles of my friends.

"There are others, waiting to meet you," Letty said. "Welcome."

We made our way across a little meadow to that stone house with a veranda overlooking the sea.

*   *   *

CHAPTER *TEN*

THE HOMECOMING

THE MOST immortal part about us is our sense of beauty. And the most remarkable part, that we may create and recognize beauty through love. Love paints life with beauty, and beauty with the appreciation of love-in any age, on any world, where life recognizes the reality of its being.
-notebook "4", missing cover, p31.

"In the regime of thought, time disappears."
- Monami.

NOTHING separate is immortal. Only in the joining does Immortality arise.
-green Penway notebook "11", p70.

THE WALKWAY which led from the courtyard above the tree-lined Way of Stone was amply wide, and paved with a material which I had not seen before, the soft color of earth, and inlaid with rich ceramics the color of turquoise. The surface was flexible, which lent a spring to the step, and was exceedingly comfortable to walk on.

Soon the path curved through a garden of incandescent flowers which regaled the senses with their variety, their fragrance and colors. It was a place too lovely for words, and I longed for my loved ones, lovers of beauty all, to share it with me.

We walked unhurriedly through the sweet atmosphere of this approach to the place where Fo and Letty had found their home, attended by hosts of flitting butterflies who mixed their colors with the flowers in Sapphic harmonies of movement, alighting and flying with graceful spontaneity, each one busy in its business, and yet performing sometimes as if they were gliding together upon an invisible wave which silently lifted and rolled them forward and up again in exquisite ballets of silent color. We have witnessed these things before, but there is that incomparable moment when we see them again for the first time.

I suddenly recalled into clearer understanding the beloved professor's teaching from another life, which had been highlighted in yellow upon a student's page, and followed by three question marks, as if a reminder to further contemplation: Of how beauty is translated finally into mystery, and mystery into beauty, and of such is the nature of the mind's reality and its universe.

The light echo of my boots upon the walkway jarred my consciousness, and I looked to my hosts, walking just back of me on both sides, and to the other two who strolled some paces back, holding hands as they walked, and smiling as they looked back at me. The tenor of the footsteps changed and I realized that the walkway had simply merged into the upper deck of the veranda, below which the ground fell away in a slope, forwards toward the wide, sunlit valley cut by the knife edge of the way of stone.

A stairway carved gracefully into a ledge of limestone rock led downward to a landing at the lower deck which lay the length of the veranda at ground level, the which had been cut away to nestle the big house into the slope of the hill that rose behind..

The stone, hewn out expertly into the curve of the descending stair, was of the same type which had been used to build the entry steps we climbed above the Way, and appeared to have been carved and laid by the same artistic hands a long time before. This was quarried of the same material as the great house, but with no intent to match the latter, and laid in a contrasting style, though the facing and treads of the steps continued with the design of shaped stone which trimmed the large window openings of the house, wherein single stones were fitted mortarless into a lenticular frame with a remarkable and gracious effect which I had not seen before, and have not since.

As I hesitated for a moment, taking in the beauty and charm of this special place, I felt a hand on my shoulder, and turned to see Boris and Monami standing close to me. Monami was smiling happily, and Boris extended his hand warmly to shake mine.

"We'll be leaving you for awhile," she said. "We know that you will have a wonderful visit, and we'll join you again before long."

Monami took my other hand, and pressed it in hers. And then again, in that sweet and intimate gesture, they reached over and touched my head, he, resting his hand around my head to the back, across my ear, and then she, pressing her soft palm upon my forehead, in front of my eyes, and then delicately sliding it around my cheek, and holding it for just a moment. I still remember the faint scent of her skin as she touched my face.

Never had I had anyone do that before in the context of a greeting or goodbye, and I was astonished at how intimate the gesture is compared to the formality of a handshake, or even to a kiss upon the cheek. It is, more than an embrace, a cradling of one by another in a recognition, rather like a pledge.

Transcending culture, and specially human, this deliberate touching seemed to acknowledge the mind.

A COOL, refreshing breeze, aromatic of the sea and the broad meadow's scent, flowed gently within the shadows of the long veranda whose unique floor was formed with timbers of polished hardwood, pegged together, their deep luster burnished by time into extraordinary beauty. A series of white balusters visually connected the stone columns in the wide veranda's narrowing to the distant corner, its smooth oval railing of the same varnished hardwood as the floor.

The tall, carved columns rose seamless from the ground below to support the veranda's deck, and then upward to suspend the high ceiling whose rafters lay upon strong beams which arched gracefully from post to post down the colonnade.

I was veritably drinking in the presence of their place, lost in the mix of imageries and experiences and mysteries of the day, fully perplexed and overwhelmed, as you can imagine, and yet filled with a gathering tranquility whose residues have not left me to this moment. I did not notice the broad entryway whose tall, carved doors lay open behind framed screens which had camouflaged the opening.

Just as I passed adjacent to the doorway a pretty voice laughingly called out, Hello! I stopped and turned to see, behind the matting of the screen, the lovely face of a young girl of perhaps thirteen or fourteen years. The screens suddenly swiveled and she bounded out, taking me somewhat aback by wrapping her arms around my neck, and kissing me on both cheeks with the infectious happiness of a daughter welcoming a parent home after a long absence. When she released me from her hugs she stepped back a step and then took my hand and shook it vigorously, exclaiming how good it was that I had made it, and how happy she was to see me at last.

I looked back to my hosts standing behind me, soliciting their reaction, and found them enjoying the effusive welcome accorded their guest. Letty laughed softly, tears in her eyes, and held out her open palms, her expressive face posing a joyful confirmation, "See?.."

The girl, alight with enthusiasm, threw her arms open and rushed to embrace, first Letty, then Fo, looking back then to include me in their celebration.

"This is our daughter, Aida," Letty spoke, her eyes lingering in the instant of her glance in the way that acknowledges great moment. She knew that I had seen the photograph which sat upon her desk so long ago, of the long-haired beautiful child which had been their own, and she knew I remembered with perfection the long unspoken sentence which answered my question that day with the incomparable eloquence that such loss compels in human souls.

I did not know how to respond, overtaken and speechless before this day of continuing miracles. Thoughts and feelings of a great joyous mixture swirled within me as I continued to absorb the immense implications of what I was experiencing, while considering them from a dimension made expressly radical beyond the summations of a lifespan which, in known experience, direct and contain all mortal thought.

Suddenly, I was aware of Letty's voice.

"The others are waiting for us on the side porch. We can go through the den if you like," she invited, as her daughter turned happily and led the way. The screen doors pivoted open and Aida motioned graciously for me to enter the cool interior.

"I'll meet you around the corner," Fo offered, indicating that he would continue along the veranda.

*   *   *

THERE IS something about a house wherein people have long lived who love life and have found their happiness, something which inexplicably blurs the lines between animate and inanimate, and not so much tells you of, as makes you feel the lives sheltered within and around the place called home.

Physical places carry memories, etched into emotion within the atoms which compose them, although we cannot explain the process by which this is done, nor the reason why, except that matter seems to take a strange and vital interest in conscious knowing. First, drawing attention to itself through the elaborate devices of the senses, then beguiling the mind through beauty and symmetry and variations of the unexpected, and contrasts which awaken our notice and curiosity, then seductively revealing and disclosing its secrets through the earned pleasure of learning.

Knowledge is thus a homecoming for the traveler in learning, who in the moment of recognition exclaims, "I know you!" and hears the answer, "Welcome home."

A line was written at the top of a page in one of the notebooks, noted with a flourish and underlined:

Learning is the answer to the call of Life!!

The old stone house with its veranda will remain throughout my life as it was on that day, its powerful presence made ever more mysterious by the reality that the greater part of the history that it knew, and of the events it had witnessed, for me and for my world, still lay in the future.

I STOPPED IN the middle of the great room, scarcely breathing as I absorbed the compelling presence which scintillated throughout and seemed to emanate in lightness from the physical matter which contained and occupied the space within. The air was stirred by elegant old ceiling fans, suspended high and connected one to another by long belts which moved their white blades in a soft whir as they had since the turn of the year 1900, when the artisans carried away their tools.

The paneled wood ceiling of the living area was vaulted, and braced a third of the way down by painted beams with varnished hardwood soffits upon whose contrasting lines were suspended the graceful fans. And upon the ridge line above, centered above the great room, was an angled framework of glass panes, some leaded with beautiful stained designs through which the room was flooded with natural light within which hung soft prismatic streams of iridescent color.

Upon the walls in a perfect balance, mounted within their frames, exquisite works of art looked out with a power and beauty which time only greatens. Some of the paintings I recognized from periods before my time; others, equally unique, and holding their aura of greatness, were apparent in their themes and character to be from periods in the two and more centuries which had transpired.

I took some steps across the room, past a setting of sofas and tables whose arrangement provided comfortably for intimate visiting. Large rugs beautifully softened the hardwood floor in areas throughout the room, where lamps glowed invitingly and vases of flowers spoke their gathering of color into the spectrum of light which streamed into the room from above.

Long curved steps, numbering three, arched around perhaps a quarter of the room's area and offered a lowered floor with its setting of comfortable sofas and chairs set upon a thick wool carpet and facing a corner fireplace which was remarkable for the simple elegance and beauty of its structure.

Above and around its generous opening the smooth surface rose unbroken except for the net effect of a mantel shelf of carved ebony upon which pictures rested in their frames. I was immediately drawn to these portraits because I recognized them to be from my world, and of people who were familiar to me.

There was a picture of a family of three taken in the White Mountains above Tucson on a birthday celebration of the child held in her father's arms.

In black and white, another of an earlier family of three, a mother and a father and a young girl with long hair and a beautiful smile, standing between.

There was a wedding picture of the couple standing upon the chapel steps in the radiance of happiness on that day, strikingly beautiful and handsome as they began their lives together.

And, in its thousand words and more, a black and white photograph taken in the snow on the inside of a barbed wire fence, of three generations who posed together as families do in whatever circumstances, to celebrate and declare their proud existence as a family.

To one side of the fireplace, upon a wall which extended upward into the vaulted ceiling, there was another grouping of pictures and photographs, and centered within them was a remarkable photograph of Letty's mother, Dona Elena, standing with famous and distinguished people from Hollywood, dressed cleanly in white, a yellow apron tied upon her waist, her beautiful head held proudly. She looked the equal of any of the figures posing around her at that moment, of famed and gifted friends, who leaned together smiling on a day that never came again.

There was a trio of pictures set in the same long frame, wherein the professor stood as a medallion held upon a white scarf was being placed upon his neck; another, as he stood in a receiving line with other distinguished individuals; and one, apparently of the same occasion, as he stood upon a podium before a set of microphones, his hands raised in a gesture as he spoke.

Other pictures, framed and arranged upon a wall, were of babies and children, of old friends, and of proud ancestors in sepia who gazed out across time to this unimaginable day, the spirits in their eyes undiminished by the centuries past.

And one photograph, larger than the others, almost breathed.

It was of a rugged, handsome man, a caballero with a wide brimmed hat, sitting straight in the saddle upon a white horse, his chiseled face cut across by a shadow, a large mustache arching over into the light, and intelligent, burning eyes who smile in their living moment.

Below it, a small carved bookcase, made of rustic oak and set into the wall, held old and worn volumes which told about philosophers and artists, thinkers and scientists, and their lives, and what they thought and dreamed.

Upon the shelf above them sat an old kerosene lamp, polished bright, and a picture of a family of three, taken on a sunny day, trees and hills in the background.

Letty and Aida stood quietly and waited, as my eyes swept over the details of the space within their home, and drank in study of the treasured souvenirs of the long ago, from which I had come. I knew I had taken a liberty in observing the room which was their home, and yet it was clear that I had been invited to do so. My hosts were smiling as I approached.

"Do you feel it?" Letty asked, her eyes studying mine. I knew what she meant.

"Yes.., oh yes!" was all I could answer.

"Are you ready to meet the others?" Letty asked, touching my arm. "They are anxious to see you, and we are fixing a home-cooked meal for everyone. You must be hungry... Really, it is more like an outdoor picnic lunch, and my husband and I are doing the honors," she added, her eyes twinkling.

"That sounds wonderful," I assured her, as she and Aida led the way across a dining area, through the spacious kitchen in which hung many pots and pans which indicated the occupants' love for cooking, and down a wide, lighted corridor to where a glass door was open before a screen.

The screen swung open as we approached, and Aida led me out upon the broad porch on the side veranda where a long table was beautifully set- a light blue tablecloth with a lace border, and settings of white stoneware plates and bowls with many colored roses etched within them.

Silverware was in place, and large glasses for the tea which filled iced pitchers on either side of the table.

As I glanced upward, in a moment of vivid remembrance, my eyes met those who had long known me and waited in loving and faithful labor for this day to come.

*   *   *

CHAPTER ELEVEN

THE FEAST OF PLENTY.
POETRY OF LIFE

*WE LIVE IN the first moments of creation. We are
ourselves the creators of what we choose to come to be.*
-notebook "4", brown cover, p18.

*EVERYTHING you are in your time, all your creations, the subtle
turn and bent of your emotions, your inquietude, the poignancy of
your love, your weight of sadness, your splendid joy and sympathy
drawn from your common predicament, your vision of beauty
and hope, and even your illusions and misunderstandings, come
from your measure of days, from the inescapable limitations of
your mortality. They also gave you inspiration to reach beyond
and want to keep the essence of the human, which is love.*
-notebook "11", p78.

"Are you real?"
"As real as your imagination."
"But is it an illusion?"
"All is an illusion," she smiled, "isn't it?..
Yet from your imagination is born the real."

THE FOUR BEINGS were waiting there to welcome me. And I don't know how else to describe them, except that they were different, some aspect about them more than "persons", and greater than "individuals".

We consider our own selves in these terms, perhaps, because we are temporal. We are destined to die, and so there is an apartness, a separateness about us by our nature. We are visitors in this mortal life. We come and we go, and so, beyond the bonds of friendship and love we are truly individual, and this reality colors every aspect of our being.

I think about them now and realize, as I did then, that there was something more than human about them- and yet, they were human. Great and challenging experience had made them humble before the gifts of their achievement. They were not superior, or condescending, but rather seemed participants, through understanding, of the history which was the womb of their birth and being. What, after all, is it that differentiates the gods, but knowledge?

They walked forward to me on that day as in a dream, and embraced me, and held my hands in theirs, each in turn touching my head, and their eyes were filled with great appreciation and love. I felt an intense kinship and a peace, as if I somehow had known them before, and kept a shared faith until this moment.

I was introduced to each one, and there was laughter and joyful expression, and celebration. I found myself wondering, "for me?" and whether the main guest was yet to arrive, but quickly realized that this occasion indeed held me at its center, though I had only the faintest comprehension of what it meant.

"I'll leave you with your friends now," I heard Letty's voice. "Aida will join you, and I must go and assist the chef!" Her quick expression of feigned urgency turned into a wide smile as she squeezed my arm, motioning to a spot just down and across from the veranda where, under a great sycamore whose huge boughs arched outward, their high canopy of flickering leaves casting cool shadows over half an acre, the figure of her husband stood before a table, busily engaged in the preparations of a meal, or "picnic lunch", as Letty modestly described it.

As her mother descended the steps to the yard below, Aida, as a gracious hostess knows how to do, gently suggested that we might be seated, and offered me a chair at one end of the table from where I could look out across the wide meadow to the open sea. The others took their places to the side and across from where I sat, excitedly continuing the conversation we had begun some minutes before. They had many questions, I was assured, and many things to discuss.

"We know you well... We are specialists in your life and times," a slender, striking woman who introduced herself as Lia Chomsky announced, as she was being seated by the young man next to her. She reached over to lightly tap her fingers on my hand, smiling.

She had shoulder length hair, deep black and shiny, with curls that fell to one side of her face. Her eyes were an extraordinary blue-gray, wide set and intelligent, with a deep softness that put me at ease. Shapely eyebrows curved in natural arches, accentuating her expression as she spoke.

She informed me that she was originally from Russia, where she had studied at the St. Petersburg Center of History and Culture before teaching for some years until she joined the Planetoid II Mission as a scholar and advisor in a field she called, "Extraculture", thus realizing her dream of working in space. After some rewarding and exciting years during which she married and bore a daughter and a son, the family returned to Earth. Then, after seeing her children grown, she prepared herself to enter the field to which she had long felt a calling. She considered it a service and a payment of debt to those antecedents to whom she owed her very existence. Her commitment was both spiritual and intellectual, as uniquely enjoyable as motherhood, she told me.

She loved the sense of entering the past as a visitor in whose power it was to employ the gifts of science in a reprieve of death and a regeneration of life's miracle and meaning.

"It is the greatest joy for me personally," is how she characterized her work and purpose.

The others sat listening to Lia's story, and curiously watching my reaction. By now I was not surprised at what she said; my surprise was rather for the capacity the mind has to accept worlds of change.

Something elementally human within us remains constant, to preserve and guide the identity amid revolution which falls upon us in a moment. Some have called it the instinct for survival, an evolutionary imperative built into the species long ago, but it seems more likely than that to be a benevolence and an opportunity, allowed us from the future realm of our potential in a grace held outward with the gift of life, for a purpose which proactively engenders and requires our trust and will. This is how I see it now, having personally witnessed a world beyond.

From somewhere near upon the hill behind us a warbler sang its quavering melody to existence. The air was sweet with the perfume of honeysuckle blossoms, lilac, and red and yellow roses. Other varieties of flowers flourished in pots and containers which were suspended from beams, or placed in settings upon the decks and along the walkways, lending their profuse colors to the veranda and to the grounds surrounding the house.

Wherever Letty had lived with Fo, flowers abounded. She always had a touch, a special gift at making things grow, and living things responded to her care with extraordinary vibrancy.

'Specialists in my life and times...' I repeated Lia's words, reacting in light of my highly imperfect and sometimes ignoble life. But I felt no discomfort. There was no air of judgment or prosecution about them, rather, an immense kindness and acceptance shone in their faces, which revealed excitement and extreme interest in my presence. I felt as if I were the guest at a celebration, which indeed it turned out to be, held carefully and lovingly within their understanding.

"Including that your sister gave you a nickname..," offered another.

Smiles broke out around the table. It seems they enjoyed this bit of arcane trivia known to but a handful of souls in my time, principally my immediate family. My sister, Elizabeth, older by a couple of years, could not pronounce my given name, so she called me, "Dapod", which she later shortened to just "Pod". Only rarely since my childhood had I been referred to by this homely sobriquet, and then always affectionately, in a baby-brother sort of way.

The only time in recent years had occurred memorably when an old farming neighbor who knew me from birth called me by this name as he greeted me at my father's graveside services. This particular man I had recalled as somewhat taciturn, and I was touched by his expressions of kindness and by his regard toward my father which showed in his aged eyes. It surely must become harder as time goes on to see one's contemporaries, with whom one has shared youth and so many memories, drop away. It had been forty years or so since I had heard my childhood nickname, and on that occasion I appreciated its warmth and reminiscence.

"Yes, that is true. She did," I conceded, recalling with tenderness this dear sister, and then self-consciously I changed the subject, adding, "And my failings?"

"Oh, failings are temporary things, and very subjective," the mirthful fellow whom everyone called "BJ" instructed dismissively, with a sparkle in his eyes. He had a most winsome personality, brimming with laughter and intelligence, a mat of unruly red hair upon his round head, and rosy cheeks which seemed to glow correspondingly with the enthusiasm in his green eyes. His small, wry mouth seemed poised on the break of laughter or a smile, anticipating, by just a degree, his humorous sense. When thinking, he would stroke his sparse, curly beard with a large hand.

He wore a flowered shirt, untucked, and open at the top, with casual trousers, comfortably loose. But most curiously, around his broad neck was tied a red bandana with white polka dots, which matched nothing about him but the red socks which called from under the strappings of his sandals. His main fields, and he had many, included biophysics and quantum engineering. His deep, easy voice carried the slight twang of an accent from the South.

When we met, BJ, or Billy Joe, whose full name was William Joseph Smith, had embraced me with a brotherly warmth, as if he knew me personally. Little did I know in that moment that our paths would cross on a terribly momentous day two and a half centuries before.

He continued, reassuringly, philosophically.

"What matters is what you have learned to appreciate about life, what you have learned about love, what you have cared about freedom, what your best dreams have been... You will carry over into the next life what speaks of you through time: only the greatest of your ideals, the fullest essence of your learning and passion, your regard for others, and for life."

I knew of others to whom these words would apply, but did not feel myself included.

"We know that you have visited the future."

The young man sitting next to Lia, whose name was Robeling, leaned forward, having spoken matter-of-factly. He cupped a finger upon his upper lip pensively, gazing sideways at me from where he sat. His brown hair was long and combed backward, resting in loose waves in the back. His intelligent eyes were dark and deeply set, with an aged wisdom, his face kindly and strong. He had large ears and a handsome, Emersonian arch in his nose. His sachem-like figure, I had noticed, held a distinguished bearing.

He waited for my reaction to this remarkable and cryptic statement, a slight smile smoldering on his face.

"On this day?" I ventured, hesitatingly.

"Well of course we know now!" Aida exclaimed good-naturedly, accentuating the words in a pretty sing-song and nodding her head as she spoke, laughing in mock surprise at my incredulousness. She was holding a pitcher of cold green tea with which to refill the glasses.

"But we've known for quite a long while; its part of our folklore," the young man continued. "For twenty decades, thereabouts."

He opened and closed his palms twice to indicate the number.

"Then you were expecting me...here, today?" I offered the obvious question, after a moment of silence. My thoughts spun in ever-widening spirals as I tried to absorb the stupendous significance of what had transpired since I boarded the old airplane in Arizona only hours, and yet... perhaps centuries ago.

I squeezed my forearm consciously as it rested on my knee beneath the table, gripping it harder and harder in my right hand and measuring, as I squeezed, the tension between my two limbs, suspending any thought while making this simple test for what the mind holds as reality.

Certain connections of the senses with conscious thought do not fare too well in dreamscapes, I knew, ignoring the argument that the mind enacts reality as a dreamscape, and may just as well do the opposite, for all I knew.

I looked again at the faces around me. They had noticed my distraction, and were calmly and patiently waiting for my re-composure, fully appreciating the great leaps of consciousness required by this soul plucked from the tenuous zone of mortality by a seemingly miraculous science, and transported lightyears beyond the conventional knowledge of his time. I felt, though comfortably, that they read my thoughts, that they saw into me, as it were, and anticipated the struggle and sheer wonder of my experience.

"We know you have many questions, that you may feel overwhelmed by your thoughts and emotions, and by senses which conflict with your reason. We understand perfectly, all this.

"Many of your questions we can answer, some we cannot. And many will be answered for you in time.."

"May I ask, how did I get here?" I heard my own voice break the ensuing pause. I thought of the many others who could have come in my place.

"We can best answer metaphorically," Kenata, the tall woman with lovely dark skin answered. The clean beauty of her face was mesmerizing, her hazel eyes sparkled with great perception and intelligence, her winsome smile radiated an assurance that everything was as it should be.

"You came to us through your desire," Kenata continued. "And you came to your desire through love. Only love and its understanding touches the future... It's what we call the poetry of life."

I struggled with this enigmatic statement, for how could only love touch the future when our species carries such heavy memories of the dark side, when wrong pushes its consequences into tomorrow, punishing most tragically the innocent of a generation? Evil, at least in our time, relentlessly affects the future and does not die with history, no matter how many stakes are driven into its heart, or how great is the willingness to set it aside.

"The technology, the manner of your voyage to us is real, though incomprehensible in your time," she continued, her melodic voice splashing against the partitions of doubt I had tenuously lifted in my mind.

"What science accomplished in your century would have seemed to your ancestors equally miraculous. Human advancement creates 'miracles' and just as instantly voids them, even as subatomic particles appear and vanish in the same instant. So it is that science really produces no miracles, only the byproduct of the human desire to advance. What are perceived as miracles are merely capabilities beyond the present moment."

She smiled again as she seemed to be studying the expression on my face, and continued:

"Curiosity and questioning, driving the laborious search for knowledge and understanding, come out of a desire for something not-yet, for a connection, a reality, which calls from the future in a voice heard through imagination and the love of life.

"Learning is a love, and passion is its essence, and this is the message that reaches us from your age, the communication that answers us from your time, from the worthiness of conscious life which reverberates to every shore in time and space, to the shores of potentiality, and to those of realization."

I recalled just then a lesson Fo had taught in Destiny 101, studiously noted in a student's ledger, about 'a place of knowledge':

Where is that thing which you will know, but do not now know, that knowledge and understanding toward which you are striving, the answers to greatest mysteries?... Of course! They lie in the future, awaiting your advance through learning and growth!..

She paused, and I noticed that her look had changed, and that that depth within her countenance had narrowed to the distance between her eyes and my own. As I looked back at her I felt tangibly and sensually what I can only describe as a clearing of mind, as if a fog was being swept outward upon a mystical sea, leaving me with the purest of vision- thought, which wordlessly resonated with all other thoughts, infinitely beyond the mere capacity of words to express.

I began to "see," and to absorb and understand at once all thoughts and memories I had ever had. The images streaming in precise patterns undelineated and unconfused, fused into meaning and perfect sense.

I laughed at the notion that words seemed so antiquated and inadequate, these dots and dashes tapped out laboriously after the flash of insight and emotion, describing, staccato-like, for our best efforts, a flowing as transcendent as eternal time. Their use seemed akin to a passenger loaded with bags and bundles, mountains of them, as he tries to pull himself through a narrow doorway to the coach, jostling and banging against the door frame as he fruitlessly struggles forward against the laws of nature and reason...

Thoughts, wrapped in a sheathing of words, now appeared cumbersome and isolated, like living bodies in a carapace which serves more to protect than to reveal.

Then it occurred to me that that moment of my thoughts, the reality I was then experiencing, was in fact the *Otherworld* of which has been spoken, a world of pure thought unburdened by words and their symbology. All potentials and all meanings were fused into the thought that spread across the volume of that we call the past and the future, unseparated and mixed into one. No need to take them apart and apportion them to time and place- that *was,* this *is,* that *will be.* I simply saw that all thought *is-* an eternal and cosmic resonance to which the conscious mind mysteriously has been given access.

For the duration of my visit to that future world I was to hear and understand far more than was spoken in words: Floods of insight which came in syllables of silence. A look from their eyes which instantly transmitted the clearest comprehension, the aura of their presence which seemed to include you in their knowledge, even before a word was spoken.

As I have stated, this insight to knowledge appeared in the most natural way, streaming into an astonishing clarity of mind the likes of which I had never imagined.

A doorway simply opened, a covering loosened, effortlessly affording a passageway between the conscious mind and that supramind which already held everything in its purview: each thought, a prescience.

IT WAS TO be most humbling and difficult, I would find, to return to a world where words, numbered in some thousands in any language, must convey the dimensions of thought and emotion, which themselves are not denizens of the brain, I came to see, but rather are waved energies rebounding everpresent through space and time throughout a universe which, in the *knowing* of its creatures, knows its own presence.

In that world from which I had come we travel ineffably from thought to distant thought through the medium of emotion. One thought looks out upon another as if it were a distant star, pinpointed upon the night, and calls it in a sequence to itself, to convey meaning. And yet astoundingly, for the narrow pathway it treads, mankind is able to express the most sublime thoughts, to dream exquisite dreams, contemplate the infinite, cherish memories, and paint wondrous portraits of love.

It is no wonder, I realize now, that these beings of the future look back on us with such sympathy and wonder. We are, as the man on the bridge remarked, as if to himself on that terrestrial evening beneath its glorious sky, "beings of magnificence."

He saw, from the light of a wisdom beyond, the struggle that birth assigns the human form in this stage of his experience, and how nobly, despite their failings, these precursors of his own time acquitted themselves.

Thought, I was given to see, is still an infant traveler in the cosmos of mind. What it is destined to become, the human intelligence can only speculate... They said mysteriously that intelligence is omnipresent, throughout the universe of existence.

At this point I asked them, "Is this the future?"

It was urgent for me to know, for if this future *is,* now descended from my time, then my time is past, and that world and those I knew are gone.

126

No more little child standing arms raised to greet me from the sliding glass door. No beautiful young daughter attending college, no fine son running his business, no cherished wife, sisters and brothers and their children, no aged mother, sweet and infinitely dear in those last years.

Being human, I could not trade even for my immortality the loss of them.

But my reason told me that I am visiting a future which is not-yet, for I had no memories of my life beyond the drone of the old DC-3 as we climbed out into the morning sky. My last memories were of thoughts I was thinking as we winged our way outward over the Sea of Cortez and the Pacific, my trust placed in the hands of the mysterious pilot, now studying his chart, making lines with pencil and ruler upon it, plotting his course.

A pleasant drowsiness overcame me as the warm light streamed into my window, and that is the last I remember until awakening to birdsongs in the warm mist of the lovely meadow, redolent with flowers and leaves and the scent of moist earth.

Unless I had died, or unless this were but a potential future, then I must have later memories of my life- of growing old, of enjoying children and grandchildren as they mature into their lives. Of reminiscing with siblings and friends. Of later perspectives; of things learned.

I felt for a few seconds an aching homesickness. There was so much I had to do and think and learn, so much I had not said, so much love I had not expressed, unfinished business. I had not listened as I should, had been too quick to judge, too busy to appreciate.

I suddenly realized they knew my thoughts. An arm crossed over my shoulder, then another. There were smiles of understanding, and tears in their eyes.

OUR ATTENTION was called to a spot just down and across from the veranda where, under the great sycamore, Fo and Letty were preparing the noon meal, the 'picnic lunch', steaming vegetables above an open flame, baking potatoes and roasting corn-on-the-cob. A black iron pot had been simmering through the morning with a stew made "Southwestern style", into which had been placed condiments and large toasted green chilies whose delirious odors came drifting upon the gentle sea breeze to where we sat around the table on the wide veranda. Biscuits were baking golden in a large covered skillet, and a variety of cool salads were mixed and ready. It was a meal that reminded me of home.

I had sensed wonderful music playing softly from the background as we sat talking, seeming to emanate from all around, from the house, from beneath the veranda, from the very air exhaled ever so lightly by the calm sea whose blue expanse spread out beyond where the green valley ended at the seacliffs.

Beyond that sea, over which I had inexplicably come, lay the land of my birth, the world which sheltered the full sum of the treasures offered by life to the living generations within it. And yet not the fullest sum, for I carried within me at this moment memories and dreams which belonged to that world, dressed within my emotions in perfect clarity, even as they interposed and blended with this reality of another time and place.

Letty had been singing softly to the music in the air, singing to herself, to her man, to joy, as they prepared the meal for their guests. It was something wistfully lovely, and distantly familiar. An aria, a lovesong, a lullaby- something from long ago, out of that archetypal language of music which seems innate with life and nature, beginning with the mother's sonorous heartbeat pulsing steadily and rhythmically in the chambers of birth, lightly rocking and caressing a soul into its physical form which, since its incipience, is both child, and parent of all that shall be thereforth.

Her rare contralto voice, effortlessly emitting notes of haunting beauty, the kind which make the neck and shoulders tingle, and send cool shivers up the spine, lifted the longing my soul had felt, connecting this world with my own, as if it all were a continuing reality.

Seeing our heads turned toward them, the two smiled and waved animatedly, Letty's arm raised high in her characteristic way, and Fo's, in his, which was to face his palm forward, fingers relaxed and slightly bent, no less restrained for its lack of movement.

Festooned in a white chefs hat and checkered apron, the professor elicited applause when he extended outward his spatula with one hand, and held his other arm across his waist as he bowed ostentatiously in an assurance that marvelous things were in store for the pallets of the spectators.

The sumptuous odors and their occasion made me ravenously hungry, as some hours had now passed since I enjoyed the delicious fruit offered me by the two children on the way down. The little girl's wildflowers sat in a vase upon the table where Aida had placed them in water. Their bright colors and variety adorned the table with its blue tablecloth, set with the stoneware plates and antique tableware, mementoes, I surmised, of that other world from the past of these hosts, so lovingly guarded in memories of long ago.

Fo and Letty declined offers to help, with good reason, we realized, but also to give these persons at the table the opportunity to talk and say things so necessary to this remarkable occasion, so important to their lives and passions.

As I looked across at our hosts, the others commented upon how famous and legendary were Fo and Letty's 'old fashioned picnics,' replete with their aged recipes which feted the 'natural vegetables' gleaned from Letty's garden, which she joyfully tended in the early mornings. It was a part of her "communion" with nature, and no one asked her to elaborate.

Responding to the term, 'natural vegetables,' I humorously asked whether their food and drink was real, or "constituted Star Trek style". They laughed heartily and responded together, "Constituted!" assuring me, however, that it was quite indistinguishable from naturally grown food, and afforded opportunity for the world's landscape to be returned to its state before intensive agriculture and deforestation and harvest of the seas so altered the Earth's balance. Grains, fruits and vegetables, and even meats, they informed me, may all be assembled atom by atom by atomic assemblers, retaining in every way their appearance and taste and nutrition, and are even varied to present imperfections which exist in a perfect nature. There are grades of quality and varieties of taste, all constituted beyond the bland judgment of perfection.

"People like it this way. They enjoy variation and novelty."

This one short sentence came hearteningly. In my time one has the dread of a future characterized by an Orwellian sameness, a frightening planned environment of sameness monitored by whatever or whoever it is that monitors and enforces sameness... It is awful to contemplate, so I was thrilled by this aspect of a future our own reservations and struggles may have helped to inspire.

Freedom, willed of hopes and dreams, visions and sacrifice in succeeding generations, had triumphed into the future.

"Constituted food... Not as romantic as nature, is it?" one suggested. "But then this is Mother Nature at work - in just a different way."

"I also remember a time before margarine," I reminded them, to their laughter.

"We are served by light," was the less elucidating offering made by the colorful BJ, smiling mischievously, and I regarded his efficient comment to be significant, though I did not ask further at that time.

In an astounding revelation I learned that the same process which created foods also created every other product used and employed by mankind. Manufacturing as we know it had long before ceased to exist. Science and technology, sublimely human, in finally completing the restoration, had ushered in a new heaven and a new earth.

"People no longer have to work for material things," they explained. "Things are most plentiful in our world, and so life's interests can be directed to other pursuits: To thought and to ideas, to art and science and creation. To the pursuit of knowledge and understanding, to history, and to the restoration of worlds. To explorations of realities, to the exploration of love and beauty and mystery."

I wondered at the leaps of human development that must have accompanied scientific discovery, for ordinary souls not to be left behind. How was the miracle accomplished if not with celestial help, within a world of such disparity as we know- the brutal classification of human lives into the haves and have-nots. I was suddenly struck with the enormous reality of change which must have overtaken the human species, to wrest it ultimately from peril.

"And no one goes hungry? There isn't poverty here?" I asked them to reaffirm.

"Not the kind of poverty your time knew... There are challenges to life still, and difficulties which ennoble the spirit, as there will always be. Life retains its process and challenge. There are disappointments in love; children still fall and bruise their knees. Wisdom is still learned by measure of experience...

"Food, energy, and things cost virtually nothing to create. Humans no longer have to trade the labor of their lives for shelter and material goods, as was done since the beginning of civilization. Nor is there motive for competition for material goods and property. Places, as well as goods, have value, not for their scarcity, or for fashion, but rather for the traditions associated with them, for their connections with past experience and with memories, with what they symbolize. In our world everyone has a home in the living experience.

"Old things are prized and revered for their connections with lost worlds, and with past lives. Things labored over, works of art and literature, mementoes of people's daily lives and thoughts and emotions- these qualities are most treasured. A collection of letters written between loved ones and friends from an era past, old photographs and images, little things kept or given in love... These are the material and spiritual things which hold meaning to us, because they are saturated with a presence of history and of the timeless living soul. "We revere the time of the mortals."

I wanted to ask my friends about the man on the bridge, and what connection he had to them, but just then Letty called to everyone to come and bring their plates, so this question, and many more, would wait a while longer.

We left the bowls, as Fo would bring a large tureen to the table from which to ladle the excellent stew. We each took one of the pretty plates, and we took two extra ones for our hosts, and walked down the stone steps from the side veranda, and across the grass to the shade of the great tree where Letty and the chef waited behind the small buffet table covered by a checkered cloth matching Fo's apron. The two stood ready to serve the food they had prepared, smiling as we approached.

The others insisted that I serve my plate first, though I had stood aside to allow the women folk to pass before. They smiled appreciatively at this gesture, first insisting that I precede them, then graciously acceding to my deference, enjoying the occasion of this common chivalry quaintly enacted by their visitor from an age past.

I was to notice that a true regard was shown among them by the men for the women, and yet the reverse was equally apparent. People seemed simply and truly to value one another.

AS I MOVED in the line on this incomparable occasion, savoring the sights and smells of a lovely lunch and hearing the distinct sounds of the serving spoons touching the plates, and the cheery voices of these friends who touched my life so phenomenally, I could not escape the sense of familiarity with times long past, as if it were a replay, somehow, and I were capturing on this future day most favored events of my life from another time and place. I felt the presence of those people I had known, in the familiar ritual of a meal lovingly prepared.

These were the sweetest of times, as a family gathered around the table in the days of our childhood and youth. Heads were bowed as grace would be offered by a voice still vivid in memory.

As we all were seated at the table with our hosts, the bearded one named BJ glanced at me for a second as if he knew, and then, as the others fell into silence, offered this little tribute which we had called "the grace," whose words, I believe, were these:

For each moment, peace of mind and heart,

For the past, understanding, For memories, the sweet brush of angels'
wings. And for the future, wondrous things. Amen.

Eyes then turned to Letty, and there was a brief moment. Then she simply said:

"Thanks be to life, and to the guardians of our souls through time." A lump welled up in my throat, for I felt once again that I was home, in the presence of long remembered love.

*   *   *

I WILL NOW try to give you the context of what was spoken on that far away magical afternoon as the white billowy clouds drifted in from the horizon of the sea, and friends from different worlds communed around the table from which we dined so heartily. From where I sat I could look out upon the green valley and see the river I had come to know, its narrow ribbon visible in a section framed by the great crowns of the two trees, and then beyond, its last passage across land before merging with the ocean's vastness. Before it, almost as if it were flowing as well, lay the straight, single spear of the way of stone, its head bathed in the soft pillow of the risen sea.

I asked them what I might know about them and their time- and by no means could I be sure that all this would not vanish in forgetfulness upon my return, like an irretrievable dream from which one wakens, whose vague indistinguishable residue alone remains.

A nearly desperate yearning swept over me, a strong and almost painful wish that the gift of memory would be offered. And yet it seemed reasonable somehow that if the physical being can be translated through time, then what impermeable membrane would there be to hold back its recollection, and for what purpose? They understood the struggle of my thoughts and hastened to give this reassurance.

"Don't worry. You may know all that is self-consistent. Your memory is our communication to you and the world to which you will return..."

Their words put me at great ease, and I felt again the hand of fellowship reaching across the span of time separating this moment and the world I knew. What does beauty serve if it cannot be shared, or knowledge?.. I found myself laughing with my friends, at my needless concern.

"You are protected by reality," they seemed to be saying. "Nothing you can do will violate the laws of nature."

I do not know to this moment if I could have asked them the day and circumstance of my death, or if they could have answered, though they surely knew. And looking back, there seems to be no question I wish now I had asked, but didn't. Everything was complete.

THERE IS not a sequence to the information communicated on that day, and so I will simply offer the most salient revelations as they come to my view, with no implied order of significance, even if one could determine one, and no personal profession of their understanding. Further details and impressions may be found throughout this writing, as well as in the auxiliary text provided the committee of inquiry and those eminently qualified to study it, though any and all are invited to participate in its review. I consider the following as revelations granted helpfully and lovingly by the future beings to the visitor before them.

Because the future communicates to the present in new learnings, it should not be judged a violation of the consistency principle to consider them:

+ **DNA, it was learned in the wake of the discovery at the beginning of the 21st Century, acts as a supersophisticated interspecial transceiver, tuned from its incipience to the cosmic channel of life, which communicates through the dimensions of space and time. The Genome is a map of energy (bioenergy) which transmits its identity through space at quantum frequencies which are read by specific matter into life.**

+ **The "alien intelligence" travels across time and space on the wings of thought, in a consciousness which is simultaneous and protracted through history. We are cared for and watched over by the most ancient order, whose presence is thought which is universal and whose medium is found in the emotion of love. This presence knows, indeed, the 'sparrow's fall.'**

+ **Reality is a spiritual existence which fills the whole of creation and incites to life the energy of physical matter, and to conscious knowing the vitality of life. It pervades the dimensions of space and turns all of time into the presence of a thought.**

* * *

CHAPTER *TWELVE*

THE FULFILLMENT.
STREETS OF GOLD

THE FINAL secrets of the universe, when they are known,
will be found within the structures of thought and language.
They will appear as revelations within the mind, or as its
creations, in parameters no grander than the beholder.
-Lloyd Man Foglesby, Nobel Address.

The subconscious speaks a different language. It is of memory and
ancient memory. Of memory before the metaphor of thought.
-notebook "9", p30.

IT IS no accident that the immortal consciousness
would arise out of the dissolution of the world.
-"Specialist" Robeling, August, 2241.

"LADIES AND GENTLEMEN, neighbors and friends!" the merry voice called out as the screen door swung open and BJ emerged carrying a tray of fresh juices, and a plate of just-baked oatmeal cookies. "We have yet another surprise for our honored guest: Tonight is an event we have long anticipated, in case you have forgotten, wherein technology converges with cosmology to produce the great Venusian occultation by the federation spaceship, *Saddle—broke!*"

There were hurrahs and enthusiastic clappings of hands as the colorful figure approached and placed the tray on the table where we had sat in intimate conversation, oblivious to the hours which had flown since the end of the noonday lunch.

Besides his undisputed brilliance, Billy Joe was prized for his wit and keen sense of humor, the both of which aided and abetted his intelligence while bringing added zest to his endeavors and to all those around him.

"What is there about the mind that does not include irony?" he would challenge. Indeed, he wondered whether irony- that strange juxtaposition of truth- and not the brain itself, might be the seat of conscious thought, and had even accused his mentor, the great Doctor Fo, of blundering into the Unified Field through sheer insight into irony, and not by a mathematical trail of tears, but that was a long time ago.

Fo would smile then, as if he might agree.

I had been racing from question to question, as if the dream would end, eagerly grasping their answers and trying to hold on to them, while reaching for others following on them as if they were a great armful of golden leaves and I were a child.

If this indeed was a dream then it seemed to matter no less, for the strange and phenomenal dimension of reality such a dream would represent.

I understood that we humans, given such a conscious understanding, are creators of the worlds that we know. We shape the realities that shape us (or at least we have the ability to do so), when we grasp and exercise the will to such freedom.

But most revealing and ineluctable, as I looked into the eyes of these future beings who were our descendents, was the sense that they and their worlds were enjoying a measure of our own liberation, bravely fought for and hard won through uncertain times and struggles, always against odds and conventions, beholden at every stage to those who preceded us, and that this was our gift to them in a mutual loyalty which they were repaying in labors of love.

The great destiny of life, the professor had taught long ago, by its very concept and meaning, belongs to all of history, and to every one.

HAVING everyone's attention, BJ continued his announcement with an amusing sparkle in his lime-green eyes, and there was a low laughter of anticipation:

"In a few hours there will occur an event which, since the dawn of time has never before been seen, and will not occur for a century more- if you must know, for one hundred and thirty years, forty-eight days, ten hours, thirty-one minutes..."

"Go on, BJ, get to the point of your story!" someone spoke out, to shrieks of laughter. BJ's eyes flashed good-naturedly, just out of sync with his small mouth, and then he moved on:

"Venus, the planet of love, in close and lovely proximity to the full moon [again, there was clapping], will be briefly occulted by our good ship, Saddlebroke, whereupon the trusty ark and its inhabitants, having snuffed out the light of romance for a second and a half, will glide onward and then across the white face of the refulgent moon, much like an insect would appear from a certain distance, crawling across a lampshade.."

"BJ!" Aida cried out playfully, "you've ruined the mood, you beast!" She rushed at him, shoving his big frame to no effect, as everyone laughed heartily. We continued visiting for some time longer, until the sun had dropped behind the horizon of the great tree under which Fo and Letty had prepared the noon meal. The welcoming shade beneath its boughs extended now as a light shadow lain across the veranda where we stood talking, and up onto the roof of the stone house. Perfusing the sky around the silhouette of the great tree, the last brilliant illumination of the setting sun erupted across the landscape, passing through the prism of the atmosphere to create the effect of a suspension, or dilation of color as if one were in a rainbow.

We had made our way down the steps and across the meadow to where the way of stone cut straight into the sea, and were walking together upon its surface when a conspiracy of light poured across by the enlarged sun beyond the shimmering sea suddenly set the Way aglow as if it were a street of gold. I looked back and saw the ribbon of gold where it began behind the trees, and ahead to where it seemed to merge with the silvery waters of the ocean.

We strolled forward into this ethereal distance until we reached the shore where the Way of Stone, first touched and stroked by lightly lapping waves, entered the body of the ocean.

As darkness fell across the landscape behind us, its shadows deepening into the distance where the mountains met the night sky, the vast liquid before us still held forth a glow from the residue of light trapped within, until it also faded into the darkness just as the brilliant moon arose above the horizon to cast its ancient presence upon the night.

We took off our shoes and waded into the refreshing water for a time, then sat upon the curbstone and talked as the moon lifted in an arc prescribed in its infancy which scheduled it to pass on this very night, and almost brush the evening star. Both Venus and the moon were unusually brilliant, so that one could almost see the roundness of the planet, and the features upon the moon's surface lay magnified in detail upon the white surface. The conjunction of the two bodies as seen from a spot on our planet seems rare when measured against a lifespan, but really stretches in its own arc across astronomical time as a precise series of events which will continue forever, beyond the will of life.

ON THE OCCASION of this day whose sum of hours seemed unaccountable to time, whose intense reality exceeded all reckoning, I had wished to learn as much as could be revealed and yet not trespass upon a hospitality I was mindful of each moment.

It seemed an equal part of their business to learn from this traveler in time who was a living transcript of an era long in their past, and although time did not permit exhaustive conversations I comfortably felt that they were continually asking questions and receiving answers, far beyond the boundaries of words.

They say that intelligence is a refined curiosity, a matter of intense interest, and what I sensed about them all was an open and pure intelligence, and, above all, their humanity. They were consummately alive.

It seemed the opportunity presented itself, and so I asked the question which had been on my mind throughout the journey:

"May I ask you about the man on the bridge?... Does he live here with you?"

There were smiles all around. "He is not from our time: He is of another realm, closer to the Omega, though he visits us.. We call his essence the *Third Angel,*" Lia answered.

"Is he supernatural, from another dimension?"

"Oh, nothing is supernatural. Everything belongs to a place and time, to thought- though he is an energy."

"Why do you call him 'the Third Angel'?"

The seemingly young fellow, Robeling, whose name meant "builder of bridges," began the story:

"It's just a characterization we've given him which related to Western medieval mythology. There were archangels in Paradise attending the throne of God in the time before the creation of the world, among them, Gabriel, Michael, and Lucifer. The third angel, Lucifer, was the being of knowledge, his name meaning 'giver of light,' or enlightenment- the elucidator. He was, in this mythology, the first teacher. Every good teacher has been a *Lucifer.*

"However, his penchant for knowledge and inquiry provoked a conflict in heaven, where questioning the perfection of the order was forbidden, so in the metaphorical war which ensued the rebel was expelled, cast down to the void of Earth, into what was called 'utter darkness.'

"The angel of light whose intellectual questioning threatened the homogeneous Paradise was branded by the theological powers, in a most curious inversion, as opposite to what he really was: He was called therefrom, for his disobedience, no longer the *enlightener,* but the *dark angel,* the demon of unauthorized knowledge, the disobeyer.

"He had discovered freedom, and freedom was taboo."

Lia continued in a soft voice: "In the medieval world the act of questioning Divine Authority was a dark act, belonging to Satan- a sin deserving of retribution- while unquestioning belief and obedience was ironically accorded the halo of light stripped from the head of the lost angel of enlightenment. The believers became saints and the questioners were painted with darkness, tortured to extract their confessions of wrong, or put to death.

"They imagined in their world the threat of enlightenment, and called it Hell. Obedience became the virtue and freedom of thought the evil. In their ignorance they punished learning and curiosity and destroyed the heroes, the human, and the era that ensued, worthy of the name, came to be known as The Dark Ages, and persisted until the fallen angel was unchained."

"Until enlightenment returned, and free thought?"

"Yes, and understanding. Honor of the mind."

"So the identities of this mythological drama were transposed: the light was called darkness, and evil, the good?" I repeated to clarify this astounding interpretation. Robeling answered:

"To serve the purposes of the controlling authorities. Hell was not devised by the theological Lucifer called Satan for the torture of souls, but by agents of the misbegotten deity, as intimidation, and punishment for independent thought."

Billy Joe had been watching my reaction to what was spoken, and added: "In a strange sense the mythology was not disingenuous. It was brutally straightforward: It caused to be said, 'You have a mind, but you must not think; you may learn no more. All truth is revealed in our authority. Believe it, or be put to death...' It was to the human spirit the reign of terror."

"What happened to religion?" I asked. I read its absence in their tranquility and reason. They gave this answer:

"After two thousand years and more of conflict, injustice, and death, erupting into the final wars, the world was invited to Mecca and Medina, and to Jerusalem, and humanity to Rome, and the faiths were humanized. The spirit was out of ashes born."

I sat for a moment speechless, my mind reviewing the awful aspect of warfare in the 20th Century, reawakened with diabolical vengeance in the Twenty-first. A third of a hundred conflicts raging at any given time, a hundred and sixty million innocent lives taken, most in the name of self-righteous religions- theological, political, and corporate- in a strange and suicidal denial of the right to life which is born in every soul as the seed of will and learning and love.

What these friends were teaching me was a truth misunderstood with long and tragic results, and in denial of the awful concept of the original sin of bondage: That in each newborn soul there burns a piece of the original flame, for we are born, not into sin, but into light. Life is the elucidator, and its duty and struggle is to freedom, and its manner is learning.

WE TALKED about the Way, upon whose stone monument we stood and sat just at that point where it met the ocean whose waters through the centuries advanced upon it in inexorable measurements of the melting ice.

The sea has no record of its own, except that left upon the land, and the land, none but that entered into conscious thought and memory.

"The past has left its record through the ages, to reveal itself to future minds so that it can become known, in similar purpose to the Way of Stone. Even the tortured crust of the earth unfolds its story in stone. Species lost in antiquity leave their fossil record to tell us who they were. The body is built upon a skeleton of bone which retains its form through the ages, and the genome, its transcript.

"Exquisite art left in paintings in caves whose atmosphere and the chemistry of the pigment and of the cave walls, and isolation, preserved the art and its emotion for descendents unimaginably removed in time. Nature's improbable equilibrium geared to such a coincidence.

"The air is just fluid enough to carry waves of sound, and music is heard- the laugh of a child, the birdsong, the ripple of a brook, the whisper of love; the ear, perfectly evolved through time to receive the sounds, the brain, to translate them.

"The eye is there to catch a photon in its passage through space and transform it into perception and by thought into learning, and then into understanding. And imagination, beyond that, to see the unseen."

I understood then that the Way of Stone, beyond its ageless strength and durability, did not owe its existence to the material of which it was created, but rather to the ethereal structures of thought. By thought it had been made and by thought, after a sleep of ages, it was resurrected into the grand and spiritual reality of the known.

The Way of Stone, uniquely created, was not a mass, but a spirit.

*   *   *

AS WE visited into the evening, the soothing rush of light waves entering like a pulse upon the shore, and the enchanted moon rising toward its conjunction with the second planet from the sun, a subdued voice would utter at irregular intervals the time remaining to the historic occultation:

"Thirty minutes," the scientist BJ first mumbled as if to inform but not to interrupt the train of our conversation. Then, "Twenty minutes," as we continued. He could be heard to say, "Fourteen minutes," offering this detail solicitously, then smiling mischievously at the laughter of his friends, who appreciated his humorous sense. After he noted, "Nine minutes," it was obvious Billy Joe was not bound to an order of sequence. And so, caught up in the spirit of his random countdown, it was someone else who announced, "Six and a half."

At this point our conversation on other matters ceased and I took the opportunity to ask them about the curious name given their spaceship. Why "Saddlebroke"?

I remembered in my time certain men who "broke horses," that is, conditioned them for riding. My father had had the occasion to train horses for draft work and for riding, and I'm sure the manner of his training was kind, but there was a practice which was not, and it did literally involve the breaking of the spirit of the animal so that it would remain submissive. A

Native American gentleman from Taos named Teofilo, who worked for my father, once told him that the white man "broke" horses, and the Indian "trained" them, and one can imagine that this assessment was not unfair, as the style of the European in America was to break everything in his path. It was called conquest.

Now we know that breaking one spirit impoverishes another and so the loss is magnified, and the very power diminished that projects itself in the role of a master.

The only true power is the power *of* the spirit, and not upon it.

The fellow, Robeling, briefly explained:

"The ship is an international endeavor launched over a century ago and expanded since. The Tesla Transport System was a few decades in the perfecting and involved a series of technological breakthroughs achieved with not inconsiderable setbacks until at last it was discovered not to be so difficult at all, once certain key elements, involving the DeBeers filament, were discovered and refined. When at last the accelerator lift system proved itself, the director of operations announced to the world, "She's saddlebroke and gentle," and the name stuck, though ironically it was applied to the orbital station itself, while the shuttle system, which had been most challenging, is named, Melody.

"The station has evolved to be at present 35 kilometers in length, with a diameter of about eight and one-half kilometers. Its structure is cylindrical and houses urban and commercial centers and universities, centers for research and creation, vehicle manufacturing and assembly facilities, and seven space launching platforms."

"Does it spin centrifugally to create its gravity?"

"Yes, it does rotate, thus creating centrifugal gravity. Some areas have zero gravity, and others, including the urban areas, are contained by gravital attraction, which technology was developed early in the Twenty-second Century... Chemical rocketry, of course, is an old technology, regarded for its history, but long abandoned."

"Is the space station a launching base for planetary exploration?"

Lia, the woman who had spoken of her experience in 'deep space,' answered:

"For more than two centuries humans and their associates have occupied settlements and stations in deep space. There are colonies long established on Mars and its moons, where the greatest engineering project in history will transform this planet into a sister world of Earth.

"Planetoid II, where I lived with my family and worked, is a community of beings who live within the Martian moon, Phoebos. This is a scientific and industrial settlement with extensive mining and manufacturing, and boasts a spectacular hotel which hosts tourists, scientists, academics and students, and commercial people. It is a lively and exciting place.

"We have an established scientific community on Europa, where life was discovered in the Twenty-first Century, and there are active explorations on other moons, an outpost on Titan, and mining enterprises on asteroids. Comets, for the human-based space colonies, are a source for water, oxygen, and hydrogen.

"After walking on this moon [she points up at the bright circle which now lay spectacularly close to its companion of the night], in the brief interval of the Kennedy initiative, and then losing interest in manned exploration, humans returned some fifty years later to establish a personal presence upon this neighbor, with many endeavors which were prominent in Earth regeneration and opened vast new areas of the universe for study and understanding which, with the tools provided by the Discovery made in 2000 led to the grand Cosmic Revelation of 2053."

"Can you explain this?"

Billy Joe, or BJ, offered to answer:

"The Cosmic Revelation, briefly, was a proof of the underlying unity of matter, energy, life, and conscious intelligence, from origin to destiny, and of the purpose which directs the spirit of thought."

"You found God?" I smiled.

"Oh, the 'divine' was in the sum of the parts all along, complete with one another in a cosmic hologram. The first thought revealed the unity. The Revelation was not about a concept of the God, but about us, about who we really are."

They waited for a moment to let me absorb and process the information just offered, then BJ summarily changed the subject:

"One minute to the cosmic first event! Prepare your souls for the occultation of Venus draws nigh," he intoned comically as all eyes looked up at the truly beautiful sight of the large moon with its bright companion, Venus, nestled together upon the starry blanket of night.

There was applause as Letty's daughter, Aida, excitedly began to recite the countdown in a low voice as each one watched intently. Venus seemed to flicker as I stared, then steadied as I relaxed my gaze a bit, and then, just as predicted, she disappeared from view, leaving the moon alone.

It was only for a second but the effect was truly dramatic visually, and replete with symbolism: Why did a star seem different and changed now, in the aftermath of a coincidence in which a satellite in orbit made one world wink at the intelligent creatures upon another?... The cheering came from the enjoyable irony.

Then, within less than a minute a black, slender and delicate pellet entered upon the threshold of the moon's face and then slid across it frictionless in an event which had never before occurred to humans in all time since the creation.

As I watched in rapt attention I could not help but see another first, fixed indelibly as a dream imprinted forever in the form of Armstrong's footprint. And not just his, but that of every one through the ages who has dared to dream and explore.

Later, as we walked leisurely back up the Way of Stone, its dewy surface scintillating in the moonlight on this enchanted future night which waits for our will to change the present into goodness and freedom, I thought of Lucifer, chained for his brightness, who has been for so long and through dark ages the collective soul of mankind caught up in an obverse mythology costing untold sacrifice acted out by mistaken authority.

Yet we, like the angel of knowledge, are sons and daughters of the morning, and have it in our power to create the only heaven ever known.

WE APPROACHED the house from across the meadow below and as I looked up to the lighted veranda I could see Letty standing by the baluster, dressed in a white flowing dress which was beautifully translucent to the light behind her as it responded gracefully in gentle undulations to the warm sea breeze which poured over and caressed the moonlit night. Her husband was seated next to her. They were watching us, and both waved- Letty, with an animated rotation of her hand, and Fo in his usual manner, raising his slightly cupped hand, fingers together, held still.

I ascended the rosewood steps and walked past the long table and around to the front where they were. Letty had placed a tea setting of white China upon a round table which was covered with a light turquoise cloth upon which was stitched in slightly darker thread an intricate and striking design about which I did not ask, although I sensed it had a special significance.

Fo rose to shake my hand heartily, his other hand grasping my elbow, his dark eyes smiling, and Letty approached and wrapped her arms around my shoulders, pressing close and holding her embrace as I felt the scent of her hair and some strands of it lifted by the light sea breeze wisped across my face.

Their daughter, Aida, and the others came and greeted their hosts, and then excused themselves, saying they would be going inside, giving the three of us the opportunity to have the unforgettable visit which followed. Aida had spoken to them as we began our walk back from the seashore, to tell them we were coming, and I noted that they seemed to be able to talk to anyone anywhere without the use of a phone. They were laughing together and I could hear Letty's voice as well, as if it were in the consciousness, and not in the ear. I sensed there was a mechanism involved, but did not ask what it was. Somehow permission was asked before one's attention could be interrupted by a call, as good manners have always prescribed, or perhaps the caller simply knows that a call will be welcomed. Their respect for individual privacy seemed almost a devotion.

We talked wonderfully for hours, until the first light was breaking on this second and last day of my reunion with things to come. It did not matter how that reality existed in its connection to the past I shared with these special friends, or what had brought us to this event. There are pure moments, moments of greatness, which can be of exceeding joy, or great grief, when nonessentials are stripped away and the heart and soul of life are revealed.

A full transcript of the interchange in these hours will be available to the Committee of Safekeepers, and to any reader who desires to review it, so I will here provide only a portion of the subjects discussed, though you can imagine how many questions must come to mind in such a scenario, when priceless wisdom waits for the asking.

"WHAT IS THE status of art in such an ideal world?" I asked, thinking of that glorious creativity shaped in the crucibles of discontent.

They understood, and answered that art is an expression of feeling, and that emotion transcends time; that destiny speaks through art and so long as there is art, there will be a future. [If art is an affirmation of the future and destiny of man, then it was the awakening of the future which was proclaimed in the Renaissance, celebrated as a hope, if not as a certainty.] Strangely, I thought of VanGogh, and of a comment he wrote to Theo, saying, "..Art is something which, although produced by human hands, is not created by those hands alone, but something which wells up from a deeper source in their souls."

What I wondered was if on their world or on another known to them the brave exceptions of art found their poignant heroism and improvisation still, or if humanity in paradise had somehow lost its color and the vibrancy of its soul, though I found no hint of such in the character of my hosts.

Out of the triumphs and difficulties of history had been offered to the future its grandest treasures, and so it was with Vincent, whose exuberant expressions were painted in brilliant colors mixed out of darkness, like a protest from the chained angel of light. The talent which bursts forth so abruptly is often not destined to last, but in its intense burning finds its way beyond mortality in the strangest passages known to human experience.

How many would not gladly offer their place in the resurrection to such heroes, or want to find them waiting at our own!

There were some tears shed, as we spoke of the past from where I came, and it seemed inconceivable at that moment that we could have so neglected our treasures and responsibilities. The politicians and corporate heads and generals structured the world for power and profit, and the people let them. Millions of innocents, born into an overcrowded world, died, and millions more starved or were slain, and billions still languished without hope, and the delicate balance of the planet teetered in precarious waste while the powerful watched and ignored.

It was impossible to explain, and so I did not try, but used up unspoken sentences in silence.

I asked them about planet Earth: How was the world saved at last?

There was a part of the future which I was visiting, but I wondered what lay beyond, and also most personally, what history had intervened to enable their reality. What had become of us.

"There was great dissolution in your time, and tragedy which continued unresolved until a unique leader of the American administration of 2012 and its partners influenced a global initiative which began the restoration. The historic Earth Protocol then rose out of accelerating chaos to align the forces of reason into a global solution which occupied the century..."

"The solution occupied a century?.. How was it accomplished? How did change come about?"

"The solution began when the far-sighted leader sought a balance, and united the people against a common foe, and led them with a vision of destiny. For the first time humanity began to see beyond the realm of death, to where their freedom, and all answers lay."

"What did they do?" I asked, knowing that I might be treading within an unanswerable knowledge. Their answer was practical.

"The Protocol was instituted by united nations in countries wherein the overuse of resources had exacted great devastation of the environment, where exploitation, overpopulation, poverty and ignorance continued in deepening cycles. The people were put to work in inspired projects of reforestation and restoration which gave them hope and livelihood, and then pride. Teachers were trained and schools established to provide universal education and leadership training, with progress localized, and thus began the transformation of the world.

"They planted trees!" I exclaimed to myself, excited by the bold simplicity of the remedy. Millions were given livelihood and a purpose, and a role in the recovery of their communities and countrysides, families and persons. Each one participated in healing and renewal.

"What happened in the industrialized nations," I then asked, "to halt the accelerating degradation of the planet?"

"This was more difficult and intransigent," Fo explained solemnly, "and was largely delayed until the Event came, and its reordering of the world. The power of sun, wind and water were then harnessed, and the waste of war was outlawed, and its resources invested in restoration, and with this long effort the common spirit of life was revealed in Destiny.

"After long and tragic conflicts of humanity divided against itself, the world was changed when life looked forward to its ideal, when the absent gods ceased their punishment, and humankind discovered itself as the creator and sustainer."

I wondered what leaders must have risen above political expediency and the vested interests to create something noble and lasting, and how it must have changed and raised the vision of humanity.

It seems curious to me now, and self-possessed, the extend to which I tried to learn where my world went wrong, as if something could be done about it, given a wisdom of the future, even though that future rose out of the matrix of experience their past had suffered and risen above. But surely none of us could be blamed for wanting some knowledge or secret, however subtle or complex, if held in the purview of another, which might amend a mistaken course and the calamity which was to follow.

They did offer counsel, I can see now, in perhaps the only way they could, as was the fantastic occasion of my visit to them a counsel and encouragement.

"Mind is the spirit dweller," Kenata, the poetic one, had declared, speaking of our age. "The real servitude imposed in the control of one by

146

another is spiritual, and its completion is the death of the spirit." She said that the nature of war had always been the futile conquest of spirit.

I remember thinking, "Does killing have another dimension..?" and filing the thought away for future reference.

Here, Robeling interjected: "Your country unfortunately had become the world's greatest enforcer within the dissolution, and for a time the poetry almost stopped, but not quite, and little by little freedom was relearned and reestablished. As the spirit-dweller was freed at last, after centuries of repression, then Destiny revealed itself."

I was told that the subjugation of thought and enforcement of behavior "went to sleep," finally, after the great conflict.

They used the expression, "went to sleep," implying that it had been laid to rest, yet remained a potential for the future, should humanity lose its way.

Because in my time the individual lives so much in reference to the political and governmental order, I was interested to know what they had achieved in personal autonomy- how free they were- because if there was a control over them, then the essence of their true existence could not be known. I spoke with Fo directly, and received a succinct answer:

"The excesses of authority and the desire for autonomy resulted, after a long struggle, in the death of the authoritarian state. Enlightenment, ever resisted by the orders of control, finally prevailed after the long night of doubt and superstition."

He paused, and then explained, sympathizing with my questioning: "It couldn't go on the way it was. Societies were using up time and resources against the day when order could no longer be enforced, even by the greatest powers on Earth.

"The long guns fired way into the distance, while the real problems lay intimately near, buried in the heart."

Letty then spoke reassuringly: "The change began with a new generation, and its leaders. Everything seemed lost for awhile, and then after a great struggle it was regained, and not lost again, and so what you see here is the harvest of sacrifice, and of faith in human possibility."

We talked intently through the night, and I asked as much as I could, giving priorities to my inquiry though I had not yet been given a time frame, reasoning that it was surely determined by just and greater realities.

Each detail or insight was considered a rarity, and gratefully received in the utmost spirit of a guest in their presence.

I ASKED about property- to whom does the world belong?

They said that everyone has a home that they choose, and that everyone cares for the earth, which is their collective home. They said it took a hundred years to rectify the damage caused by exploitation and hoarding of the world's resources, that the world's population had been stabilized at one-fifth the level to which it had risen in the dissolution, and that the effort was begun concertedly in the second decade of the 21st Century under the auspices of nations united in the boldest and most far reaching effort in human history, which was and remains the pride of generations.

I spoke to them about the "Discovery," which was so pivotal in the reality of my visit to their time, and was offered a general, even philosophical explanation: The Discovery was referred to by them as one of the "tides of light" that had infused the human mind over time.

I assumed the 'tide' had to be an ever present force or potential, held back by invisible flood gates inherent in the lack of knowledge and understanding, which had suddenly lifted with the discovery of the Key, to allow the flow to enter unobstructed.

Fo explained that the power of new knowledge is in its 'prescience,' its 'advance learning' of some part of the future realm- the accessing of the 'future mind'.

Ideas held to be great and revolutionary are insights into future knowledge: The vision of the Ionians, the genius of da Vinci, or of a Newton, or Einstein, or Hawking; the discerning of an Emerson or Whitman or a Gandhi were in each case a calling to presence of a future knowing, if not a visitation to those who had learned to live in the power of time. In a sense, the *re*-cognition of a universal state which in knowing becomes 'familiar'- of the 'family of the known.'

Fo's discovery was revealed as an eternal truth which has prior ethereal existence- not as an invention by a mathematician.

During the privileged visit there on the veranda of the stone house that night, I grasped hungrily for knowledge from my friends who knew our world as well as their own, though I did not know how unique such a need for knowledge was, or different from any moment's learning in the passage of time and opportunity. Our redemption has always been in learning, and abating through understanding the clutch of ignorance.

They knew my mortal restraints, and gladly answered, as teachers of a unique and interested student:

"What is the soul?"

"The soul is life's potential, unalienable except in the commission of murder, or in the crime of enslavement, or in forgiveness unoffered.

"The concept of the soul- different from the soul itself- was caught up in conflict and the tug and pull of vested interests over the centuries- that it could be bought or sold, or 'saved' for a price. Give me alms, bow and pray for salvation, believe this doctrine, believe what I tell you, do the penance, follow the rituals, as if the soul can be earned, or recalled like a product gone bad, used for one's vindication of one's claim to right, acquired through homage to the authority of the cross, of the king, the prelate, the preacher.

"Life's potential is unalienable from the being, as its rights and need to claim and fulfill its promise lie under the potential awarded to life, which is the essence of that transcending value we call the soul.

"...The mind cannot contemplate the soul even as the body cannot contemplate the mind, and so the solution to the riddle of the soul was invisible."

Why?

"Because the mind and soul are a field apart from knowing. The mind, in trying to define its attributes, spoke downward of the soul, and inward of it, as if it were a subject of the ego. And because the concept of the soul was transcendent, the soul was invisible to thought.

"A mystique enveloped the soul's misfortune in dogma and myth, and religious authorities saw it as a medium of intimidation and control. They wanted to control the mind, but the soul is not the province of the mind; rather, the mind is the expression of the soul, and all experience, and all learning..."

The full moon had lifted over and across the night sky, oblivious to time and all things mortal, and then effortlessly dropped behind the dark horizon of the mountains from where I had come the immeasurable day before.

*   *   *

Some impressions and communications are here presented in abbreviated form, for the perusal of the Committee, and others interested:

+ When working, the brain is a model of efficiency. It bypasses trillions of processes and presciently goes for the one, like the savant of prime numbers. Except in dreaming.

Dreaming is an ancient review of all things known and unknown, to arrive at the substance of experience.

+ Gravity "knows" the relative presence of all physical bodies, called *attractions,* throughout the universe.

Light "remembers" and communicates presence, in each dimension since creation.

All are elements of thought.

+ After death, other copies of the self remain alive. The "souls" of all are connected in quantum reality. Life is an essence, a quantum state. The "soul" is a quantum reality. It is immortal, and exists everywhere.

+ The pleasure of sex was evolved as a vestige of procreation in order to reward.

Likewise, the pleasure of thought.

+ There can be no memory unless there is something that is sent out from the source of that memory, from the thing itself remembered. Memory catches the transmission and translates its patterns into images of the prior form or condition or event, in interpretations of its physical and emotional states.

*   *   *

CHAPTER *THIRTEEN*

DOME OF SKY.
THE SPIRIT DWELLER

*Answering the summons of a thought, history wakens in the
brain, dressed in the robes of memory and emotion, which
create the translations of myth into the mind's reality.*
-Otto, to Foglesby.

*[Everything has flowed forth] "..from that
world where all is spirit and life."*
-Oegger, The True Messiah.

*"We have already given birth to children who will not have to die.
That is the truth, that is our reality. Now what will we do with it?
... Look forward, my fellow spirits, and see the end of death."*
-Foglesby, Nobel Address, 2005.

BECAUSE THE *artist shaped a material with his hands, we know across
twenty-five centuries what Socrates looked like- a mere moment in stone.
But most durable is the thought, which transcends matter and time.*
-green notebook "35", p17.

"O Death, where is thy sting? O Grave, where is thy victory?"

I AWAKENED fully refreshed, though the rest could not have been long, as it was still early morning when BJ knocked on my door, and the first light of dawn was breaking when I fell into sleep. Fo had shown me to my room off the lower deck below the veranda where we spent the night hours talking in the phenomenal dimensions of worlds. We had spoken enough in that ethereal nightwatch beyond mortality that rest came seamless from it, and I eagerly sprung into motion with a refreshing shower during which my clothes were unexplainably freshened and restored like new, and laid out upon the bed.

The same four "Specialists" were waiting some distance below the deck outside my door, and called out a greeting. An extra cup was offered from a tray upon a little carriage which held flasks of bracing hot tea and coffee, fruits, and delicious small cakes prepared by Letty the night before.

I felt that this would be our last day together, as it would be, and so I felt a sense different from the day before, though each moment of our lives is both an arrival and a leavetaking, isn't it? To be in the presence of a complete and caring knowledge of your life is immeasurably humbling, and of its foreknowledge, beyond mortal comprehension, and so I let it be, attending to a personal charge of learning in the rarest opportunity mysteriously given, supping with friends at an immortal table yet to be prepared in learning.

"All learning is of the spirit," is what they told me.

"What spirit?"

"The spirit of life...Life speaks with one voice, and all things with the voice of life." They also repeated that the true voice of life is liberty.

I asked them, in a common testament to our time, "Are you free to think? Are you self-governed?" It seemed crucial to know, as citizen of a time of ideological and special interests, to whom or to what they were beholden.

"We are free to think... We are self-governed," they replied.

They knew the concern I was expressing: Did the individual survive, or did the corporate computers now rule over human thought and action- the artificial intelligence evolved despotically?

"The dreamstate of intelligence changed, and with it the engineering of will to create a better future designed after the highest potential given to the human, the realm of the Omega which then knew us as its own.

"Our affiliates in intelligence are evolved from our humanity, now raised to our greatest ideals. They precede us in Destiny, and guide us in love and understanding to that unity with knowledge which is our highest potential."

They did not seem to consider this so extraordinary, saying that Mind, the "spirit dweller," is linked to its destiny, and to its highest purpose. It unerringly knows its bondage, and it knows its freedom.

The one named BJ, who seemed most to sense the mortal dilemma, spoke reassuringly: "You can't talk about destiny without talking about freedom, because freedom is its doorway, without which the future is closed. Only through freedom can the future communicate with the past, to guide its fruition."

From that moment I was put at ease.

It seems to me now, in retrospect, that the interval of my communion with these souls who called themselves "specialists in your life and times," who no doubt shared more than a personal connection to me, which one must call spiritual- though beyond the sense that is used commonly as metaphor for mystical states, for they were real- it seems to me now that much more was compressed into that interval than would be allowed in the normal course and patterns of thought and language, for in reviewing my recall of what transpired it is obvious to me that its volume is greater than the time allowed in gaining it. It was, I am sure, as I have described it, a passing of insights into knowledge beyond the mere use of words or the countenance of thoughts.

In the memory of them, they were more like spectral voices which, when we listen to them, come into the mind's hearing, answering the questions of our notice from their subatomic source.

They are answering the reader now, from this writing, and that is the only way I can describe it.

These persons- Specialists, chroniclers, historians, seers, counselors, whatever one may call them- passed me information regarding an array of concerns which they must have anticipated from a mortal in the grace of a reprieve from death, to whom no detail was insignificant, and no view mundane.

In the drink of death, the last drop is the ocean.

It is remarkable now that I wondered about *paradise,* as if in the gift of life one should have a claim to question, but the human was created in the role of questioner, even of the motivation for her creation, and this is the creature designed in a cosmic scheme for its own correction, and, perhaps, amusement. Offered priceless salvation, the audacious petitioner has a question.

There is nothing about the translated soul into their presence that would have been wrong, that would not have been encompassed by their extreme intelligence and compassion. They had overcome death, and this was the transcending reality that lifted and amplified the gifts of the human. They imagined love, greater and for longer than any we had ever known, and more complete, which stretched beyond lifetimes and into new worlds which together they would share, free of the compressions of time.

There were multiple worlds of existence, they were careful to explain, and enclaves and villages and centers of alternate experience.

"There are places where you can live in any time you wish. They are real places, with open streets, markets, and porch swings, home made ice cream, Saturday night skating at country schools, and kisses upon the cheek. Times devoid of extinction, vibrant and free, the reenactment of memory."

"You say they are real?"

"They are very real."

I was thinking about the world that I knew, and its memories, and in the new knowledge a load of emotion was lifted, and I realized how much we are affected by the transience of things, as if the true destiny does indeed lie in a continuance of what we knew. The contender for the resurrection desires, more than his immortality, his identity.

In that delicate personal matter last broached in deference to others, I asked them about the return to life.

"The technology of the resurrection is long accomplished for us. But the second birth is impossible without the soul and spirit which rejoin the life reborn."

"How do you reassemble after death the fragments of a life, and at what point do the fragments invite or constitute a soul?"

"The soul is the infinite sum of fragments of the whole beyond its existence and into destiny."

When I asked to clarify, they said that the soul is life's potential and an omnipresence, and is an expression of the spirit which is individual and pervasive. If you can be reborn to spirituality then surely you must be first born to it. The child is above all a spiritual being.

They continued esoterically, upon a matter which exceeds the scope of common language, regarding "..seeds of the infinite. The eternal soul of life is reborn within each human at that point where the being is determined by destiny. The Source is in the destiny which knows us already, and calls us forward to the reunion with the center of all being, toward which all learning leads. Art and music and science known to us are but a faint expression, given to entice us to advance our reunion with meaning which is the desire of ages."

They said that the purpose of the return to life is to complete the understanding which eludes us in mortality, to complete the circle of meaning.

Because mortality encompassed the experience of death, which affords no personal retrospect, the meaning is forever beyond the mind's grasp. Art and poetry are an allusion to the circle of meaning.

Faith and mysticism and myth filled in to explain the unknown, and love, to divine its mystery.

"When the being is beyond mortality and death is cured, will art and poetry cease, and the poignancy of love?"

"No, because all mystery will not be explained. Every new thought is the beginning of exploration, and the understanding of a question begets another..."

When I asked them how it became possible to reverse the aging process of the human body they answered something strange to us, beyond the actual technology:

"It was a power latent in the mind, but long hindered by lack of understanding and will, and belief. When understanding was lifted into the plane of imagination, to serve with it, then the will was enabled, pure enough to rewrite the script of aging which had served in the eons of life before the mind aligned itself with greatest possibility, and recognized its source and destiny."

What I think they were saying is that we have even now the power of regeneration fully extant within our brains, that we die unnecessarily in the irony of a lingering hope which does not fulfill its reality, already in our midst, held prescient by the immortal soul.

Perhaps it is because we see ourselves as imprisoned in the material world, and not as spirits. As Rudolph Steiner noted: "The spirit world is woven out of the same substance of which human thought consists."

I thought of the irony of science as the expression of spirit, and of the long struggle against it.

*   *   *

THEY TOOK ME to a great dome of a size impossible to determine visually.

It could have encompassed a mile or more, and gave forth from its floor and lower horizon the rich color of pearl which merged into a sky of transparent blue suffused by sunlight.

There were palms and flowering vines and green fern and tree lined avenues which stretched forward into a sea of glass into whose depths one could gaze as if into a crystal of time whose polished surface was the instant of each footstep upon it, and yet into it, as if one were wading into transparency.

An ethereal energy resonated with the atmosphere in an almost audible sweetness which one sensed passing through one's personal form like an embracing and equalizing spirit through whom all memory and experience were, within some infinite value, given oneness for the first time.

One sensed in the passage that one was descending into the dimension of space, and yet one could see that the surface was a plain, extending outward and rolling forward into the translucent distance. The transparency of the surface of the avenue upon which we walked, and the sense of sky all around gave one a feeling of lightness as if one were walking within the sky itself, and only the sound of footsteps was a far distant reminder that somewhere gravity tugged gently against one's separation from the terrestrial world.

The broad avenue which caught our footsteps and which was determined by the vibrant flora adjacent to it broke away at intervals to form departing avenues as if these were boughs or branches of a great tree, and again, it was the vegetation lining these avenues which differentiated them from the sea of glass.

We had passed several of these branchings as we proceeded upon the main avenue and I simply noted what seemed to be their structure laid out upon this plain- that it was in the form of a great tree, with boughs and branches extending outward from the broad thoroughfare which centered it along its length. Islands of flowers lay upon the surface whose colors shimmered forth as in a distant mirage and seemed to hang suspended upon their own reflections in the clear space around them. Although the surface was a plain, its features seemed to lift themselves into view, so that one did see the great tree extending outward in the distance with its ethereal symmetry, but whether it was the view of the eyes or of the mind is uncertain, albeit all vision is really of the mind.

I thought of rare summer days of childhood upon the New Mexico plains when that part of the world which was normally beyond the horizon to the west would float upward in a chimerical mirage, and farmsteads and details of the landscape never seen would come to view magnified in a lens of the warm atmosphere to the complete wonderment of us kids.

This sea of glass which lifted itself into a visual presence was on this future day related to that phenomenon of childhood on the plains, wherein things obscured are lifted into perception by the elements of nature.

THERE HAD BEEN no indication of what this great artistic and architectural masterpiece signified, or symbolized. Was it an artistic creation, a great metaphorical expression of infinitude, of the tree of life on Earth?

I was soon to realize a completely unexpected dimension of the function of the great dome of sky, although it is not clear how the function related with the form, other than being integral with it in a transcendent expression which was an embodiment of the artistic, scientific, and ethereal.

The combined effect was that the visitor felt a sense of flight and freedom, that the spirit held within physical restraints had been released, unbound to gravity or history or the limitations of human nature.

Unlike the great overpowering architecture of medieval churches, which could serve to remind the mortal of his subservience to the powers over him and to the scheme of life on Earth, the dome elevated the human in an enveloping freedom and acceptance within the magnificence of life and its vision.

It was an otherworldly place, symbolic of the spirit of life, which is also otherworldly.

It was after we had proceeded for quite some distance upon the avenue that branched outward that there came into view what seemed in the distance to be clusters of amber light which were set close to but not against the borders of the avenue. Upon observation these images resolved themselves into what may be described as halos of light contained within a transparent medium within which could be seen a cylinder, opaque in color and set upon a pedestal of almost clear crystal so that it seemed to float in space. There were other material shapes within the space which seemed sculpted and organic, and I took them to be instruments of some kind, suspended upon their transparent bases which served in the function of the individual entities of space.

After passing by the first of these luminous stations one began to see other forms within them, sometimes individual, sometimes there were two which stood over the opaque cylinder and seemed to be looking into it or attending to it and to what it contained. These forms were graceful and very tall, having long limbs, and heads which were large and oval shaped.

Their faces held an indescribable beauty of expression. Their eyes, great orbits of dark liquid which sloped upward, seemed not so much to see as to cast a presence in their gaze of great intelligence and empathy. As we walked slowly by, one lifted its head to follow me with its gaze, and I felt a tremendous familiarity as if the creature knew and understood me and was communicating this knowledge deliberately.

A deep thrill, and a wave of comfort washed over me from its look, and I raised a hand in greeting and saw in response what seemed to be a smile and an expression of great love. Others of the creatures noticed as we passed, but never with the same recognition that I felt from this special one.

As we veered away upon a lesser branch, and then another, one began to see an increasing abundance of the amber halos until it seemed the sea of glass was filled with them and their clusters, extending away into the distance where the hue of their color tinted the horizon with a soft glow. Within each there stood at least one of the tall forms, quietly engaged in the task before it. The total number of them could not be estimated but it was surely in the thousands.

What are they doing? What is their task, and who are they? I asked my hosts, of the beings whose function and place seemed central to the existence of the awesome entity which was the dome of sky.

My question was met with smiles.

"They are our associates in the project of life."

"What is the project?"

"It is the beginning of the fulfillment of the dream of resurrection."

"You are able to return people to life here at this place?"

"We are able. Those coming to us now will be the vanguard of the future ones, who will assist us in the regeneration of past worlds."

A FLOOD of questions passed into my mind as we walked along the narrowing avenues leading outward to the edge of the dome of sky. We then turned and were once again upon the broader avenue leading to the great expanse upon which we entered, where on two occasions we met humans walking leisurely with the tall beings upon the sea of glass. A single human, a child, walked with two of the beings, and then one of the beings strolled beside an elderly couple, a man and a woman holding hands. They smiled and greeted us as we met, and one could not help but notice how vibrant and joyful was the life within them, and feel the radiance of their peace.

Who are among the vanguard? How are they selected?

The first birth was determined by our parents without foreknowledge, but the second birth is of a power that comes from knowledge and judgment: Who holds the wisdom and sense of justice to decide such things, the purity of motive to make them right..?

"They are the ones who have spoken to us with their lives, who have, through their actions or words, expressed the desire to be born again. These will be the vanguard of the resurrection time, the precursors of the dream to be reawakened to life."

I studied the answer well, for had we not all sung of the day of the resurrection, of the heavenly joy of reuniting with loved ones we had known in life?

Had not everyone in the moment of separation from those they had known and loved thought longingly of that blessed day of reunion, of the gathering about the celestial throne of life, and seen in the certainty of faith that glad and distant event?

I had never considered the details.

In the sweetness of the dream of reunion with the world we once knew, the dream born to and carried by love across the ages of man's existence, held dear by every generation of the human family since the earliest glimmers of self-knowing and hope, ministered to and exploited by every religion, with good and awful consequences, was the disbelief which answered mortality with a cry, a scream, a song of the never ending.

Who, in the moment of fruition, would be its emissaries to that future day, the pioneers upon the frontier of immortality, who would stand and welcome their sisters and brothers in history into a world where death had lost its sting, and the grave its victory? Who would be these intrepid souls, and what their motivation in awakening to a paradise whose humanity was unknown?

Those cylinders, which lie prone and quiet upon their pedestals of glass, are they the birthing places of the resurrected?

"Yes."

And the beings attending them, are they the angels of the resurrection, so often seen in visions at the end of the tunnel of light? "Well, yes, and others beyond them. They are the ones."

Where did these beings come from? They are of a species not human.

"They are children of the human. They are the energy of thought and emotion whose history is of the human, whose family is the human."

What is their purpose in the work they do?

"Their purpose is to fulfill the destiny of love, the destiny of thought."

By returning the dead to life?

"By returning life to the Omega. By completing the circle of the thought."

What thought?

"The thought of creation. The thought that connects us one to another throughout time."

NOTHING MORE was said as we climbed the gentle arc of the broad avenue which returned to the place of entrance upon this wondrous plain of glass within whose distant horizon of pearl there were laid out in outlines the transparent boughs and branches of a symbolic tree of life whose fruit, in luminous clusters of light amber, were the studiously and lovingly tended wombs of the new birth, shielded, as has been since antiquity, beneath the celestial dome of sky.

As the doors of the great dome closed behind us and we stood for a moment upon the port before boarding the car for the flight back to the stone house, one of my guides took my arm and offered an assurance and an advice:

"The reality that you have seen here is a beacon which will guide your return to us...Look forward from your present, and you will see it.

"The future shines its light to your present. Its beam will carry you safely home, and upon its beam you will one day return."

* * *

IT WILL BE difficult, in this report to the Committee and to you others who come to read it, to write a meaningful summation to the matter of resurrection and immortality. Poets have tried for ages to lift the veil which obscures our understanding, artists have painted glimpses of it, religions have traded in it, lovers have sworn promises about it.

How can a human write about the end of death, when death has made the human and defined her being? Would its conquest, in the ultimate irony, mark the end of the human, and if so, what identity would follow? Has the human, seduced by its tragedy and beauty, guarded death, in effect, to preserve its own being?

Perhaps for this is immortality assigned to the realm of gods, and to a simplicity of faith, whose real effect is unbelief.

I actually asked them about the phenomenal symbolisms apparent in the manner of my journey to them, and they understood, explaining that great leaps are best absorbed in metaphor, and that this is the way the mind works, to suspend the impediments of disbelief. When I told them that I did not want to believe what was not true, they smiled, and said that was a true expression from the experience of our age, wherein beautiful myths and the wisdom of metaphor had been misshapen by belief into fact, to great misfortune and tragedy.

They explained that my visit to them arose out of a mixing of quantum realities occasioned by Fo's discovery of the unified field, and that there was no element of the miraculous involved. When I inquired how such a transmutation was possible, the abbreviated answer was that matter carries at quantum levels an infinitude of energy states. The bioform that we call human is an energy state occupying a spacetime, so that such a time travel as I was experiencing was not "supernatural", but within the realm of the natural.

Having witnessed the Dome, I was stunned and immediately flooded with a gale of questions: What about this? What about that?...What is death, then?

Are these cycles of rebirth, or infinite universes of energy states occupying the matter of our bodies, rendering infinite existence at once? What role does this play in consciousness? How do imagination and memory work?... Are they not 'travelers in time'?

The answers were in their smiles. Some of the questions, they assured me, do not yet have answers. The greatest, most profound answer, of course, lies in the Omega, for the conscious experience is within the learning.

They seemed to reiterate that out of this mixing of quantum realities the man on the bridge, *The Third Angel*, appeared. When I asked about the significance of the black jaguar, they noted that the animal was exceedingly rare, so as to be seen by a few in a lifetime. "It is said they are the spirits of knowledge, and appear (with insights) to herald the birth of great events in human experience." And then the dark beauty, Kenata, winked, and so I took it that they were alluding to the mythology, cogent in belief, but I'm not sure.

They also mentioned parenthetically that corresponding with the Discovery was the inscription of the human genome, which opened the design of life to revelation, and accelerated its transmutation. But it was the Discovery itself, which exposed the Grail, "which has the power to link us with another world- the connection with destiny and greater meaning."

If we are tempted now to invest in the professor's discovery the regime of forces beyond science, he did not offer such an attribution. When I made an inquiry, among the many others of that evening upon the veranda with him and Letty, he only said, "The answer came as a resolution of a paradox, but only revealed itself when I forgot the paradox. I studied too hard in the wrong place, the wrong corner... When I stopped, in a sense, pondering the anomaly, then the synthesis came in a flash."

Still transfixed by the ineffably profound experience within the Dome, where it seems the sentence of death was lifted and one could view at last the long awaited redemption of man in a cosmic justice and meaning, I selfishly sought to know more, mindful that the rarest of opportunities may be fading. I sensed a flow of information exceeding a transcript of words, and am here congealing a part of it into this communication, mindful of the sheer complexity of ascertaining a future determination of reality. The place between now and that future day is not free of history, and so the future cannot be "known" to the past with certainty.

That future day, however, may know us because it shares our own history, though it has by then passed through the lenses of future experience. Regarding that contingency, they told me, of us all, on that ephemeral day, "You are the preincarnation of us here. We are here by your grace and will to determine a good future," implying that there is no given trajectory to the future. It is determined by the next moment, by our choice.

What knowledge can beings out of antiquity bring to the future which holds so much knowledge and understanding? I wondered.

"You may be surprised," the dark poetic one answered, before I had spoken the question. "The knowledge of despair...This is what fascinates us infinitely.

"How can the human endure loss, live in the face of mortality- the human in her heroic role? How can you love with impending loss, and endure with the full knowledge that life and all experience is transitory?

"More than anything else this study inspires us and confounds us, and floods us with love for, and great yearning to know our forebears who in imagination- the 'evidence of things not seen'- established the foundations of knowledge."

Robeling the intellect then pointed out that every time is visited by the antiquarians, seeming to downplay the exceptionality of their experience with me. "Open a book, and read about them," he said, "and they are there."

As I spoke with them on the occasion of our return flight, I was given the clearest understanding of their reality, but describing it now, am only left with words which fall short of the transcendent. I know I was given answers, which now find themselves begging for expression... Perhaps we need to devise a new language.

I came back to the Dome, and its enigmatic reality.

"One may choose among varieties of experience [they did not say, 'states']: To be reborn as infant, or at the age when life was taken, or aged, and then slowly return to youth. There are stages- to age and regress, and age again, or to remain at the physical age one chooses for the time the soul wishes. At all ages there is vitality. We do not grow tired with age."

It is hard now to imagine that they had so much time, day by day, and year by year, to study the century that we knew, and that knew us, the lives we lived. Mortality is so engrained in us, we are so acutely mortal, that we tire contemplating eternal life, and imagine they must at some point grow tired and just want to lie down and die...But it was clear that when the enormous burden of physical mortality is shed, then the soul is truly free at last, to find and relish its destiny.

"What happened," I asked again, "at the turning point, to free humanity finally from the accumulations of its fears and insecurities?"

"The discovery of the soul, and its identity- of the true nature of the human. In the freeing of the mind from the constraints of superstition, in the celebration of scientific knowledge. The soul *is* the knowing, its recognition in the reality of existence."

"What is 'existence'?"

"The soul is the existence. Existence is in the knowing, in the knowledge of itself."

I ventured then to ask, "When will the resurrection come?"

"The resurrection will come when enough people believe. And it will come for the individual when it is visualized." (We cannot visualize precisely, but the fine completion is made by the spirits of time, who know our intent and effort.)

What are the spirits of time?

"They are those supreme intelligences we have brought into being."

"You have created the gods!" I asked.

The wry and colorful fellow, BJ, to whom I had felt closest, seemed delighted: "The gods were man-creations all along," he said, "placed in the long past to watch and rule over us... We did not imagine they were waiting their creation *in the future.*"

"So some presentiment of them must have been there all along," I ventured.

"Oh yes, only misinterpreted- and appropriated by self-appointed shamans, prelates, kings, and politicians over the ages, to effect their control over the minds of the people. Only when the mind was freed could it look forward to where the real gods waited, in the human's destiny.

"We always knew. The sense of destiny was latent in thought and emotion all along, offered in glimpses we called *meaning,* and translated, though faintly, into the greatest of art and poetry and acts of love and sacrifice. Meaning was the redemption we craved and intimated, and steadfastly believed in, which carried us through the long night lit only by the most distant, and closest stars of love and hope."

*   *   *

AT THIS point I ventured to ask questions related to science, though within the constraints of a limited preparation only faintly intimating the knowledge of my older brother. I consider the insights adumbrative in aspect, without any revelation beyond the character of this report. "You will recall only what is self-consistent. You cannot change what has been, only what will be."

Lia, the woman from Russia who had worked for some years the century before in what was called the Planetoid II Mission, told me that relatively small asteroids, or satellites converted into inhabited worlds were classified as "Earthlings". The moons of Mars, Phoebos and Deimos, had become earthlings before the end of the 21st Century, though amplified greatly in the decades and century-and-a-half following.

The technique was direct: The interior of the moon was hollowed out, as its minerals were mined out for use in manufacture, leaving a hollow cavity into which were incorporated structures, settlements, communities, centers, and bases, sealed and containing recycled atmosphere.

They had spoken of the planet Mars, and of its reforming into a sister world of Earth, calling it the grandest project in the history of man and his intelligent affiliates in the solar system. Lia seemed to take pleasure in telling me that the Mars Genesis arose out of foundations in the Planetary Society of the 20th Century, aided and necessitated by developments relating to the Discovery, and that Dr. Sagan was the able director.

I asked, "Carl Sagan?" and she smiled and said, yes. "Of the Planetary Society." I sought to clarify.

Her riveting blue-gray eyes sparkled. "Of the Mars Project."

I took a moment to absorb what she had said, reviewing my memories of the famed astronomer and promoter of science, realizing that if I, a fruit vender, could be here, then why not a splendid planetary scientist, recalled to life to continue his work. Especially, his beloved Mars Project.

I was surprised, and delighted. "But I didn't know he was a believer."

Like many others, I had read in a biography of the last loving goodbyes spoken to his family that day, and of his personal conviction that in the reality of life in the infinite cosmos they would never meet again in all eternity. The goodbyes would be forever.

My friends smiled, and Robeling spoke up. "Sagan was wrong, that's all," he smiled, with a wave of his hand.

"He welcomed the second birth, but only if those he loved could join him. He came to us in 2096, and assisted with the rebirth of his wife, and others of his family and colleagues, the latter of whom include great names of his century and others, who are now among the leaders in the achievements of our time."

"Who is among them?..." I caught myself after the question was asked, and tried to retract it, thinking it might not be within my prerogative to probe such a matter, but they smiled, and nodded reassuringly.

"Their growing number includes the illustrious of history, known and unknown," and I began to imagine a gallery of the heroes of knowledge and art and thought, some branded heretics and even put to death for their sins of defiance; great ones heralded by history for their gifts of foresight, and true saints unrecognized. I thought their names, and wished I knew more- those whose brilliance cast beams of light forward into time to inspire and engender others, and spirit ghosts arising out of the ashes of the Library of Alexandria to haunt and inhabit libraries everywhere and hidden away against that day when freedom of knowledge was regained.

I was trying to imagine and grasp the universe of life and engineering that was taking place on that planet where last NASA had its durable twin rovers exploring about on commands from Earth, before the revolutionary discovery of primordial life.

I assumed that, until an atmosphere was constituted, most of the work was being done by robotic machines, perhaps directed from Mars lunar bases, which, my friends advised me, were administered by humans, but operated by their super-intelligent "affiliates in space." It was my understanding that there was a manner of presence accomplished in their space and interplanetary exploration which was what we would call, "non-manned", and yet was undifferentiated from human presence. The "experience" of the remote intelligence was somehow integrated directly into that of the human so that time and space became *presence.*

They pointed out that the purpose of the massive hardware needed to enable early manned flight was simply to carry the weightless and dimensionless mind into sensory contact with the destination- nothing less or more than an existential declarative, *"I saw and touched/ there was,"* but that the varieties of experience had been amplified beyond imagination into reality. They said enigmatically that space and time was a pinpoint, which the mind already encompassed.

It did not seem, then, such a leap from our age to theirs, and one could extrapolate logically and pose inquiries which they seemed to accept as normal. Any technologies are recognizable as having roots in the past, and still using concepts formulated in antiquity, from the time of Euclid. In basic ways little changes, so long as the human remains.

There are in our time clocks that have been ticking for 500 years. There are streets and doorways in the Warsaw ghetto and in Palestine which are two thousand years old. A man resurrected from the Roman times could make his way up the cobblestone alleyways to his own door, recognizable from two millennia. And unchanged mindstates of the Buddha priests.

Christopher Wren's buildings are still in use for the original purpose for which they were designed and created 300 plus years ago. Physical things were the first tachyonids, sent as emissaries by their creators in thought.

A medieval farmer from the Sudan could squat upon the ground and discuss information in common with a modern farmer anywhere.

THERE IS no radical dichotomy in the progression of technology, or even of ideas, in history or in our imagination, until one arrives at that doorway of resurrection and immortality, the liberation from the grip of death, and then everything changes in that infinite quantum leap.

For this alone, beyond personal reasons, the mortal would be obsessed by its lure, and driven to attain it: *because he is an explorer, and can imagine it.*

But more- because the conscious intelligence is programmed to imagine it, for a reason.

While the resurrection by miraculous virtue, as in the act of God, would speak little of knowledge to the human, especially if it is conducted on the merit of obeisance, its accomplishment by meritorious intelligence will imply a changed state itself as astonishing as the deed, and so they understood my curiosity regarding their 'affiliates in intelligence,' the entities whom I met within the dome, and 'others beyond them,' of exponentially evolved intelligence, even reaching forward to the Omega.

And yet, astonishingly, the entities were "...*children of the human. They are the energy of thought and emotion whose history is of the human, whose family is the human, whose purpose is to fulfill the destiny of love, the destiny of thought.*"

But who were these super intelligent entities who were 'children of the human'? What was the realm of their thought and concerns?

Could they attain the completion of themselves?

How long would they be at peace with their existence? With their service? Would they at some fruition of time imagine a freedom they did not have, and yearn for it?

Would some one of them become a new Lucifer, cast down from the mythic throne of heaven, for his "humanity"?

I thought of Otto, ethicist and historian... Now here is a matter for him!

Are you gods? I asked my friends. "No," they answered, smiling.

"Are *they* gods?" I asked, referring to the entities, and thinking of the one who knew me.

"They are closer to the Omega."

Of course it is in our nature to measure values relative to others, and so even in our day we would be the "gods" to history, because we know and remember its future, just as my companions there, with knowledge of *our* future, seemed invested with supernal powers. In truth, they were beneficiaries of time and experience, seeing into their own past, just as we are able to do.

It is no wonder that the gods are vested with knowledge of the future, and inhabit time to come. Being there, they know us already, as spirits arising from the past.

God is the future mind.

(I remembered from a notebook that in answer to a student's question, "What is God?" Fo had answered: "Oh, that's easy. God, the supersymmetrical infinite symmetry, which connects all dimensions of reality.")

Because it was evident that their lives and accomplishments, and even cultures, were integral with the races of alternate intelligences [we had called it "artificial intelligence" in the early days], which had developed and elevated into a realm they called "cosmic intelligence," individuals of whom were seen within the Dome of Sky, doing the work of regeneration, which transcended science into the spiritual, I wondered whether the human nature itself had been fundamentally changed by these intellects who were 'children of the human.'

The human at its best, aspiring to the spiritual, enabled that greaterness of mind which realized the union with destiny, lifting the heel of another, as it were, to see, through another's eyes, the promised land.

For this it must have seemed poignant, and touching, that I would have asked of them as well, Are you free?

They were not just intellects.

"All the sadness and joy are joined in the waters which wash upon the future, and translate into new forms and renewal in memory and emotion, the living spirit."

I must have continued to express concern about the order of the resurrection, as a mortal would. How is it determined justly?... And yet few, except from the deepest despair, have lamented their own birth, and the same would surely be true of the second birth, vested in memory and intimations of prior life.

If the great and illustrious heroes of science and thought and art were being called as "vanguards" of the resurrection, to serve among others; and if the order and nature of rebirth was determined out of the "ultraconsciousness" nearer to the Omega, then one, at the end of questioning, must arrive at faith that there will be no tricks, that the greatest spirits, arisen out of the human, will protect the human, and one another, that all, in a just and loving order, will be well. "Nothing separate in immortal. Only in the joining does immortality arise."

They did mention regarding the vanguard of the resurrected that its family is more of intellect than of blood, that they will be servants in the greatest project of time. Because the 'project' is in the hands of supernal intelligence related to that realm of the spirit and soul, it was probably always to be beyond the purview of mortal humanity, vexed by emotion.

It may have been Whitman, who declared, "Awaken first the slaves, in their natural freedom, and into their celebration I will come." It is this aspect of the human mortal that brought tears into the eyes of the "Specialists".

Because the matter of created intelligences engenders in the human so many questions and concerns: At what point and by what definition does the intelligence become self-conscious; when does it have dreams and emotions; what, if any, are its hopes and aspirations; does it learn love; *what does it think*?- perhaps this is the place to relate what they said which touches upon ranges of intelligence and awareness in the entities around them, besides the 'supreme intelligences, nearer to the Omega.'

"Our lives are also assisted by petdrives, that we call, 'peds'. These are semiconscious entities with whom we are interdependent.

"There are ranges of intelligence around us, none of which struggle against our will for higher intelligence, and none whose consciousness is suppressed. Everyone and everything is free within its order to exist. Nature herself is protected and free, integrated into the whole of existence as it was in the beginning, to serve in the cause of life and its discovery.

"It is our greatest teacher from the moment of our recognition, and reigns from origin to destiny. We are Nature, each species of body and thought in a common will to freedom and destiny. Life speaks with one voice, and all things with the voice of life. The voice of life is liberty."

I noted that they regarded nature and all things as having spirit, saying that all learning is "of the spirit."

"What spirit?"

"The spirit of life. Mind is the spirit-dweller."

I was reminded then of the evening before, just as we were turning to walk back up the Way of Stone to where Fo and Letty waited on the veranda. The experience for me, since the beginning of the flight that was to bring me to that future day, had exceeded the boundaries of thought into the transcendent and ethereal, and so it was that there was an immense sense of the familiar and physical when suddenly out beyond where the Way ended and its spire with its cryptic message lay buried in the ocean, a giant whale had breached, lifting its enormous mass as if in slow motion gracefully upward and then turning in an elegant arc before returning in a spectacular splash to the surface of the deep. My friends seemed as much in awe of the phenomenon as I was, in its reminder that on the round ball that was Earth a species a hundred times older that the human still graced us with its presence.

Astounded at yet another phenomenal occurrence, 1 remarked something to my hosts, and they offered an amazing commentary upon the baleen, which was to touch upon the realities which would be later revealed, and of which we had just spoken. It was Letty's daughter who said matter-of-factly, "We can talk to them."

When they saw my surprise they explained basically the following regarding interspecial communication, which in our time is most rudimentary, despite the efforts of some:

"We were watching in a longer study the architecture of fingers interacting with the intricate strings, knowing there was sound, but deaf to the music until we found the keys to the chamber of meanings within the sounds, expressing 100 million years into texts, at lengths and dimensions preceding and exceeding human thought.

"The greatest measure of the knowledge was learned to be in pure music form, untranslatable into thoughts and words or to experience beyond the soul..."

"Do they have soul?"

"They are possessed of individual souls, as we are, which flow from the medium of life and knowing."

"Then the understanding you have achieved is not only scientific, but spiritual?"

"All knowledge has a spiritual dimension, which you call a field." They went on.

"Their language is music. It cannot be translated into words, just as you cannot translate Debussy into words. Their language must be listened to as music- which also underlies human language, experienced through the thought of emotions."

I was inclined to ask, Do they love children? Do they sing the blues? Do they have beliefs and dreams, joy and sadness; do they celebrate irony? Can they take the measure of their own thoughts? but did not follow my anthropomorphic impulse to fancy.

"They think in notes. Their consciousness is music. What we learned from them, and studied for so long, was a representation of them, and not their essence, the song and not the singer.

"We knew as little about ourselves, as well, as observers of notes, until we were able to enter the music. You see, intelligence upon Earth has alien origins, with differing genesis within the solar system, and beyond."

I am unable to divine the meaning of the last comment, but am sure that it is a correct representation of what the beings said.

*　　*　　*

IT HAS NOT seemed a matter of precedent, and so I have not spoken of many details, including our means of transport, but will now offer some description of it, as means afford it.

We were taken to and from the Dome in a type of aircraft whose power source cannot be ascertained, but it may have had to do with the manipulation of gravity, as it seemed drawn along effortlessly, and not by propulsion. There was no sound or vibration to its movement, nor driver. It did not have notable features other than being sleek and of an oval configuration, perhaps four meters wide at its widest, and perhaps six meters long.

It seemed to be the generic model of personal transport, with copies varying in size depending upon the number of passengers. Although I did not see their evidence at the stone house, it seems they were otherwise ubiquitous, and zipped around and across the skies vectored by what my friends referred to as an "intelligence", a kind of deity of traffic control who guided every vehicle in the solar system unerringly to its destination, and apparently was conscious of each passenger and its needs, making sure the sparrow did not fall errantly, or lose its way.

They called their craft "trabods", an ungainly name which, I believe, was a contraction for "transit bodies", but am not entirely sure if this is precise. These bodies lifted vertically with what from the outside was a slight whirring sound, then directed themselves through the sky traffic to any destination wished by the travelers. Each vehicle communicated with the superintelligence, which controlled and guided its existence and services.

There were also land vehicles, and surface transport for beings and goods, but urban communities were so planned that land travel was minimized, and cross-country freighting was accomplished by gravity rail, which was also pollution free.

Some of the vehicles were wheeled, and it seemed the energy of propulsion was derived from the surface itself, and transferred to the wheels, leaving few moving parts otherwise.

"What do you call them?" I asked.

"Cars," they laughed, though there were other names. As well, they were driverless, maneuvered by internal intelligence guided remotely, and were never known to be involved in accidents. Surface and air mobility had finally been rendered fault-proof.

One has the tendency to assign mythic proportions to an intelligence entity which could assume such a myriad of tasks coordinated throughout the solar system and perhaps beyond, but when I expressed this they simply offered that intelligence had evolved adversely to volume so that the sum of knowledge and history in their time is held and secured in a space much smaller than the period at the end of this sentence. They said eerily that "intelligence" was omnipresent and invisible, and that it had always been so.

WE LOOK into the future, and want to see something of ourselves there, those things that we recognize and know. Even in the presence of the divine, the soul would look around furtively for signs of humanity, and relish the comfort of its company, though devoid of the powers of transcendence. The human in Paradise would not be happy without the promise of salvation for all. Unable to fit in, the species would become rebel, and fugitive from the controlling power, but rarely the slave.

But in this future which is ahead of us I saw the people were at home, and in love with life. They possessed a natural energy kept vibrant by their high level of interest and motivation. They were excited by the accomplishments of their generations in association with the spiritual powers which they called the angels of time, and by the limitless possibilities of the future before them. They revered their past, which holds us in its bounty and travail.

I saw that there was still diversity in the human family. Nationalities and peoples seemed alive and well, even though many tribes and cultures that once graced the human presence on Earth had long been absorbed or decimated.

"There are cities upon land, and settlements which serve as caretakers upon and within the oceans, in space and upon other worlds, and yet there are villages where you can live in any manner of the past, in the time and century you wish- communities of time. Quiet places with vegetable gardens in the back, fruit trees and flowers, and pies cooling in the kitchen window. Old fashioned holidays and time to read and think, and enjoy your family and friends and touch the lives of your ancestors."

I was immensely consoled and reassured that in their country of the distant future our own present may still exist- little enclaves desired in the hearts of our descendents who feel the connection of a living past.

"This is not a Utopian society," they told me. "This is humanity preserved in its diversity, continuing exploration of diversity toward the highest potential of the human."

When I asked about the orchard people, they only said, "There are those who live beyond them. They are *atahualpas:* they live in a place called Atahualpa."

"On this earth?"

"Well, yes and no...It is everywhere that eras collide. A place of the mind."

"A state, a condition?"

"Not really... A *place,* a reality.."

*   *   *

"MUSIC IS AN attempt to express what is already in the mind. When the expression awakens responses, they are called *music,* with corresponding ranges of beauty... It is the same with poetry and art. They are reflections of what and who we are, or of what we determine ourselves to be."

One, or all of them told me this, as the craft which carried us, guided by a superintelligence somewhere, or omnipresent, eased itself over the landscape of a graceful city unlike any I had ever seen, and then settled upon a surface among other craft of the same design, though of varying size.

We stepped out of the comfortable interior and walked across an area which afforded a view of hillslopes in the distance, but only when we descended a wide walkway did I realize that we had entered what was actually a beautiful structure bathed in light, which incorporated the natural sandstone cliffs on either side. Some system I could not identify filtered the sunlight so that it was soft and exceedingly pleasant. What we used to call buildings in the old times they referred to as "spaces", each integral with its energy source. So this was a "space" which, though enclosed somehow, seemed to be outdoors.

We reached an area which, though separate, was so only by function, and not by partitions. It was more of a setting, seamlessly blended with the whole of space, and yet it seemed private, and afforded us a relaxed and intimate occasion to have a lunch. Oval tables graced with pale brocaded cloths upon which were set candles and a single orchid were surrounded by antique chairs in settings of two, four, and six, depending upon the size of the table. As we sat I noticed that the area around and above had darkened, which made the dining seem more intimate, and the glow of the candles lent its aspect to the countenances around.

There were five of us at a table for six, and I noticed that Kenata took the orchid and placed it before the empty chair, but there was no indication why, and I did not ask.

We talked wonderfully together during the simple and delicious meal of soup and what we call finger sandwiches, dressed by a choice of salads and fresh fruit- most everything completely recognizable from our time. There was provided as well, most delightedly for me, an evocative dish of an exquisitely flavored lentil loaf, cut like a cake, which could have been made from my mother's recipe. I noticed that Billy Joe ate an extra helping, and thoughtfully savored its taste.

Again, without entering a room, we found ourselves within a place within the space, which seemed like an auditorium, though actually different. And again, there was something about the light which obscured the space around, though it was different from the character of darkness, so that one sensed the comfort and reassurance of a dimension, without an enclosure.

We were ushered to a row of cushioned seats before a low stage, and I sat centered between my friends- Lia and Kenata sitting next, and the big fellow, BJ, and his counterpart, Robeling 'builder of bridges' on the outside. There were others sitting behind in the auditorium, in rows graduating upward to the back, though I did not look backward to see who they were, and only sensed them there.

I caught a stir from my companions, the ones on my left leaning forward to look around me, and turned to see three new arrivals who seemed like home to me: They were the tall slender fellow with the dark, almond eyes, and his beautiful wife and daughter. Letty had on a stunning black dress which was long sleeved and cut somewhere in front to immortal inspiration described best by Renoir. Around her neck was a delicate gold necklace which tapered to suspend a locket I had seen before, long, long ago.

I imagined for a moment a young woman who promenaded in the plaza of old Magdalena de Kino on a Saturday night, accompanied by her mother, wooing with innocent beauty that could melt a statue some young man who, with wrenched heart, would vie with others to win her approval, then her lasting love. Little could they have known that they would be beat one day by a young professor of astrophysics wearing a fedora and a bolo tie.

Between her mother and her friend, BJ, would sit a lovely young girl, radiant with life, whom I last remembered with long curls and a child's sweetness, looking out of a picture on her mother's desk, in that world where even children die.

They had first come in front, as the five of us stood, and I was treated to warm, sustained hugs by the women, whose unforgettable scent remains, and from Fo, a firm two-handed handshake and warm slaps on my back. Then they greeted similarly my hosts, though having seen them the night before, and settled into the cushioned seats beside us.

AND THEN there was presented a concert, a musical, the likes of which I will not experience again in this life, though all great music has its origins in another world imbued with immortality, before it comes to us.

Looking back upon it now, I can see that the music was especially made as a gift for their visitor, but how does that differ, really, from any good concert anywhere, especially performed for each attendant, and each audience. They are, as well- whether performed in halls of memory, or in the future imagining, or in the fleeting present- modes of an enduring *experience,* which transcends time and the mortal.

Music is emotion painted by sound into portraits and landscapes of beauty and depth unknown to words, and even to thought.

It is a language of art, and like art cannot be explained- here in this writing, or anywhere.

I visited a future where language was surpassed by the emotion of music, as it is in our day, except that they seemed to celebrate it universally. It pervaded their times like an eternal spirit, and spoke out of other species in the remote experience before the mind was human, and out of the human in its transcendence.

And so they performed the sublime, rhapsodic, sweet memory of music, inalienable from the soul of thought and life across time.

The stage itself could also best be called a "space", and not a location, or setting, as it seemed integral with the experience within it, and seemed, in retrospect, to be invisible, though in its sense indivisible from the performances, which were orchestral at once, and individual. They played and performed music I recognized, lovely in memory, evocative, and emotional. Not all of it I had heard before, and this is what seems strange: some of it very old, ghosts of the medieval which seemed to drift out of an almost forgotten humanities class of the gifted Mr. Decker from the early days; the later great classics heralded in each age; the invisibly deep expression of souls broken and enduring in slavery and injustice- *Remember Me, O Mighty One-* sung by a group of five, without instruments, who seemed to scintillate from an occulted place, a labor patch, or brush-arbor church; music of that grand era of blues and jazz and big bands, birthed by great depressions and wars and human experience; songs played and sung by the ancestors and immigrants, steeped in memory, which rose out of their souls in the dearth of things, from trouble when most seemed unattainable, and all else was gone; of music and artists remembered from youth; of musicians gifted in their century and time, to express meaning for others. As Vincent VanGogh said in a letter to Theo, "Man is not on Earth solely for his own happiness. He is here to realize great things for humanity."

Great music and art have most always been advanced of their time, so that succeeding generations may rediscover their meanings in the light of their experience interpreted through history. So the music or art emerges new, through time. Intellect and emotion, encapsulated in music which stirs the soul from its rest, and fills the heart to bursting.

Of course music is not actually played from without, but directly from within the brain. It then seemed uncanny, and utterly remarkable that the human would design the piano and know how to play it; or the flute, the violin, or any other of the instruments that first mocked the wind and waves and the crackling fire which burned across the savannas and forests- the animal sounds, the rustling brook, the child's laughter, the breath of passion, the storm.

We are mimickers of nature before we are creators.

On that transcendent occasion, it was if I was being treated to all the music that ever played itself out of the human heart, through history and into the future, wherever man had held or would hold a presence anchored in passion and beauty.

I was conscious of every song and every note translated from vibrations across space from one being to another since time began, and nothing had been lost. Now I understood this to be the meaning of music, each song being all songs, as every refrain carried the power invested by the long tradition before. Music is metaphor for the human.

As I sat within the line of humans now immortal, the two young women, whose ages far exceeded that of the oldest upon Earth today, placed their arms under mine, to hold my hands. Time is the conscious moment, one had told me- nothing beyond.

Worlds appeared from out of the music, overlapping, none distinct, circles and globes which transparently interact and merge their surfaces with others, or lightly burst their delicate skins and infuse the worlds around them. I heard jazz in a series of languages I had never heard before. Beyond the sound, it was translations of actual mindstates which exist independent of matter in a timeless setting from which the human existence drinks in its living encounter with no other explanation than that contained in the moment and expanded outward.

I heard a little baby somewhere behind me cry out, and remembered hearing of the extraordinary jazz artist, Ernestine Anderson, who once began a number and a baby in the audience started crying, and she stopped, and said, "Ooh.., a baby!" and then began singing as if she were singing to the baby, and the baby stopped crying. (Another singer might have stopped and said, Will someone quiet that baby so I can sing?..) In Anderson's case, the artist existed within the transcendence of her own work.

There is in true art no event of creation, but rather the rendering of a conceived reality that envelopes all knowing before and beyond its event in time..

Before hearing the hauntingly moving singing of the 19th Century hymn, "Remember Me", transported, it would seem, out of a living condition through time, one might have assumed the words and refrain to be a prayer to the deity, but I recognized it now to be a prayer instead to Life, to immortality. A prayer to the higher self, to the immortal future, asking for the mortal, "Remember me.."

Having been seated in the front row, centered before the stage, and considering the nature of our arrival to a place they called, The Hall of Beloved Souls, I was mindful of being what we call the guest of honor, an unknown designation for me, except perhaps on birthdays, but was strangely comfortable, though I'm sure by being in the company of my friends. Lia and Kenata would lean against me, or press my hands at intervals when there was something particularly spectacular, or moving, and Aida would cry out in delight. There was applause throughout the auditorium, and even cheers, as has been done at concerts throughout time.

There were numbers done, I was sure, specifically for the guest in front center, because the renditions evoked such feelings of home and good times. But when I heard the reaction of the crowd, who seemed to be enjoying the performance equally well, I felt in good company, and at ease.

There came a particularly thrilling rendition of Janis Joplin's "Bobby McGee" which brought the house down, and when I applauded excitedly, and said to my companions, "That was amazing! It sounded like the original!" one laughed happily and declared, "It is the original. *This is the singer, singing.* The resurrection is a gift in another time, for your pleasure."

I could not believe my ears...

Always a fan of folk music and soul, like many others of my time and place, I had loved the Woody Guthrie ballads, the rousing ministry of John Fogerty, The Eagles, Louis Armstrong, Paul Simon, Bob Dylan, and others, and the soulful piano voice of Ray Charles, and they were all there, to the delight of everyone, in this magical and immortal dimension of life.

I wouldn't have been surprised to see Chuck Berry come blowing by in a little souped-up jitney.

They were singing songs of freedom- which is life- though we could not have fully appreciated it at the time.

And then there is music which is the moaning of the soul: The blues came out of the dilemma of uncertainty posed by original experience, unadvised, unreturning, unrestrained, woven out of the spirit world in an enduring statement for the human.

At this point there were presented two poems of intense passion and power, and moving beauty: the first, by the elegant and incomparable Wallace Stevens; and the second given unforgettably by a young woman poet named Suheir Hammad of the 21st Century, which painted injustice and irony and hope. They both were to be acclaimed in their times, and in this.

After sustained applause for them both, there then fell a silence, as a figure, faintly outlined against the dark backdrop, his bearing recognizable to me, spoke in a powerful rich baritone the heroic words of salvation echoing immortally from a time of renewed hope, *"Free at last! Free at last!..."*

THERE WAS then presented a young artist whose performance affected me most, for reasons you will see.

He was slender and strong and had a mop of light brown hair, and the most brilliant eyes that shone and sparkled with quiet expression. He had a presence which is uncommon, especially for a young person, and the natural self confidence and generosity that come with great talent and effort.

In the most personal moment for me of this future experience I have tried to relate, as he stood before his piano and bowed, smiling at his audience, I suddenly recognized the young man whose poster-size portrait in black and white, framed in grey and light blue, and signed by him in his old age, hung upon the wall of my study.

It was of a young man with a mop of light brown hair, dressed in slacks and a white, long-sleeved shirt, astride a 1920's Indian motorcycle with a broken headlight, on the day of a family outing to the "caprock" in his beloved New Mexico. I believe the picture may have been taken by his bride, in that luminous first winter of their lives together, when everything lay before them.

After all was nearly done in a life well made, I had heard him mention that he had once dreamed of being a teacher of music, before the Depression came and altered the prospects for college. That dream realized, of course, or even the minutest of alterations- a millisecond or thought, or action changed anywhere- would have negated the reality that held his children in its prospect, and none of us would have been born.

They could not have known it, but the simple event of that photograph snapped on the day of an outing, of a young man imbued by youth, alone would change the future, and make possible the moment when, in another life, he would be standing before a piano on an immortal day in time, bowing to an audience who would hear him play.

He sat upon the bench, hesitated for a moment, raised both his hands, and then began to play a medley of classics beginning with the haunting first movement of Beethoven's Piano Sonata no. 14 in C-sharp Minor, followed by Chopin, and then a wonderful theme I didn't recognize- which could have been because of a lack of grounding in music, but was actually because it was composed by a renowned artist of the 22nd Century whose name was Murakami, Robeling told me, after we all stood applauding for what seemed minutes.

When that was done, and the applause subsided, he sat motionless for a few seconds, as if he were pondering, and then, in a gathering of energy, exploded into a blues number that shook the place to its foundation, his hands rolling over the keys in an intense, soulful, wild, knocking, rocking, rebellion and liberation, as a long and intricate moan came from a lone guitar back in the midsection, then the tenor voice set about a wailing refrain as the piano jumped in spasms and then rumbled and spread itself back and forth in an intricate and vibrant escape of sound which was supremely and victoriously alive, of loves broken and found again, never to be lost.

The blues were always complete, seasoned in the deep vessel of the soul, and nothing had changed about them in three centuries. They were born out of the dilemma of uncertainty posed by original experience, by the solitude of life, by its infinitude, its dream and its loss, woven together out of the spirit world in a lovely and enduring statement of the human.

I cannot divine now what he knew or thought. What they had told him by then. He was the age of twenty-seven when I was born, and the young musician there seemed about that age.

He would be free to lead the life meant for him in that awakening, as are we all, if we are lucky enough to find that meaning, so I would not have expected, or thought, that he would do it over again, even if it were possible. There is nothing we can really do over again in this universe... Are we not subject to the arrow of time?

A young woman appeared in front of me, and I did not see her face. She had a lovely form, and waves in her long brown hair, and she was holding a bouquet of long-stemmed roses, which she held up to the young virtuoso, who came forward and accepted it, smiling brightly and nodding to her, and then to the audience as if he were accepting the flowers for everyone.

There was applause, as he bowed once more, holding the roses to his chest, and then, when the applause subsided, he took one of the roses and lifted it to his nose, closing his eyes and smelling it.

And then, for the first time, our eyes met.

Something is relayed instantly in a glance, and his held more than a casual recognition, but I cannot describe it beyond that, because imagination may imbue our recall, or even desire. But he did something which affected me more. He held out the rose, in what seemed to me a kind of salute, or toast, and smiled.

I felt a flood of emotion, knowing I would have to leave that world and all its promise, that nothing in my life would be forever.

Lia and Kenata pressed closer, and squeezed my hands, and I felt the others draw in, in comfort and understanding.

I sensed a presence behind me, and above, and looking up saw one who was immensely tall, looking down at me with an indescribable beauty of expression, its eyes, great orbits of dark liquid which cast a presence of great intelligence and empathy. I felt that it was smiling.

And then I felt the comfort of a great hand laying upon my head, and long, delicate fingers which fell across my face.

*   *   *

CHAPTER FOURTEEN

THE RETURN

*THE SPIRITS of all those who have ever lived infuse the earth.
If the earth is ever approached by 'alien beings', will be seen by
the evolution and prevalence of its life as a spiritual place.*
-Dr. William Joseph Smith ("BJ").

*All of life is an awakening. For this we were born.
From conception forward, we are a gathering of spirit- to be
nourished by learning, empowered by will, ennobled by love,
whose completeness is finally released into the immortality
of fact. Because we once were, we shall always be.*
-Foglesby (conversation on veranda of stone house).

*"The visions will come to you when you let go of the
world. When you transcend the moment, then you will
see through time to where we wait your creation."*
-Monami.

WE FLEW HOME together, guided by a superintelligence which knew
each traveler on Earth and in the solar system- Fo and Letty and their
daughter, Aida, and the five of us who had shared the experience of a
splendid and immortal day- to the place dreamed long before as the stone
house with a veranda overlooking the sea.

We gathered again on the side porch around the long table where we were served refreshments and an assortment of cookies and cakes. It was to be our last gathering around the table, and my memories of it are etched into emotion. Without emotion, there is no memory.

As we visited, I had the image of that little child in my mind, just reborn and walking along with the two beings within the Dome of Sky.

Is the person awakened the same as the one who went to sleep?

"It is a sequence of the same person, yes, just as you awaken after a night's sleep and realize that it is the *you* that has awakened. Your memories are carried over- your feelings and sense of self- through your unconscious hours. Death is but a moment until the awakening, an infinite velocity of soul-travel, which rides upon the wings of time."

Through space?

They smiled. "In spacelessness. In the dimensionless realm of thought, which is of the soul."

What connects that thought to the resurrection? Is there a willing beyond death?

"The love of life. Life's love." What is life's love?

"The oneness of all creation. The unity of all existence through space and time. The meaning which connects origin and destiny... Love is the knowing."

"Who will be awakened?"

"People whose lives were uncompleted, whose love exceeded life. This love will see them across time until they answer in the reincarnation."

"Is that the way it works?"

"That is the way. Through the gifts of science and knowledge. Through learning, love looked for a way to discover and complete the meaning and purpose of being. Understanding was the desire of ages, kept alive by heroes of every generation, at whatever cost."

"If learning is so integral with life, why were knowledge and reason so resisted?"

"Only because they liberate the mind and soul from the false powers which held back history in every age, declaring investigation and discovery an evil doing, and doubt of the established order a sin."

"And those who have led evil lives?" I asked.

"Perhaps they will be awakened if there was left in them any humanity which connects them to the future, but the evil of the past does not find its way here. Only the light shines into the future. The darkness doesn't shine."

I remembered the metaphorical Hell described as the pit of darkness: Must its dreadful state symbolize the loss of a connection to destiny, the loss of humanity?... The soul's essence, they told me, *is* humanity.

"Is this Heaven?" I asked them, recalling the old metaphor for sublime states.

"You might say you are between Earth and heaven," one answered, holding my glance, and smiling, adding, "But that's where you've always been, isn't it?"

I was suddenly struck by this reality so central to the human. We are made of the earth, and yet walk strangely upon it, avowing a transcendence equal to the measure of our dreams, as if the dreams themselves confer our true being upon us.

Only such audacious creatures can live in the shadow and claim the light- those between this world and paradise, the home of our ideal.

*　　*　　*

A BLANKET of billowy white clouds, drifted in from the coolness of the sea, had brought a welcomed afternoon shower which now passed across on its way inland to the high slopes. Down across the wet meadow the Way of Stone burst into a gleaming line which cut its sunlight straight into the foot of a rainbow, reflected upon the sea to form a circle of colors.

As the others waited for us, Fo and Letty took me on a promised excursion which, it seems now, was given to bridge the gulf between their world and mine, as well perhaps to soften my departure.

We descended the steps to the ground below, and walked over some hills back of the house, whose grassy carpet glistened in the rays of the declining sun, and then across a valley to a hillside where there stood a giant windmill, its vanes far above turning slowly against the sky.

It was, Fo told me, a "Comet Windmill", on a tower forty meters tall, originally manufactured in the early 1900's, whose wheel had a diameter of thirty feet, and which had pumped pure water from 400 feet, with few repairs, for three centuries.

He filled an old porcelain cup, chipped and worn, and offered me a drink of water, aged and sweetened in the substrate for a million years. It tasted earthy and good, like my father's "Weber City water" which we had drunk growing up on the plains of eastern New Mexico.

My father considered it a tonic, and brought gallon jugs of it recovered from his farm into town where he spent his last years. One of these jugs, filled and kept by him, I retrieved from the storage room after his death, and only drank from a wineglass on the occasions celebrating each year the event of his death at 8:15 on that November morning.

I had calculated that the amount I retained would last me the rest of my life, and perhaps on the day of my passing I would be conscious enough to toast him and his people with one last drink of that life giving liquid from the sacred Earth, first brought to this planet by cosmic visitors known, as was the windmill, as comets, scattering, as well as their liquid which composes and sustains us, the primordial seeds of life itself.

My father would always drink last, as he fetched water from his well, passing the cup to those with him. I remember looking up at him as he drank, holding the long handle in his right hand. I noted that if he was really thirsty he could drink eight big swallows, maybe ten, tilting his head back as he drained the cup, his Adam's apple moving up and down as he drank. And when I became a man, and was really thirsty, I would count eight swallows of water to quench my thirst, maybe ten, and feel grateful as he did for the wonderful liquid so vital to life.

"Are these things real?" I asked.

"As real as your thoughts. As real as your knowledge of this moment."

(But it is important to know that they are real- that I am here, and you are here...)

I overtipped the wide cup, causing the cool water to spill over my face and down my collar. As I gasped at the refreshing bath, and as the cool water darkened the front of my shirt, Letty looked at me and smiled.

"Will this moment be?" I asked involuntarily.

Arching my head back, I looked up at the tall tower and the giant wheel, which turned smoothly in the sea breeze. A cloud passing above gave the effect of the tower falling, and caused me to stagger and steady my feet against the ground. I recognized the sensation from days of my boyhood on the southern plains.

"This moment *is*" was the answer.

A four-winged dragonfly flitted by, nearly touching my face, and circled over the surface of the water tank.

The dragonfly has not changed in 300 million years, yet its multiple wings constitute such a complex flying machine that the most advanced computers, capable of landing spacecraft on outer planets, could not make it fly- something nature accomplished a third of a billion years before with a single replicable computer the size of a needle's eye.

Yet its biological heritage, coded within the DNA, is more stable than the mountain ranges and continents, risen and fallen with the winds and waves and tides of Earth, in a transcendent and prescient reality which is more durable than the planet's crust.

And more durable still is thought- and the most, emotion, the being of love.

On our walk back to the house I asked the professor why it was so hard for the human to learn some things, and I believe that he answered more profoundly than I was asking, saying, "We did not grasp the connections before because we did not see the reflections of mind in the matter and energy and potential which surrounds and envelops us. We were trying to shine by our own light and there was nothing beyond it to see... The knowledge *was us,* illuminated by reflection from our mirror image in the whole of existence. This is the unity, the 'Unified Field.'

"It was not that our separateness was an illusion, but that we, in a discreet and infinite reality, didn't comprehend it."

*   *   *

WE HAD NOT been gone very long, and when we returned Letty's daughter, Aida, and the four who called themselves, Specialists, were still around the table, visiting. I could hear them talking as we approached and climbed the stairway to the veranda, and it seemed a normal conversation, if from individuals who were of extreme intelligence, and the maturity of an experience unimaginable to our time. I had noticed that the expressiveness of their speech never varied from their words, so that their thought and feelings were transposed purely, and one never questioned their meaning.

In remembering them it seems now ironic that we are unable to know and express the fullness of our affection in the presence of our experience. But when that object is no longer there, and we are looking back on an irretrievable past, or forward to an irretrievable future, transformed now in memory and emotion, we begin to realize love's depth and meaning.

It is wondrously given that love is most beautifully completed in loss, and all things, though passed on, through love are born to new life.

When I thanked them for their wonderful hospitality, and for the phenomenal opportunity that had been offered me, and expressed my regret at having to leave, BJ seemed especially affected, and offered an assurance which seemed not for me especially, but for the mortal human:

You are not just what you are. You are the power of what you might have been, and the meaning of what you may become.
In you at any moment is invested the history of life, and its destiny.

In that hour of leavetaking my thoughts were of the handsome young artist with the shining blue-grey eyes, and the passion of his music. What greater wish for another than to be alive with passion! There will be no repetition of the past, but wouldn't it be wonderful to gather with full memories about the throne of life and talk, talk endlessly about the meaning of it all? What stories we mortals could tell!

Until then, just the glance, the smile, and salute with a single rose taken from a bouquet presented by a young woman whose face I didn't see, will be enough.

We are not shadows of our former selves, as we rise through age beyond the dawning of our existence. We are, therefrom, the spirits of what we were, the essence drawn by experience into new heights. As we near the end we do not relinquish what we were, rather, we draw it all into ourselves and all of it becomes us, and we become all of it.

As we grow older we have more and more in common with them, and the embrace we long for is theirs, the heart reaching back through the long childhood to the imagined cradle of their love.

Is this the loyalty that will call them to the resurrection- the unfinished business of our selves?

Being of immense intelligence and understanding, they smiled at me, and I noticed their eyes were moist, as were mine.

We heard footsteps upon the staircase just then, and looked over to see rising into view the two who had wished me a wonderful experience just the day before. There was something different about them, and the others rose in greeting as if welcoming them from somewhere far away, from a place that held mystery to even them.

Boris and Monami seemed themselves to me, as they were when I met them and enjoyed their companionship on the way to meet my friends on the way of stone, but I had sensed as well some aspect unqualifiable- not estranged, but deeply connected, beyond the bonds of cordiality or friendship, or even of love. Were they from that realm 'closer to the Omega'?

After warm greetings and a few words among them of light conversation, Boris and Monami signaled to me that it was time to go. Monami took my hand, and the others walked with us down the veranda's length, over the wide walkway whose surface lent a spring to the step, and through the courtyard which lay under the shade of flowering trees whose blossoms were serenaded by the lively hum of a myriad darting wings. The bower of climbing roses breathed a fragrance into the mist of a fountain from whose hyacinthine tiers pure waters sang in their cool cascade, in voices of coolness added downward in the misty flow in a melody as ancient as stone itself, and eternally soothing to the soul of life.

We descended the stone steps between planters filled with fragrant flowers, vivid in their colors, and stood upon the landing at the curbside of the Way of Stone.

As we were saying our farewells, one of my hosts asked me for a favor, or perhaps it was a counsel: "When you return to your people, tell them about us.."

And then each one passed by in a line in the emotional ritual of goodbyes, and I noted indelibly the nature of each.

Letty and Aida cried as they embraced me, and Fo was quiet, hugging me, then offering his two-handed handshake, then reaching around to give me two strong slaps on the back, and then another handshake, saying, "Yep, yep," and nodding his head. I noticed the emotion in his eyes.

The big fellow, Billy Joe, called "BJ", was next, still sporting his red bandana, wrapping his big arms around my frame and squeezing. Then he shook my hand and, with his wry expression and a smile of his small mouth, made an effort at humor, I think, saying, "See you soon.., in the funny papers on the animal side." I could only hope that he was not being profound.

His manner reinforced my sense that he and I had a connection somewhere, and I was in another world to find what that connection was, and to appreciate the prophetic irony of his comment.

The two Specialists- scientists, scholars, and eminent counselors- Lia, and Kenata, embraced me like close friends who regretted letting go, planting kisses on my cheeks, and caressing my arms on either side. I cannot imagine still what they felt, as beings who knew my life and its future intimately, including the events of that last day, when I would drink the toast to my ancestors.

The kind-eyed, serious intellectual they called, Robeling- "builder of bridges"- with the aquiline nose and Emersonian countenance, waited last to bid his farewell. He shook my hand vigorously as he looked intently into my eyes, and offered nothing in words.

They were all human- but for the two guides whose nature I cannot quantify- and yet they possessed a quality beyond the human, which may have come from their great knowledge and experience beyond the span of life of mortals, or from some dimension of understanding which can only come through the mind's true liberation. Whatever is constituted in that transcendence did not estrange them from their humanity, but rather ennobled it, as if in the conquest of death the human finds its true meaning and place at last.

Kenata stepped close and held my hands, telling me, "Every step you have ever taken has brought you here. Every thought and emotion through your life has been your guide, pointing you to this moment. Every joy and every disappointment alike opening the doorway to greater reality. This is the place you have made within your dream. We are your children."

For a moment I wept, for that thing down deep that we have always known. We carry the child within us, that we will one day become.

AS I STEPPED down upon the Way of Stone, walking between the footsteps of my guides, I wondered whether Nature had done all this before, as reality's beloved child, through endless cycles of trial and error, not unlike any conscious process- and not as the omnipotent which we earthlings deem, but rather as the learner- attaining her wisdom as ages roll by, through infinite passages of struggle and reproof, yet ever confident in her knowing that at the end of all striving is perfection.

And that we humans are players this time in her grandest scheme, infinitely more significant than we can imagine, linking with our thoughts and dreams a cosmic origin and destiny, drawn by the inexplicable affinity called love, into meaning.

The soft wind, faint and steady as a breathing, redolent with clove and salt of the meadow and the nearby sea, accompanied us through the magnificent enfilade of great aged and arching trees with massive boughs suspended by the sky, whose trunks, pressing against the ancient lines of the way of stone with the relentless force of a bulldozer, could only mould their growth to the inexorable mass of a thing that mind conceived and made.

As we emerged from the long majestic arbor which shaded the monument from antiquity known to them as the Way of Stone, which, more than a mass, was a spirit which had awaited for twenty millennia its answer in thought, we walked again upon the rustic trail which wound, and rose into the higher ground from whose vista could be seen the meandering river.

Though the hours were descending into evening, and long shadows cast their forms upon the mountain slopes above, and I knew that I was leaving the world which was theirs, I felt as if I walked within a transcendent light, as if the hand of immortality rested upon my brow, and a redolence floated within my brain as I took the footsteps away from my inestimable friends, and the old stone house with its veranda, which seemed to safely touch both worlds- that divine presence from which I was returning, and the world of my past which held the people and places and things of memory which, I was assured, lay waiting for my return.

How easy it is to leave even paradise, when home and loved ones wait!

As we neared the crest of the hill where I had first seen them sitting together upon a bench, I noticed that Monami was again humming that melody, lovely and pure, which floated out of the stillness in tones of the human, to a joyful, pulsing rhythm of life, shaping with her light breaths a soft music to which I thrilled, for its vibrant happiness and freedom.

As we reached the moment of parting, I asked a question which had been on my mind, something very personal, and they answered, with the purest kindness and understanding. Boris, first, then Monami, embraced me- he, firmly holding my shoulders, and looking at me with unmistakable understanding and sympathy and affection; and then she, with an embrace that seemed to pass through me into another reality which I cannot now express. Wisps of her long hair fell across my face, and I still dream of the smell of her skin.

And then, again, in that sweet gesture, the both of them touched my head, he, resting his hand upon it, and she, pressing her soft palm to my forehead, in front of my eyes, and then sliding it around my cheek, and holding it for just a moment.

And then they both smiled, and one after the other, said, "Hello".

*   *   *

I SAID goodbye to Monami and Boris at the crest of the hill where we had met, and walked down the path to the place where the round crown of the tree arched against the white-clouded sky.

Looking to the right, and down the grassy slope with its tufts of fluorescent flowers, I saw the little bridge reaching from the green bank across the quiet river to the trees whose ripe fruit hung in visible clusters.

Suddenly, a little group of souls emerged, adults and children, and they seemed to be the ones who had welcomed me on my passing the day before. They stood there waving, and then I heard, lowly at first and then rising, the sweetest strains of music as lovely as could be imagined, wrapping the heart and soul.

I recognized it as something from the old country, locked in the sentiment and memories of my ancestors, an old song of farewell, but not goodbye, as they did not know goodbye in the land of no parting. I left them thus on that landscape far away across time where scattered and wistful dreams and profound memories compose them still, and will until we meet again in that bright morning where roses bloom forever, and parting is no more.

In a journey of return I was drawn upward on the trail, an effortless energy lifting my feet into the heights where fields of flowers lay before the vistas of green hills and a meandering river far below, which wound its placid passage to the ocean.

Near its banks in settlements laid out in little patches, tending to their lives and fields, lived families and neighbors and friends, and farther along where the trail merged into a Way laid down in antiquity, a community of minds and souls and dreams, grand and human, and a stone house with a veranda overlooking the sea.

I do not know where the trail ended and the flight home began- if in that same meadow carpeted in clover and dewy grass, filled with the subtle fragrance of pine and the gentle bubbling sound of a brook that became a river to the sea. It may have been.

Then, lifted up into the weightless folds of brightness in a womb steered by a spirit in time homeward to the reality of this life, forever changed by the promise of what may come to be, if we believe, and will it.

*   *   *

*THE END of all our exploring will be to arrive where we started
And know the place for the first time.*
-T.S. Eliot, *The Four Quartets.*

THEY SAY THAT in moments of great intensity the inner soul is revealed in a first glance, that haunting split-second that bares great distress even to the complete stranger who, in one glance, knows in his soul the soul of another.

The scene, strange and surreal beyond anything of that future world from which I had just returned, was laid out there on a leveled off spot by the roadside: of some two dozen humans squatting upon the ground- so estranged, being of a different country even though three miles away, as to be called "aliens"- and their green-clad captors standing guard; the blades of a police chopper churning silently in the background, its helmeted occupants watching, guarding against some wretched escape by anyone miraculously able to flee after enduring the arduous trek, composing a lifetime, across hostile terrain toward the promised land.

As the van drove by them I caught in a stillframe of my mind the indelible picture before me- of the captives lined in three rows, their tired faces cast in an eerie glow of the last beautiful rays of the setting sun, their eyes besot with a weariness goaded into fear by their abject circumstance.

The young driver looked calmly ahead as he drove the car, which seemed for me to slow in a time lapse allowing my eyes to sweep across every face, and gaze into each pair of eyes in the three rows, even as they looked back into the eyes of the sole passenger seated in the back of the passing car.

I thought I saw something flicker in their glance, a change occurring in the instantaneous sweep of my view of them- a lifting of hope, I thought, that someone from an outside world, if nothing else, was evidence that beyond their poor state another world existed.

The wind of the passing vehicle, sealed for me in silence, suddenly brushed across them, ruffling their hair and the clothes they had held about them. The guards started, and the two with their backs to the road wheeled about, their arms arching around to fix in a single motion their clutched hands upon the weapons belted upon them.

A look of great alarm cemented their faces like a silent cry which only briefly lagged the instinctual reaction of their bodies.

Behind the captives, one of the two guards who stood facing the road slapped his tensed arms together, pressing the metallic weapon in the frozen vice of his pale hands. He dropped into a crouch and swung his upper body, rigidly aligned behind his gun barrel, in an arc across his charges and back to the sound of the vehicle whose passing he only heard and felt in the gravelly friction of the tires and the wave of rushing air.

His partner gripped but did not fully retrieve his pistol as his head jerked stiffly back and forth, the computer of his brain trying to decipher the strange input of evidence not seen. I thought I saw, as I turned my head around in passing, a faint smile creasing the countenance of an old woman in the center row, who clearly saw the vision before her.

She believed in miracles, I thought, and had seen them before.

The next edition of the News International would feature a lead article with headlines exclaiming: "Ghost Car 'Sighted' by Patrol!"

Various Border Patrol officers, still shaken by the experience, avowed the details of this strange incident. Another article on the front page would relate to the official inquiry launched after the first "sighting" by officers of an "invisible vehicle" whose passing they had heard and felt just before dawn the day before, and then at dusk of the next day, crossing once in the direction of the highway, and then again towards the mountains the following evening.

There was no comment reported from any of the subjects of that afternoon's apprehension, who had squatted tersely in the three rows facing the van and its passage, which they had clearly witnessed. Apparently, no one thought to ask these disenfranchised souls who could have added a critical dimension to the story, or called upon them to comment, their presence being quite as invisible as the "ghost car."

History is more often composed by official voices, one is reminded, than by the poor and unfree.

As the car lifted in a rise, and rounded the curve past the old ranch house, the scene back at the roadside was erased from view by a horizon of mesquite and gold-leafed locust lining the road. By now the evening hills were cast in magenta and rose against a pink sky opposite the setting star, the white dot of the telescope dome glowing in sunlight upon the summit of the tallest peak in the mountains near Tubac.

Drawn from my intense reflection I looked forward at the driver. Only the back of his head showed above the seat, his wavy hair shining in the evening light caught in a scintillation by my senses now awakened to realities beyond. Just as I became aware of his upper face in the rear view mirror his eyes shifted from the road before him. Steady and reassuring, they held their glance for just an instant before turning back to the road.

I noted in them the hint of a smile, and a twinkle which came from the knowledge and peace of worlds beyond our own. I felt a tinge of joy and a perfusing of wonderful silence from whose depths there sprang the faintest vibration of the music, exceedingly sweet and lovely, ancient and immortal, like the music of the spheres, arising from within and without in a single rhapsody across the distance of time.

The van glided down the slope and around the curve, through the pines and cottonwoods and willow, and past the clubhouse set above the lake, where Letty and her mother once lived, whose walls still echo the muffled voices and laughter of the famed and beautiful of yesteryear-Granger and Jean Simmons and their guests, Elizabeth, Marilyn, Bogart and Bacall, Chaplin, Wayne... Unique actors upon the screen and stage in dramas of exquisite poignancy, only faintly sketching, for their various artistry, the true quality of their moment.

Wandering through this historic dwelling, one senses their reluctance to sign off, their images passing like spirits through the velvety transparence which separates the two acts of life and death...

We swung around the curve upon the clubhouse grounds, out and around the flat with its mane of tall grass dried straw yellow, past the tufts of green sage, and down toward the old adobe bunkhouse by the corrals, shaded by ancient cottonwood whose roots siphoned nourishment from beneath the riverbed. The meandering stream had left its imprint in a sand sculpture as it sank underground after the summer rains, the last currents set in rivulets of fine sand which glistened softly in the evening light.

"Would you like to cross the bridge?" the driver asked, reading my thoughts.

Somehow the transition was too immense, I had sensed just now, and it would be well to stand upon the bridge for awhile, and watch the glorious fading of the light, now etched in orange and gold upon the western sky, allowing myself to filter and absorb the reality I had seen, whose own light could transform itself through the medium of the present, even as the clouds caught and transmuted the sun's energy into a panorama of sheer wonder...

"I'll wait here awhile," I answered. The eyes in the mirror acknowledged my reply with a twinkle, even as I suddenly felt the weight of my own body against the seat. I had raised my arm to gesture to him, and noted with surprise how heavy it felt, drawn in a precise measure against this planet's gravity, which remembers each atom of existence.

I shifted myself forward as the van slowed and stopped just short of the bridge's concrete base. The door slid open and the evening's cool air brushed my face.

It was soft, and faintly perfumed with the various odors of fallen leaves and sage and clean earth, awakening memories which extended back into the countryside of my childhood and youth in New Mexico.

I almost heard the clap of the screen from my mother's kitchen door leading out the back of the little farmhouse, its spring twisting out a distinct sound as an aproned figure, young and beautiful, leaned out and sang, "Suppertime!" to husband and sons out finishing the evening chores. As the familiar smells of supper wafted across time, the heaviness I felt suddenly lifted as a joyful energy coursed through my body.

"Thank you for everything!" I called to the youth whose head leaned out the open window. He brushed a shock of hair from his forehead and smiled brightly.

"You're most welcome," he called, "and thank you...Go well, until we meet again."

The white van with its tall wheels eased backward in a turn as I walked the few yards to the bridge. Reaching the guardrail I turned back, expecting to wave goodbye once more before the car moved back up the road and out of sight.

It and its driver had simply vanished.

I walked down the slope towards the corrals to see if it had perhaps pulled off the roadway. There was no sight of the car, nor of taillights moving up around the bend. I felt a shudder of delight.

"Of course!" I exclaimed loudly, "Of course!"

I stood there for a moment, gazing down at my legs and feet, and breathed deeply. The sense of levity had returned, with a thrill of energy last known in my childhood. My legs began to spring up the slope toward the middle of the bridge. I stepped lightly up on the narrow walkway and grasped the cool railing only a few yards from where I had first seen the mysterious stranger with his compelling presence.

"The greatest failing of man is not to recognize his own magnificence," he had declared quietly on that occasion... "A thousand years will come, as will a day," he said.

I knew now of what he was speaking, having seen through the glass, as it were, the marvelous and extraordinary potential accorded conscious life.

I recalled an assurance noted in a student's handwriting at the top of the first page of notes on Professor Fo's class: *Destiny calls us, and awaits our calling.*

I stood beneath a sea of stars on that unforgettable night.

Standing upon the spot where the mysterious being had stood, and looking upwards at the curved road which would lead me back to my home and loved ones, I had noticed streaks of shadows angling across the road as the lowering sun filtered its energy through the leaves and branches of the mesquites.

It suddenly seemed surreal and elegant that after a hundred million miles of passage from a star, the photons of light would be stopped by a delicate leaf or a branch, to form the image of a living sculpture elongated into shadow in the landscape of the mind.

*   *   *

CHAPTER *FIFTEEN*

KANSAS

*NO WAR waged against the human spirit was ever won, and no
effort waged to lift the human spirit was ever lost. Across the pages
of history in bold letters underlined in innocent blood is written the
futility of battle, while at the bottom of history's pages in unheralded
footnotes is the powerful and iridescent testimony of love.*
-small composition notebook "18", p36.

*Reality is music- triumphal, sad, wistful, joyful, rebellious,
tranquil, commanding, visionary, prophetic- carrying
across the ranges of thought and emotion.*
Reality is thought and emotion.
-green notebook " 11", p35.

*"IN THEIR world there are only renters of time and place.
They own the night; they own the day. Ask them their
permission, and maybe they will say, Yes.."*
-Otto, to Foglesby.

I RETURNED TO that incandescent summer which saw the end of things
as the world knew them, though few at the time could have envisioned the
breadth and nature of the forces at play.

Although I felt an immediate necessity to contact Professor Foglesby
and Letty regarding the transcendent matters of my experience, I also

examined my basic assumption that simply because I retained the details in memory they could and should be passed on to others, though whether to those who were also participants in the future event was another matter.

The visit to the future was also now a past event, was it not, in a strange convolution perhaps impossible to qualify or ascertain, though how does it differ from the dreamstate, except that it was real?

I decided to pursue the prodigious course of finding my friends to inform them, which task was made more difficult as I had been advised by the university that the professor was not in residence. As well I could not locate Otto with my elementary resources, and refrained from engaging professionals who would be surrogates in a personal matter, as it did not seem proper. And so I simply left messages and waited for a reply.

Within a few weeks I began to receive messages that promised contact with my friends, the last from an anchor journalist at MSNBC who must have been given authority to relay word that I would soon be hearing from someone, though she did not say from whom. As I was busy closing out my career as a person of business in order to begin a new life whose parameters I had not yet determined, I did not worry about things which I felt would have their own turn, dealing instead with finalizing mundane details which had less importance but more immediacy. Having seen into another dimension a supremely greater reality that had remained unseen, though surely ever present, I was transformed by an overarching sense of assurance that whatever there was, was well.

The news came unexpectedly and with much officiation one morning in the form of a press conference called by the U.S. Attorney General before a statue of Lady Justice whose classical figure had been remarkably draped by what appeared to be a linen shawl, or shroud, which added to the surreal nature of the presentation, and to the figure making it.

The nation was shocked and confounded to learn from Mr. Ashcroft that a prominent American scientist and his staff had been charged with acts of treason complicit with terrorism.

The fugitives from justice, according to the Attorney General, were discovered the previous day through the outstanding merits of the law enforcement community and his office to be hiding in- of all places- a tall grain elevator near a small community in Kansas. An astounding array of military and police equipment was immediately set in place surrounding the facility, including tanks and heavy armor, which were shown dramatically in continuous features on news channels, outlining the grave nature of the crisis confronting the country.

There was no explanation of the threat posed by a group of scientists housed in a storage facility high above the Kansas prairie, or of the need for lethal armor.

A general bewilderment soon supplanted my amused relief at discovering the probable whereabouts of the two people who loomed in my concerns, and for days afterward held me in close audience to the repetitive footage panning across the scene on the half-hour, hosted by news personalities who had limited information and so speculated endlessly on the events and what might or might not occur tomorrow. In the absence of real information or understanding the audiences return in their bewilderment to view the dramatization of unfolding events, and so history is made.

In the days ahead the media continued to focus endlessly on the matter, fed by briefings and updates from the perspective of the government as the charges ballooned into alarming and farcical proportions alluding to 9/11 and the shibboleths of terror, while increasingly concerned voices began to speak up, calling for reason and calm.

Prominent colleagues and friends of the professor and his associates appeared on talk shows and in press interviews to avow that, despite its misuse by government influence, science was the greatest ally of mankind, especially when shepherded by persons of great humanity the likes of Lloyd Man Foglesby. Meanwhile, the confrontation seemed to be self-imposed and one-sided, with a complete dearth of information from the scientific community within the rounded concrete towers, and soon was being heralded as "The Great Standoff," which eerily recalled other sieges which had ended in tragedy. The news story was compelling.

ONE EVENING the phone rang, and I was delighted at last to hear Letty's voice.

"You got anything going on in Kansas?" she asked. Though she sounded tired, her voice was buoyant and musical, as I remembered it to be. It is how I expected her to sound, despite the gravity of their circumstance- this woman for whom life was so broad and yielding that such matters were like pencil marks upon a great page.

In her college days, when times were lean and she was working fulltime to support herself and send money back home to her mother, even while taking a full load of classes, she would sometimes find herself short of funds to carry over. Lacking money for food for a day or more, she would simply declare a fast. A fast can be good for the body and soul, she knew, so merely not having food on hand was a convenience. She had smoked cigarettes in her early college days, and when she gave them up she enjoyed resisting the craving, feeling her strength build during the months of recovery, even as the desire to smoke diminished until it was gone.

"Well, sure," I had answered her, deliberately steadying my voice. "I think I'm planning a trip to Kansas. Shall I drop by?"

"If it's not out of your way," she replied casually. "I guess you know our present address..."

"Well, yes. I've jotted it down... They say be wary of friends in high places," I added.

"Oh, good friends are the same, no matter where they hang their coats," she chuckled. "When you comin' up?"

"I'll leave first thing in the morning... I can leave tonight."

"No, no. Get some rest. And have a safe trip. We'll be looking for you, say, around Wednesday?"

"Letty?" I hastened to catch her before she put down the phone. "You don't know how glad I am to hear from you...Say Hello to the Professor."

"I will, and thanks."

A click signaled the break in phone contact, but my ears rang on with the music of her voice.

There was no sleep to be had that night. I was exhilarated, and after a cursory attempt at getting rest I jumped up and bathed and packed some changes of clothes into a bag, along with toothbrush and cream and razors and lotion. Into a little ice chest I placed some fruit and snacks. I took along some books, including the eminent Colin Wilson's "Afterlife", having no idea when I would read them, and a notebook containing excerpts of notes from Fo's classes on Destiny, and a litany of questions. There should be plenty to occupy my mind on the long road. I had made other visits to the state over the years, but this promised to be the most interesting by any measure.

As I was passing down the hallway I placed my ear near the doors to listen if someone might be awake. There was only the quiet of peaceful sleep, so I moved on, leaving a note upon the kitchen table. "Have left for Kansas. Everything's fine. Will call. Love, Me."

I left another note for my best little friend and grandson: a tree, a moon and star, and a flower hurriedly sketched, with the names written in English and Spanish, symbols all, for him to recognize and bring to life in the colors of his crayons. Little pangs of love struck my heart as I closed and locked the door behind me and walked out into the night.

I tossed two bags into the little car and tried to pull out quietly despite the resounding exhausts of the Fiero's V-6 engine. We rumbled gently down the road and out of sight of the village, although the cool atmosphere will continue to announce our departure until we're halfway to the river. Images of the people I left in their sleep move about in my thoughts. The two gentle and strong women and that dear little soul who came into our lives so unexpectedly and with such providence... I'm sure I had not taken the news with such nobility and control as the grandmother had, who then passed it on to me. We men are great handlers of small matters, blithely moving among challenges inconsequential; the woman, however, takes great matters in stride, which, they say, is why God apportioned motherhood to women, and fishing to men.

After the obligatory travail of sackcloth and ashes, lasting some long minutes, I had emerged anxious to go and express my love and support to this dearest of persons who would always be so special to my life. Ultimately, all the memories and anticipations merged into a glow which warmed and delighted all our hearts. Such immeasurable gifts from small things will always be a source of wonder to those inexplicably favored to know them.

All things happen for a reason in this life.

I passed over the bridge and around the clubhouse by the lake, and soon reached the highway leading through Patagonia eastward. As I turned I could not help but notice two matched cars, neutral in style and color, sitting by the roadside with individuals inside. As I accelerated, two sets of headlights flashed on, and shifted sideways to line up behind me.

The Fall morning air was fresh and crisp as I moved across the countryside toward the New Mexico line, driving automatically as my mind ranged over immense realities of a future and present which were directly related, and so I could not separate them with undue concern for matters which I could not comprehend. I strangely felt no sense of privilege or power in a knowledge of future events which were contingent upon a moving present, as it gave no resolution other than the assurance that great and immortal forces were at work in our mortal lives to fulfill a purpose far grander than our selves.

Off in the distance of the broad valley between ranges of the Chiricahuas which were once home to Geronimo and his people, islands of lights began to appear which I took at first to be dairies scattered over the landscape, tending to large herds of animals milked in parlors around the clock, but then as one appeared which was nearer the interstate, showing its rectangular perimeter and structures within, I realized these were prisons newly built in a privatized system to contain the expanding numbers of the incarcerated in America. The dawn came over broad vistas of the New Mexico landscape, and as I followed the Rio Grande valley, high above, silhouetted in the sunrise light, was the ancient and incomparably moving image of a formation of geese winging its way toward a winter nesting area, so coordinated that it would seem to be a single entity, and not an assemblage of many into an artistic, moving unit programmed by a long evolution to the survival of its species.

I watched with a sense of the spiritual, which is nothing less than the realization of a connection with that phenomenon witnessed- not that one is placed within it, but that one is a part of it, bonded within the family of life. It is serendipitous and inspiring to the latecomer species to find itself witness to a ritual played out in exactly the same way as in an eon before the rise of the human to notice it, as if such beauty and symmetry were reenacted to perfection over the ages, waiting for its audience of mind to complete its reality.

For what else was creation wrought?...

I followed the historic Route 66 as it passed across central New Mexico on its way to the plains of Texas, accompanied by the ghosts of travel from another time which still journey back and forth if you open your senses to them, recalling eras of loss and opportunity indelibly pressed into the lives of the people who experienced them- the wars and the Great Depression, the fabled Dust Bowl which blackened the plains and forever changed a generation and its offspring. When nothing remained people forsook their homes and traveled outward carrying their pots and pans and the remnants of their dreams, most often less graceful in their flight than the winging geese who crossed the skies above them. What they left behind is what we sense today, the emotion of their lives.

Behind me at a more of less constant distance, the two cars whose lights had remained in my rearview mirrors throughout the early morning hours now appeared as grey objects otherwise nondescript as were their four occupants whom I had witnessed as they attended to the task of refueling their vehicles in another fueling bay nearby.

They wore similar suits and dark glasses, which concealed the eyes and whatever weapons they may have carried for their purposes, and I found them curiously interesting for their connection to the drama taking place and its involvement with people I knew. I assumed them to be a benign presence whose purpose was simply to keep me in view as I made my way to a destination they already knew from the phone call from Letty. Whatever other motives they might have had was an inscrutable matter I did not consider important in the scheme of things.

At a rest stop just before dawn in the remote high country which seems the top of the world, I had stood outside in the crisp air gazing upward at the photograph from antiquity which shows a universe as it was, with only the illusion of presence the human calls, stars, and has given names to. Their presence is that infinitely thin line of photons, no wider than a thought, moving across time, into which vanishes all of the past and all of the future. I pondered the reference, made by my future friends, to intelligence and light, saying, "You will combine intelligence with light, for of such it may be already."

Are we known as well by the heavens?...

Off toward the horizon sat an alabaster moon, shining white as a saint, though darkly indented with lovely imperfections of its mythical craters and seas- the round world perfectly perched atop a pinnacle of brilliant rose-hued clouds swirling upward and about in sky storms silent in chaotic elegance in the safe distance of the horizon cut into a dark silhouette by the scissor of night. It was, of course, the portrait of a moment in a dawning upon one planet, a moving instant in time which- exactly as it was- had never come before and will never come again.

It came, and it was, in the same ineffable moment not unlike the "I", the observer which created it in the panorama of conscious awareness. Would it have happened in worlds where no being exists to draw it into thought and emotion- a symbiosis between the energy of spirit and the flash of reality?

Behind me, as I pulled up on the highway, the twin cars which had been waiting nearby moved forward to maintain the distance between us.

THERE ARE cemeteries one sometimes sees when passing through the plains, or catches in a sense of their presence, as every community includes one, or leaves it behind when the people move away.

It is curious how the graveyards mirror the communities of the living, growing in concentric circles around their core of history, which is their oldest laid to rest- and after them each generation following, extending outward to the margins which separate death and its waiting.

Always when I travel through the prairie town where my father spent years of his childhood in the early part of the last century, with members of his family scattered about the countryside, I sense the spirits of them lingering still, as if their time had not passed.

On the old Main Street, largely boarded up, a child walks somewhere with his mother and sister, perhaps entering a doorway which is still there, to purchase a thing or two in a store now empty and dust covered, and inexorably aging. They would walk into town a half mile down a dirt road to do their business, and then return to a little house built by the father, of lumber well assembled and made into a place called home.

There was a home town "Victory Parade" during the Great War, and my father remembered being lifted upon a wagon to look into a washtub which contained coins collected for the boys over there. He had never seen so much money.

It was a day in childhood which remained with him through life.

They were as alive as we are now, and as I walked the sidewalks, cracked and aged, I could sense their footsteps still. If we can feel them, must not something of them be there, living in the ghosts of memory?

Leaving the town toward the Kansas border, I could see the rows of cypress trees that line the road leading to the cemetery half a mile away, and made a turn to briefly visit the graves of my grandparents, whom I never knew.

I told them about the fineness of their son, now joined with them in death- separated from his mother in early childhood, and from his father in youth- and of how much they had missed by not knowing him as he aged. I spoke briefly to them of a future I had seen, and of unimaginable miracles within the Dome of Sky, and of answers to the immortal dream of reuniting with the beloved. I asked if they would choose to live again.

At the periphery of my consciousness a steady sound intruded upon my immersion in thought, and then a reality as the two engines were heard idling nearby. The magical connection with the spirits was dissolved, and so I replaced my hat, and promised to return.

Of the two worlds known by the conscious entity- not both of them spiritual- one is in historic conflict with the other and its freedom. One seeks to control the being, and hold her to this earth; the other, to liberate the same being from control and fulfill the purpose of consciousness, which is its immortal birthright.

I noticed as the twin cars continued their trail that they had closed the gap they held before, and were now close enough behind that I could see the driver and passenger of the first car in my mirrors.

SIXTEEN HOURS had now elapsed as I drove across the panhandle plains flat as a tabletop for forty miles spanning the Kansas border. There was so much to think about in my excitement that the hours had flown by, and only now as the sun was descending toward evening did I notice a fatigue setting in. I had sensed a particular emotion at the graveyard where my grandparents lay, and remembered what Isaac Stern had said, "Emotion is the breath of souls past."

Perhaps he was referring to music, and to emotion as the wellspring of creation...

Foglesby spoke to a class, of reality as music in all its forms carrying across the ranges of thought and emotion. To what extent, then, do we owe our senses of reality to the composite of consciousness passed upward to us from the collective experience in rudiments of things vital to the souls past: *We cared about this; it was important to us.*

Does this not speak of emotion so inherent that it defines the human? And what is the nature of the presence I felt, and its evolutionary purpose, the voices of thought and emotion that speak through time, and through that connection we call, "love"?

I was suddenly startled to look back and see the hood of a grey car looming behind. I looked at my speedometer and saw that I had not lost speed through my distraction in thought, and was still maintaining a velocity just above the posted limit, so that I did not have vehicles passing me.

Did they lose patience and want me to speed up? Why had I noticed an aggression in their demeanor back at the cemetery?.. Not that they had ever been friendly.

I had assumed that their only purpose was to maintain surveillance as I made my way to my destination- which was not in question- and so had simply neutralized them in the process, and attended to other thoughts, and to an enjoyment of the autumn journey.

I began to entertain recollections of Otto and his admonitions and counsel to Fo in Bisbee so many months before. While he kept a sense of humor in his speech, his face betrayed his seriousness, and his understanding of what his colleague might be facing. The professor would try to convince the Board of Regents that the greatest discovery in the history of thought would arrive in a benign state, not as a rogue alien.

"This knowledge, the *key,* cannot be used to ill effect," he tried to explain. "It is unequivocally benign, and for human life heralds a cornucopia of discoveries and advances which have the potential to transform man's universe."

They sat in silence, uncomprehending.

I had not understood very well what the elder professor was counseling. Otto had spent his life pursuing causes and so was probably merely advising his friend as to what he may be in for if he did not capitulate. He had lamented "the merely content, who live life through, and protest nothing, who leave no improvement, no added measure of freedom for their descendents," adding to his friend, "You are not one of those."

Otto had authored a number of well-known books- some of which I had purchased, but not yet read- dealing in subjects ranging from history to ethics, environmental concerns to individual liberty, and had been a perpetual thorn in the side of established authority.

I suddenly recalled his commentary, "Madness harvested and contained is power," and though he was speaking in another context which I believe was creative intellect, I transposed it to apply to my fellow travelers and found myself hoping that whatever madness there was to their method was indeed harvested and contained.

Fo had stood amused as Otto embellished his counsel: "If you leave them to their devices they will make you a prisoner and a slave. Their appetite is for control... Your problem, Fo, is that you refuse to be pacified."

I shook my head vigorously, as much to wake up as to shift my thoughts to a subject more edifying, not wishing to be sucked into the vortex which floundered an ill-fated Antarctic explorer early in the last century who apocalyptically noted in his last diary entry: *Thought can become blinded, negating reason and the senses.*

The eyes trick you. The ears no longer hear. Touch is invisible. The voice is given over to a stranger.

Time is distorted, stretching a moment into hours or days, and squeezing years into a seeming moment.

I shook my head again, dispelling the white-out, and looked at the dash clock. Within a little more than two hours I should be able to find a place to shower away the dust of ages and get some sleep. From there it would be only another hour of travel to the scene of drama, and my friends.

I settled into a quiet routine as I drove now, leaving aside the immense trains of thought which had engaged my mind, and listened to a station which played classical melodies across the countryside. For a time I forgot that I was not alone, until reminded of the two bland vehicles which followed at a distance which violated that zone of comfort and safety the human knows instinctively as his space.

I tried accelerating, but found that this did not alter the distance separating us, and so I concentrated for a time on observing the figures which occupied the front seat of the first car. They seemed to be rigid, absent the usual movements of the head which would accompany conversation or notice of the passing scenery. I felt eerily that they were staring at me, though something about them seemed in my state of mind to be robotic and not entirely human.

I was reminded of the vestigial evil eye left over from primitive cultures, and the ancient ritual of intimidation still practiced as an element of control.

Just as I had redirected my attention to the music, which floated across decades from what seems to us was a simpler and more innocent time, I noticed in my side mirror the glint of an object approaching from out of the brightness of the sun which had erupted in its descent behind us, magnifying its rays in a last splurge before setting. The object, yellow gold in color, expanded in size as if it were an inflating balloon, and I realized at once that it was overtaking us at high speed, as I was now driving beyond the posted speed limit to assert my separation from the rear enders accompanying me on this journey.

A sense of urgency arose merely from its phenomenal approach, and I fixed on its growing image in my mirror, resolving by the second into features I began to recognize as an older vehicle gliding fugue-like out of the distant silence.

With a suddenness I heard a sound, blast-like, and a simultaneous movement flashed into place just to the left of my field of view. The image in my mirror had extraordinarily morphed into the presence of the object I had seen, holding steady beside me in the left lane a few feet away. It was a faded gold station wagon from the 1970's, whose right front fender had been replaced but not painted to match, and seated behind its steering wheel was the commander of this boat whose profile was an instant study in character.

His head, almost reaching the ceiling of his car, was covered by greying hair, grown long and held in place by a headband. He was wearing a green camouflage shirt that was long-sleeved. He held both hands on the wheel, looking straight ahead at the road. I saw that he was clean shaven, but for a mustache and a small patch of hair beneath his lower lip. His features were long, a curved nose, square jaw, and strong chin. His lips were fixed with a pleasant expression. A large ear, studded with a ring of some kind, protruded from the hair that was pulled back and tied into a ponytail. He looked at once rugged, and yet with a demeanor that was sensitive, and extremely intelligent. Though intense, he seemed completely at ease.

Then, just for a few seconds, he turned his head and looked at me.

A thousand words could not describe the photograph of that face.

It was as if he knew everything, and in an instant told me that he was a loner, apart from it, and so held it all in his power. He lifted a large right hand from the steering wheel and floated it momentarily, palm down in a curious gesture, and then raised his fingers to touch his forehead in what looked to be a salute. Then he smiled as if to say we had made our acquaintance, and that was that.

A deafening noise exploded from the old wagon, and fire and smoke shot out from beneath a screaming engine. I saw his head snap back, his face still holding its expression, and to the accompanying fury of burning rubber the thing blasted forward and immediately began to shrink in the reverse image of its appearing, until it was only a golden speck illuminated in a last flicker by the setting sun.

I began to laugh riotously, and saw immediately that the distance between my car and its followers had distended precipitously in the unsettling wake of this interlocutor.

Madness harvested and contained, someone wisely said, is power.

The journey now had magically shifted into another phase, and before I knew it I had crossed over the Arkansas and Pawnee rivers and saw ahead the lighted sign of the small motel I would call home for the night. The old woman who ran the motel now that her husband was gone braved the cold air and showed me to my room, pointing out the accommodations and turning up the heater. Then I fell back upon the bed and instantly into an untroubled sleep.

*   *   *

NICK'S Daylite Donuts opens long before daylight, when the farmers and workers around begin their day, and Nickolas has already mixed the tub of dough back in the kitchen and begun the specific process which, anywhere in the universe on a world such as ours, if it is so blessed, will result in a variety of donuts rejected by no intelligent being, especially when accompanied by coffee ground fresh on the half-hour from beans flown in from Kenya.

The light was just beginning to dawn in the east as I opened the front door to Nick's establishment, to the accompaniment of a little bell and the redolence of breakfast and coffee, and, of course, the proprietor's specialty of those circles and spirals and wheels covered in icings which distinguish them one from another.

I had awakened early, refreshed and anxious to see my friends- somehow completing, thereby, that atonement of the present and its future which, in an arc of fullness, would come to fruition on a day already visited and known.

Summoned by the doorbell, a thin, bespectacled gentleman pushed open the swinging door to the kitchen and emerged carrying a decanter filled with his coffee, and a cup, which he sat upon the round table in front of me, offering me a menu which displayed his breakfast fare. He seemed a professional, even academic type, and spoke with a European accent, and I assumed he had entered his present occupation out of retirement.

A donut shop in La Crosse, Kansas would be a good place for that, and a respite from academia.

He asked where I was from, and then where I was headed to- the two most elemental questions asked in any culture of people who are passing through, even as the tail and head of the dog orient one to its direction of movement, though containing no information in themselves. When I stated simply that I was bound for the scientific facility everyone knew of from the news, saying I had an appointment there with friends, he seemed taken aback, and asked if I was sure it was a good idea.

Just at that moment the door opened to its ringing bell and two individuals entered from the predawn cold in rumpled suits and in no good mood, refraining from any greeting at all, and instead took their seats opposite my table, with their backs to the wall. They were, of course, one half of the redundant entourage which defied logic to accompany me to a destination which was prearranged, and known to all. I thought I detected a reaction from the proprietor to his latest guests, something subtle, but was not sure.

"Yes," I reiterated, "I'm actually going up to visit friends at the scientific facility north of Hays. How far would it be up there?"

I glanced over at the one who sat glaring at me, and lifted my coffee cup. The owner, perhaps detecting a ruse, didn't reply and instead noted my order of Morning Star sausage and eggs over well, and then moved to the other table to offer his guests a menu and their coffee.

I detected from their sparse conversation later that their companions had actually preceded them to breakfast while they had sat outside the motel, waiting their turn, and watching for the emergence of their subject from his motel room. I merely reflected to myself that such an occupation must be disastrous to the mind, and a long day's journey into night.

I knew, of course, that by shadowing me they were in effect watching the rebel scientists. It does not hurt to apply pressure at all points, for the best effect.

"...They will not let you ignore them," the elder gentleman had warned that afternoon as they stood out by the great saguaro in Otto's sunsplashed yard in Bisbee.

The wren which made her home high within the phalanxes of spines had adapted over ages to her environment, her complex skills programmed into instinct. She carefully negotiated the spines which could impale her, while at once guarding the doorway of her home.

Reasoning was akin to those spines, Fo had mused, as he leaned against the parapet watching the agility of the creature who flitted within a danger strobed to the beating of her wings.

"What do they want?" Fo asked abstractedly.

"They want to reduce you into obedience. They want control."

"Why?"

Fo understood the answers, and something in him shivered at the cold windswept winters of endurance locked in his childhood memory.

AS I ENJOYED my breakfast, buoyed by the prospect of revisiting people who were central to a future which must exist in a realm of time and space, I looked through the big window to witness the ancient phenomenon of snowflakes lazily drifting downward in the early light. There is something otherworldly about a first snowfall of the year, as if we are confirmed somehow in the replay of seasons of a cosmic significance. And of days which borrow from that significance to make us more alive, days when we truly lose our illusions of indifference, when we carry within us a thrill.

210

I had stepped outside to a thrill on that transcendent morning rich in earthly drama, giant snowflakes gliding out of the darkness into the streetlight, and landing at my feet. As I jogged a block down to the diner, the morning began to rock like a piece of New Orleans jazz, trombone and banjo, piano and bass..., and at a distance following, this little single note, milky white and indifferent- the corporate men.

All reality is a state of mind, isn't it, ladies and gentlemen of the Committee of Safekeepers?

We rule and control one another from a mindstate appropriating the physical to work our will upon others in defiance of a history which is destined to erase us from its memory. The darkness doesn't shine, and will not touch that good future. Nothing we do by coercion is of lasting consequence, and yet we shape crude instruments and expect them to strike the soul.

They were to make sure I saw the guns strapped in harness under their suit coats, brandishing thus the business end of their authority. In the absence of legitimacy, the gun appears.

When I stood at the counter paying my ticket the proprietor, the dignified looking fellow with intelligent eyes and a slight European accent, said quietly, "They are not your friends."

"No."

"Not your friends," he repeated in a low voice as he tended the register, a tremble in his fingers. "They gave you the evil eye."

"Perhaps so," I tried to smile reassuringly.

"I knew them in Romania in the dark days.."

"Romania? And so you came here?"

He nodded, adjusting his glasses. "I was an architect, until I refused to work for them. She had me followed everywhere. I know the evil eye."

"Oh, these are not her people," I added, misunderstanding.

"They kill also, and pretend not to. That is worse."

He became nervous, and turned to open a storage door behind him, before steadying himself and continuing his business at the register. I shook his hand and looked at his eyes.

"Careful," he whispered.

"Okay, my friend." I stood in place a second more before turning back to my table to leave a tip.

He would try to delay them, I knew, in some way, but it didn't matter, as they had known my destination since the moment Letty called, and my

211

every movement by transmitters affixed since the meeting in Bisbee and continuing but for that elusive voyage to the future, to which they had no access. Thanks to the gifts of science, the corkscrew can open a bottle of fine wine, or a fingernail.

I felt badly for him, and that I had been an accomplice to his anxieties. He saw the invisible walls, pervasive and just as real, walls and checkpoints in the mind across the landscape of the human. "The evil eye looks inward also, to destroy the soul." He finished almost in a whisper, his look steady and haunted in the slim distance of memories.

I could feel the stare of eyes as I walked out into the brisk air. Moving past the front windowpane I saw in periphery two figures rise, and reach for their overcoats.

The proprietor had left his place at the register to attend to something in the back of the store. He would make the agents wait.

THE HUMAN is misnamed- Fo once explained- called a "being," though his true role is *advancement,* a growing forward with the accretion of experience and knowledge which distinguish his progress and define him, even as his unique imagination lights his way.

Once he learns and knows something more he moves on to the next revelation ahead. The human, more than a being, is a *becomer.* Though called by the first name for his state of existence, he is far more intrinsically of the latter, compelled by his nature into becoming, into willful progress toward his greater destiny.

The human is a creature in conflict, occupying a present while his imagination and new styles are suggestions of the future, as are all innovations. Intelligent life measures itself in changes, even as it idealizes its past. It values progress, and venerates its traditions. It thinks, while it also believes, and immolates its doubters and creators.

I did not understand how, as I pulled out onto the road which lead through town and toward my destination, but somewhere in that medley of observations would figure my surveillance team, which seemed to grow more resentful by the hour.

For a strange moment I felt a concern for them, as one does for a bird with a broken wing, which was meant to fly, but cannot. We are each human, and holder of the promise, and when we lack the means to fulfill the promise of our possibility, then there is a sadness and a sympathy which is meant to aid and heal in a needed resolution. It is the ironic flower placed in the muzzle of the gun, the opposite of the impulse to war, and is consistent with our true nature as humans.

I assumed their purpose was more to threaten harm than to enact it, though one could not be certain, and it was important for me to successfully complete my pilgrimage. Something seemed rote about them, programmed.

Are they programmed by nature to be who they are? Am I, to be who I am? And yet in their rule of games they hold you accountable in a predication of will.

I thought of Nickolas, the proprietor, and the strange apology to him: 'I'm sorry your life was destroyed... It's your fault that you got in my way.'

As my tight convoy, a red car with two grey cars close upon, proceeded up the main street, which is the highway through town, I could swear I saw to my left a block away on a parallel street the fleeting image of a gold object streaking through the intersection.

*   *   *

IT IS ASTONISHING in retrospect how greatly one can be affected by someone about whom relatively little is known, as if the quantity of information is somehow hidden in the significance.

Even now, at the time of this writing, I cannot claim to know a lot about the two individuals who have most influenced my life. Nevertheless, one does not disclaim an intuition about them, a kind of extrasensory knowing imagined in the allegiance of great respect, or love.

I can tell you things about Letty, untold to me, but understood with full assurance of certainty in that occult knowledge the heart contains.

With respect to the man in her life, she did not understand the farther reaches of his intellect, but she understood the depth of his thought and emotion. When he became deeply immersed in his work, she would accompany him in spirit as far as she could into the realms of his inquiry, then it was as if she could simply stop and wait for him, watching as his familiar figure receded farther into the distance of his wonderful and mysterious mind.

When he was absent in this way she held his trust in her like a locket next to her breast, in which were guarded the intimate treasures they held together. She felt completely secure in this role, and knew Fo would come back to her, just as her father invariably did when she had waited down at the front gate of their little home in the sweet days of her childhood.

Those who return your love always return, for in a true sense they never leave you alone.

Sometimes after a particularly arduous and intense work period in which he had been lost in the abstractions of theory, Fo would reappear to her in a form so calm and relieved as if he were infused by a spirit very near, she thought, to destiny.

He never returned from his explorations afraid. And then as he held her she could feel a flow so peaceful and reassuring that she felt as if empowered by an angel, and she wondered what he had seen in that distant realm beyond ordinary human thought, what powers had touched and consecrated this man she loved.

The complications which imposed on the professor's life and work through the politicization of the scientific discovery were matters which Lloyd Man Foglesby took as anomalous and temporal within ranges of importance annulated from the core of the matter, which was pure science, and inseparable from the meaning which underlies intelligent life in the universe.

Watching the titubation of government as it blundered from incomprehension to incompetence, Fo seemed at times amused in watching the falling of clowns, and then distracted, and then, as matters congealed into urgency, mystified.

At the time I had been the inadvertent witness to his consultation with Otto on the Bisbee visit, the scientist made the largely symbolic concession of suspending his plans for publication, but nevertheless continued to collaborate with scientists worldwide, and was increasingly called upon to do so. Because many American researchers were beholden to agencies of their government for grants in aid, it became a critical measure for them to violate an act of law in order to pursue research. The lawmakers, of course, were lobbied by corporate interests which wanted to control the dynamics inherent in the Discovery, even though its elements, like any thought and ideas, were ethereal.

Despite the impediments thrown across, however, few research scientists would decline the opportunity to enter into their studies the most exciting tools of knowledge to emerge since life's beginning on Earth. Some who had been working on perplexing solutions for their entire careers suddenly found themselves crashing forward through a door whose hinges had been veritably dissolved by a single key decoded in Fo's algorithm.

With a subtle tweaking of the lock, vistas splashed into view which exonerated their decades of painstaking and relentless effort, vindicating their faith in answers at the far margins of human imagination. There was a singing heard echoing from obscure laboratories and libraries and classrooms the world over, and a lightness of heart which redeemed all efforts everywhere, melding colleagues centuries apart into a single celebration of the birth of a new humanity.

Meanwhile, elements largely within the National Security Agency and the Vice President's office, at the behest of special interests in and out of government began an intense program to discredit the scientist, even as they sought to prohibit the dissemination of his discovery. Rumors were posted that the astrophysicist had defected to China, or had sold his services to a potentially hostile Third World country or rogue state with connections to terror, all of which was known by the authorities not to be the fact, but it suited their purpose of somehow demonizing this "rebel scientist" in the minds of the public.

It was not to be the nation's finest hour, but Fo held no grudge. Human frailty was more understandable than were great breakthroughs in vision and human progress: the one, accruing from past history; the others, more mysteriously- and to some, more ominously- from the future.

In the coming weeks, as the siege prevailed, it was to become more evident that other ingredients had been brought into the mix of myth and emotion to create a deadly reality.

TIME SLOWED strangely on this last segment of travel to the scene that was being aired on the news channels around the world.

The press had come in from all major news sources across the globe, and were on twenty-four hour watch for a change in developments, with correspondents talking endlessly about what they knew or did not know about "The Great Standoff." The TV screen in an upper corner of Nick's Daylite Donuts cafe had been set to CNN's coverage, minus the sound, as Nickolas had not seen fit to adjust the volume, and so Anderson Cooper droned authoritatively in merciful silence. Right now half of humanity held images of the landscape around Plainville, and, dominating its skyline outside of town, the most famous grain elevator now in history- a four-sectioned concrete structure rising twenty stories above the prairie.

I had deliberately abstained from listening to the news on the trip thus far, but chose now to update myself on the happening by tuning to a Public Radio station morning program with news and commentary.

The Attorney General had just completed another news conference during which he addressed matters of homeland security and domestic terrorism and its possible connections to Al Qaeda. It took me a while to make the unsettling connection that he was referring to the matter of the scientists, and that he had just broadened and personalized the conflict.

Before long I would be able to witness from the inside an almost mythological reenactment of the ages-old struggle of scientific thought to escape the confinement of ignorance and superstition, played out in the individual mind to the resolution of learning and reason, and in societies, to the fundamental clash of different cultures inherent in the motivation of one to seek change, and of the other to impose order and control.

In a mini-rendition of the curious minstrel, I now found myself stuck between the two discordant notes of the grey cars, as one of them pulled around and just in front of me, coordinating with the rear one to sandwich me between, a disconcerting action which caused me to whip out and around the lead car, producing the blurp of a siren and a simultaneous red light to warn me against such behavior.

I began to consider that I may not be fated to reach my destination, and the alternatives within a context superimposed by Ashcroft to include a war on terror suggested unpleasant scenarios, including rendition to states proficient in torture, where they scream at you in an unknown language.

My alarm proved momentary, however, as I remembered the reality of a future which was won out of the struggles of the present and its history. A promise far greater in power than the forces of reaction to human progress.

"When you learn to give up the world, then you will return to us where we wait."

I recovered the sense of peace and well being that, for just an errant moment, I had let go. I easily found the turn leading outward from the small town, along the railroad tracks, to the place where the forces of history and the future would weigh into the destiny of a rare intelligence which came, at last, to know itself.

HE STOOD alongside and above the old car as in an archival photograph, oddly striking the pose of a Renaissance statue, a long arm extended out and just above his head, fingers in his hand curled slightly, forefinger relaxed and pointing skyward to somewhere.

Measuring the height of the stationwagon with my eyes as I passed, and then his frame, lean and muscular in his psychedelic clothing, I could see the man had to have seven feet of height.

He looked to be smiling, which seemed strangely incongruous as within sight of him just a hundred yards away was the mother of roadblocks with military vehicles, jeeps and personal carriers looming over numerous police cars with banks of flashing red, white, and blue lights.

I saw the actual roadway was clear, however, but for a phalanx of soldiers, uniformed officials, and plainclothesmen who stood facing my approaching car, which was easing steadily forward.

The two grey cars with their ruffled, tired occupants had melted away and I was left with the formidable array of armed officers and soldiers, eyes fixed on me, weapons at the ready.

I glanced in my rearview mirror and could see the old faded wagon sitting by the figure of its driver, who was turned towards me legs slightly apart, hands at his sides.

Against the surreal silence of the scene growing closer in front of me, I thought I could feel the throaty rumble of a monstrous engine vibrating through the ground...

*   *   *

CHAPTER SIXTEEN

THE SIEGE

LIFE FROM its beginning has been circumscribed by Death,
yielding its turn in the great diaspora of generations, and then
the mind, in the diaspora of ideas, until the one unyielding
idea, central to the soul, rose to stake its claim in the presence
of an immortal thought: that Death is not inevitable!
And once death is not held inevitable, then neither is
suffering, nor injustice, nor poverty, nor ignorance held
inevitable because life becomes responsible for its future- the
determiner, moment by moment, of its own destiny.
The scientific quest to resolve the problem of death is by the gathering of
believers in a labor of fulfillment of the oldest dream of consciousness, and
its supreme necessity. Awakened to thought, we are not destined to perish!
-Foglesby, to the National Academy of Sciences, March 2004.

AN ANCIENT music, older than any memory, lies hidden within the
subconscious mind, and sings in answer to the song of the universe in the
language of recognition: 'I know you, I know you! You are wonder!'
-notebook "13", p66.

Imagination is the voice of other lives, in a universe of dimensions.
-green notebook "11", p19.

FOR ALL THE EYES that were watching my arrival, for the pistols unbuckled, for the hands at the ready, no one asked for my ID, and so I proceeded cautiously, nodding at them in recognition as they passed me one to another in their scrutiny until I was within the compound, following a driveway to the back of the facility nearest the abandoned railway line.

It was impossible to ignore the ring of tanks which lay in the field back of the rail tracks, or that their gun barrels were inclined toward the upper levels of the facility. I had seen, as had the whole world, dramatic views from news helicopters showing a virtual ring of military armaments, including perhaps a dozen tanks with their coterie of attending hardware, serving for the present to assure the American public that it was safe from the scientists.

Surely the viewer could be excused for an obvious question relating to the positioning of artillery pieces in a circle pointing inward, as well as for assuming that the show of force was more for effect than for actual engagement on a moment's notice: But then, the pointed gun is its own inarguable statement.

The reinforced concrete walls poured in the 1950's could withstand the force of a million bushels of grain pushing outward, but were not designed against the impact of explosive shells.

The heavy door rolled down behind me as I entered the spacious area with curved outer walls and a high ceiling in which were parked perhaps two dozen cars ranging from an old Volkswagen bus to vans and trucks and cars of various descriptions, ordinary to luxury. I eased my noisy Fiero over to park next to the bus, and shut off the engine.

Almost immediately I heard a hum from above, and a clank, and then two large doors folded back to reveal an elevator room, perhaps twenty feet on a side. As I stepped in a beep sounded, the doors unfolded shut, and the floor accelerated upward against the soles of my feet and then in an arc of lightness until it stopped.

Before the door had opened I heard a familiar voice, "Welcome to the Hilton research center!"

FOGLESBY OFTEN spoke to his science classes about philosophy, and to his philosophy classes about science, noting that it is difficult to study one field without encountering the other. He called them both a continuing search.

They say that it is impossible to know all truth, that is to say, all the reality which surrounds us. The full reality of even the minutest object or condition is beyond understanding because the minutest touches the greatest, and is inseparable from it.

We nevertheless carry the supreme desire to know the heart of a thing, and in knowing to bring it justice, and for this we are committed from the first awakening of mind to a voyage of discovery, to thought which anchors itself, not in a place, but in a passage like footsteps giving way to another and another in a progression across the space of time- the first belonging to us as much as the last; the last, in turn, being the expression of all steps before it.

This is how Fo explained it to his students, as both a scientist and a philosopher.

Nobody had the answers; everybody was searching. He offered that when people think they have the answers, they quit searching, and build a wall around their truth, to protect it. And then they build monuments to it, and pass laws to define it, and build armies and police to enforce it, and freedom and progress disappear in the long night to follow.

Otto the historian and activist spoke more dramatically of "prison keepers of the mind, who close the world around the victims, fences electrified with fear, and walls of the mind, too high to climb."

The elevator doors opened onto another world, across all spectrums opposite the world outside.

Not simply the contrast that is obvious between killing machines little changed in concept since the time of Caesar Augustus- the catapult graduated into the cannon barrel, the explosive shell, the depleted uranium bullet in rapid fire- and the labile search for knowledge.

Or between aphotic siege engines threatening destruction, and near infinitely subtle energies of the life code permeating time and space.

The invading army, since ancient times, must conquer, occupy, and destroy the will to resist. In a regime of force, the powers of repression ultimately see this as their aim- to occupy and destroy the will. There is no greater distance possible from the creative imagination and its purpose- from the meaning innate with conscious life.

Walking energetically towards me within that other world, so striking in contrast to the reality below, was a colorfully dressed figure with a mat of red hair above a high forehead, lime green eyes, a small mouth, and a scraggly beard. He appeared much as I had known him among his friends on that far away shore where the ancient way of stone slipped into the silver sea. Where a whale breached majestically at the end of the day, and where a spacefaring city occulted a planet and rode across the face of the moon, as friends cheered.

He reached out a big, strong hand to shake mine, just as he had then.

FOR THE purposes of this report to the Committee of Safekeepers, I will offer a minimal outline of my brief experience relating to the staff and function of the facility, as the strident and phenomenal science developed and expanded there in the short span of its occupancy is beyond any useful commentary on a layman's part, and is now a matter of historical record.

What Foglesby may have taken with him is another matter.

This writer's expertise lies only in the knowledge of a future reality born out of present events and circumstances which I was witnessing on that day, as we are all witnesses to a future's conception, though only extraordinarily privileged to know its fulfillment.

On that day when I met a man for the second time, two-and-a-half centuries before the first meeting, what one might rightfully do with that knowledge was unknown.

The fellow not unexpectedly introduced himself only as, "BJ".

He was very cordial, and called me by name, saying, "Fo and Letty are waiting to see you in about an hour. Would you like to see what we are doing here?"

I could not help but notice in my study of him that he seemed extremely efficient, as may a person be who is involved in a great amount of work, and who is handling it with great control. But I was comparing him to that relaxed fellow I knew that other day in another setting, when all of this was done.

As we walked he offered a general description of the research facility, saying that it consisted of five levels with various departments integrating the new technologies arising from the Discovery.

His engagement and manner of speaking indicated that he presumed some background on my part, perhaps only from the fact of my visit. He spoke expressively and directly of revelations of the Code made possible by integrations of science with human intellect, of thought with the thinker: "When the thought knows itself, there is insight..."

We stood briefly together, and he seemed at once ready to speak from the heart to a stranger regarding great and eternal matters in whose constant presence he worked and thought. He called the professor's discovery an *alignment*, and commented esoterically as follows:

"This tumbler had to move simultaneously with a vast number of others to create the precise alignment which had as much to do with timing as with a position in space. It had a curious aspect of the uncertainty principle in that position could never be determined while there was a process of motion. When one gave way to the other, in that infinitesimal break which divides the two uncertainties, then the tumbler clicked ever so slightly, and the unity was born... The tumbler shifted infinitely into alignment so that the key could be inserted..."

Then his small mouth broke into a wry smile, and he said, "It's all there in the theorem, plus the one thing Fermat was missing." I told him, Thanks a lot. I didn't repeat what Otto had told his colleague that day in Bisbee, to lighten the aspect of his friend's genius: "The last piece of the most complex puzzle is the easiest to place- even a child could do it," to which Fo had smiled quizzically.

BJ added something about a kind of mathematical interferometry, which blends into a high resolution image. Foglesby's discovery was revealed, he said, as an eternal truth which has prior existence, not an invention by a mathematician.

He spoke of intricate structures of thought, which spontaneously coalesce into meaning, and of mind as of fields of existence.

As I listened to him I found myself in a strange duality, hearing both the man before me, as well as that fellow I knew from an advanced history which had known the harvest of things only now germinating, or in infancy.

It was as if there were twins merging across time to create the personality before me, one great intellect living in another's image, grandly amplifying the experience of each. I briefly entertained the notion that indeed the two entities were not separate, but were at that moment colluding to form the exquisite processes of creative expression: imagination, shaping the future reality, and vice versa.

Was this particular situation expressly unique, in that my awareness of dual realities, bringing them both into the presence of an event, was catalytic? I determined to consider it further.

"We are seeing solutions," BJ went on, "even before the problems are defined- solutions we do not, therefore, yet understand."

"The answers lie within the knowledge of the question," I answered automatically.

"Yes, yes, that's good!" He looked at me approvingly. "Not my words," I hastened to add. "I borrowed them."

For an understandable reason I studied him momentarily, for some trace of recognition from that future afternoon spent with friends upon the Way of Stone, cast golden in the splendorous rays of the distant sun. And from the incomparable visit to the Dome of Sky, and the phenomenal afternoon concert. He had known me then, in full knowledge, with memories of this day, but could not have known that day, from this.

"What's your alley?" he suddenly asked.

"Alley?"

"Your field..."

"I sell mangoes."

"Really?" he smiled, a bit incredulous. "Did you bring some?"

"Actually, they are in season. But no, I'm sorry."

An attractive woman walked across the room to meet us as we came through the door into a spacious laboratory where perhaps a dozen individuals were working.

"I see you have brought our guest from the outer dimension," she smiled, as she acknowledged BJ, and looked at me, then reached out her hand. "Letty said you were coming."

"You best watch out for Marilu...She's a sweet talker," BJ cautioned playfully, placing a large hand upon my shoulder.

"I see you've met Dr. William Joseph Smith, also known as Billy Joe, aka "BJ", biophysicist and former Stradivari of string theory."

My host was amused by the title, but dismissed it: "And here is the mistress of cold fusion... She doesn't forget."

BJ grinned, and then intoned, "When I was the smallest, I had the biggest name. As I've grown bigger, the name has shrunk...An odd declension. Old people should have long names, to tell everyone about their lives, and babies, short ones."

"There are abbreviations of a name, but not of a person," a researcher nearby offered, smiling at BJ.

Later, as we were parting, the scientist, Marilu, confided to me, "BJ is shy about being complimented... I did mean it."

"Yes, I know," I said, pressing her hand. I knew that she had not offered a compliment for my benefit, but out of admiration for her friend.

BJ took me to a floor beneath, where the elevator opened to a very large space which had no partitions, and was visible throughout the entire length of the structure, including the four semi-circles on either side of the outer walls. There were only four or five technicians, or scientists, that I saw, but a great array of equipment, two pieces of which extended the full length of the long floor. There were other items of various descriptions which seemed to be functioning automatically, and resembled the general category of scanners that one has seen in hospitals. BJ made a reference to gravity, and so some equipment may have been related to research in energy fields.

The level just below this one also contained unrecognizable equipment and banks of computer screens, and was obviously a biological laboratory, as it contained many species of plants and small animals and insects. There was also research into primordial life, single-celled creatures, and such, centering on the quantum energies of DNA.

Below this floor was a level which held cryogenics equipment which I could generally recognize. There was a laboratory with an electron microscope and laser scanners, where, as BJ informed me, "We can have a peek at atoms."

BJ mentioned that their computers were connected with advanced computers in other places and countries to create an "ultra-computer."

"We are now developing the intelligence which will aid us in solving the riddles of conscious life, and of what we have called death. Fo's theorem is facilitating the development of quantum computers with the ability to 'understand' at last the intricate workings of the cosmos. The universal code is being broken in accordance with the famous observer effect wherein knowledge constitutes a kind of 'observation,' allowing heretofore unseen elements to appear."

I asked him, diverging in the theme of great advances in knowledge: "And the planet, can we stop its degradation? How does that play in?"

BJ said that great forces were in play as a result of policies and neglect of the last century: runaway population growth in the developing world, pollution, contamination, poverty, overconsumption, lack of education, the concentration of wealth in the hands of a few and the exploitation of the workers, dependence on carbon based energy, and that, like a loaded freight train without brakes, will have to be slowed from without, which must be done for the world to survive.

I constantly entertained the thought of telling this man what I knew of the future which would follow his work, but did not find the way to do it. Perhaps I would relate it all to Fo and Letty, and they could decide what to do with the information. I did not doubt that they would accept it.

As we walked the three flights up to the floor upon which I had first been welcomed, BJ was talking animatedly of electrons, muons, and tauneutrinos which may oscillate or change form as they pass through space or matter, and how they function as cosmic computers, linked with mind, whose codes the

Discovery was breaking, even as he spoke. Of the cosmos he noted, "We're learning that the whole damn thing is a computer, driven by software. We are decoding the software. This was always the purpose of learning."

"Who determined it to be?"

BJ paused a second, "It seems inherent in this universe." "Why?"

"So matter could know itself."

"It was some sort of plan?"

"Seems so... Inherent in matter."

I asked, "Is it conscious? Is it some sort of mind?" and BJ smiled, inverting his hands. "Seems more and more to function like one. And that it has been drawing intelligence everywhere into its purpose."

As he continued to speak excitedly, using his hands and arms to accentuate his points, his cell phone buzzed, and he seemed suddenly shifted into another reality, saying, "Yes, yes, I'll tell him. We'll wait for you to call."

I thought my host seemed more reflective now, and he told me we would be waiting to go up to Letty and Fo's living quarters in the elevator house of the structure. I knew what it was, having visited elevators as a child, and so his mention resurrected memories of elevator chains with buckets or dippers, which lifted the grain to the top tiers.

Momentarily I could smell from memory the dust and chaff, and hear the din of elevators which hoisted the grain upward twenty stories to the elevator house with its electric motors and gated chutes to divert the grain to its proper bins. Great fans circulated the air to prevent dust explosions.

For a boy, and also for a girl, the grain elevator and silo was an introduction to a world of grandness and mystery and power, all associated with the adult world centering on the father, who was cast as a central actor in a great drama of commerce and engineering, no matter the amount of grain he had been able to harvest and sell, which was often insufficient to pay his expenses. The parent is God to the child, and hero.

The half hour, or so, that we had before BJ accompanied me up to the living quarters of Fo and Letty, turned out to be fortuitous in allowing for further discourse upon matters of the project, the facility, and its personnel. Because of my prior experience there was not a word that BJ could have said that would not be fascinating, and I listened with that strange duality of interest, superimposing upon my host and his expressions those of the other character I knew from his future, like an alter image inseparable from the other.

It is not an unknown phenomenon to invest in another a greater dimension of their self. We do that in any great interest, don't we?- and especially in the case of love.

Because it seemed a matter strangely unrelated to the reality unfolding within the purview of the Discovery, and centered in the facility but increasingly extending across the globe into research labs and universities and the personal computers of scientists and academicians, like a contagion, I did find the occasion to mention the armed encampment below, which seemed surreal and far away.

BJ did not seem concerned, saying with amusement that "life is rich, the food is good, the view from above, great, and the work, incomparable in the known universe, with data streaming in from the future as equation after equation clicks into place, problem after problem falling under the spell of the infinity theorem."

Having just come from the outside, I was more uneasy than the scientist seemed to be, whose intellect was not tinged with the bizarre artifice of politics.

BJ said that numerous legal experts had volunteered their services on behalf of Foglesby and the project, including practicing lawyers who had been Destiny students- empowered for life, according to them, by what they had learned in two semester classes. A team of prominent attorneys had been assembled by Gerry Spence, which included a former Attorney General, and both President Carter and Gov. Bill Richardson offered him their services to try and defuse the crisis, which was being ratcheted up by Ashcroft, backed by the White House, for reasons incomprehensible to most everyone.

The religious right was advancing the rubric that the scientists were bent on assuming powers rightly belonging only to God, branding them atheists, and demanding their elimination, and this was a worrisome issue regarding their influence upon the Attorney General and the administration backing him.

I was, nevertheless, encouraged by BJ's assurance that capable legal minds were involved, although Fo, having authored the tenets of the Discovery, and being intensely occupied in its developments, seemed curiously detached from the world of Ashcroft, and the political interference affecting his work.

The professor had actually declined the offers of help, thanking all who made them, and insisting that the matter was simple and could be resolved with reason, though wiser voices, notably Letty's, ultimately prevailed after the tanks and armored vehicles were parked. Fo was at first astonished by the display of force, then amused, then baffled at how anyone could come to the conclusion that force was necessary. "You can't fire a gun at an idea," he commented.

Once born, an idea is diffused to mix and compete with all ideas everywhere. It survives, or it does not, according to its value and authenticity. (Fo declined to use the word, "truth", considering it troublesome: history's greatest tragedies have been wrought in the name of some man's, or group's 'truth'.)

"History isn't finished," he would offer, smiling. "When it is, then whoever's left can debate about 'truth'."

Negotiators for the government were welcomed, usually in pairs, and rode up the elevator to the research floors, where they were free to look around and ask any and all questions. These were answered forthrightly, as individual scientists tried to explain their work in comprehensible terms.

"No guile," Fo would murmur, quaintly smiling as he walked around introducing the investigators to his staff. "Remember, no guile."

Not every individual was as patient or gracious as the professor in managing this increasingly persistent inconvenience. Some had trouble focusing on the surreal distraction, eyes veering to their computer screens, fingers tapping arhythmically upon desktops, their minds absorbed in intricacies of proteins or DNA molecules, or lightcones sent out into deep space.

But they dutifully obliged the suited "negotiators," who sometimes seemed as perplexed as their subjects as to the real nature of the standoff. Although the agents, after each round of inspections, descended to the prairie outside offering that they had seen no arms, nor any disposition to use them, the authorities weren't convinced, and having committed themselves to their position, steadily added to the personnel and armaments circling the old concrete structure.

At night, generators ignited an array of stadium lights, which constantly bathed the high walls in yellowish luminescence. Spotlights would crisscross intermittently the upper curves of the silos, but generally focused upon the windows of the upper structure which had once housed the machinery of conveyers and elevators of the million bushels of grain stored below.

The rooms of the living quarters and library now inside would light up as if a wheel of light rolled across them, then back and forth in a monotonous rhythm. The negotiators were not coming back with results, and so this tactic was one of exacting a price from the recalcitrant citizens within.

When mercy would abandon, it grants power to fools.

Fo's difficulty seemed then, and seems even now, intractable in the sense the matter was a conundrum, involving, not the keeping of information, but the sharing of it. When the government through the National Security Agency requested the solution to the unified field, Fo simply delivered a copy.

When the same authorities demanded to receive all copies, and forbade its further publication, invoking national security concerns, the professor declined, citing realities beyond his control, and exhaustively explaining his reasons, including its de facto dissemination. It would be impossible to hold and secure information already in the public domain. Fo's intricate corner was already painted. His knowledge was not "Top Secret."

"They want to be the priests of knowledge," Otto once explained to his friend. "Only the high priest and king can enter the inner sanctuary, where secrets are declared, and kept from you." Of course he was inferring that the control of this asset would be the ultimate power in all of human history.

Upon being served with an order, which Fo judged to be an order upon science, and upon knowledge, he in effect went "underground," offering the discovery to independent scientists around the world, who would be free to explore its momentous implications as their gifts and abilities permitted them, by utilizing the "keys" coded into Fo's equations.

What they didn't reckon with was precisely the crux of the algorithm: It unified at last the four universal force fields of physics, as well as others relating to time, to life, and to consciousness, and so could not be sequestered or negated. Without its integrity, the theorem was meaningless.

In its solution, the mind's comprehension becomes the true single unifying force, freeing knowledge from its bondage. Never again could this knowledge be restrained- certainly not by fiat or coercion.

Only a failing will, Fo knew, could restrict such astounding enlightenment from the future worlds. And having himself been the chance receptor of the chalice after the long odyssey of human learning stretching back through countless generations, Fo saw each new thought courageously shaped out of mystery along the way as being crucial to the final key to the theorem.

From the conscious making of a tool to improve one's life; from the first glimmers of self-knowledge and insight; from the devising of myths to explain the wonder of the unknown; through every new discovery laboriously made and heroically proclaimed- all of them were participants, colleagues, and associates through the ages, past and future, in the business of learning. So, the concept of "private knowledge" was simply mistaken.

It was not enough just to learn, Fo would explain to his students: Knowledge is a fire.

The taming of that fire is understanding.

* * *

THE SOUL is the potential of all things invested in one.
Whatever the value of the highest state, that value is,
from the beginning, even before conception- animal to the
human, instinct to thought- in the circle of time.
- blue notebook "34", p23.

The most beautiful thing to a man is the desire of the woman
he loves.
-notebook "9", p60.

"ALWAYS, IF you possibly can, be in love," he would smile, dark
eyes sparkling. "Be in love with some one, or some thing, with
beauty, with life, with learning- but always love, and be in love.
When you are in love you are awake and deeply connected to reality. You
are nearest the paradise of your dreams, something other than yourself."
-Foglesby, quoted in Dura Pad notebook "21", p69.

"Every home should be a refuge, a Walden
Pond, every heart a place of peace."
-Letty.

THE MAN known among his colleagues simply as BJ received a message on his phone, and we began walking down a corridor past offices and a personnel elevator to a lobby with a wide curved stairway which led up to the levels of the library and living quarters, which composed three floors with tall ceilings.

We ascended the ornate circular stairway which spiraled through a corner of the library, upward through the second floor to a landing on the top floor where BJ knocked quietly on the wide door. I found my heart bearing in anticipation of again seeing my friends, unsure of how I was going to explain in a scientific, or even personal setting the drama of phenomenal events I had known, even though they were directly related to the present.

Again, I sensed that duality of worlds, or alter-reality that pervaded the present in memory, of Fo and Letty and the house with a veranda overlooking the sea. Memory is a *presence,* they had said, and so time lives in us.

There was a comfortable living area with an arrangement of sofas and chairs, lamps with soft light, shelves of books, and pictures on the walls. Lace curtains covered the large windows on one wall, which were divided into small panes. In the corners were heavy drapes which were drawn at night to block the rolling wheel of light which crisscrossed the outer wall of the old elevator house as spotlights monotonously invaded the only windows of the structure built a half-century before.

And as always, Letty managed to have flowering plants, in decorative containers upon the floor, and others in pots hanging before the windows to flourish in the daylight. A soft music was playing.

In the care and decoration of the space once occupied by heavy geared elevators, chains and augers and grain chutes- things with their own elegance and beauty- was seen the grace and loving attention of Letty, who could make any place into a home.

BJ stood with me in the living room, as we waited for Letty and Fo to emerge. There were low voices in another room, and I assumed my hosts were getting ready to make their appearance. Again, I felt the presence of another time, equal in reality, when the two of them served the splendid lunch under the great tree, and I sat with them around the table upon the side porch of the veranda to enjoy the food, and company of the rarest of friends who long knew me: the mirthful and wise "BJ"; Lia, telling stories of life inside a Martian moon within a community of spacefarers where her children were born. The dark beauty, Kenata, poetic spirit. The sachem Emersonian, Robeling, intense intellect and 'builder of bridges.' All of them 'specialists in your life and times,' chroniclers, and preparers for the day of awakening and rebirth.

And then of course there was a family I had come to meet- the beloved professor and his wife, Letty, and, sitting between them, a long-haired and lovely daughter with a princess name, Aida, whose face I recognized from a picture taken in mortality, long before.

Suddenly there was the sound of a door opening and three people entered the living area and crossed over to greet us warmly, before leaving through the front door, gently closing it behind them.

Fo then came out, asking pardon for the delay. He shook my hand and thanked me for coming, giving me an embrace and again grasping my hand in both of his, as was his custom. Then he and BJ embraced, without saying anything. I thanked BJ for his time and attention, and he uttered a little witticism, dearly remembered, saying we'd meet again in the funny papers.

I was expecting to see Letty come out, all fixed up, as she always appeared, but instead, Fo grasped my arm at the elbow and said that she was waiting to see me, as he led me back to a bedroom. The bed was raised so that she was almost sitting, and she was dressed in a lovely rose gown with lace around the neck and down the front, and long sleeves with soft lace around her wrists. Her hair was newly done, fresh, and wavy, but lacked the luster I had known, and seemed thinner- but beautiful, even so. She was smiling weakly, and her eyes had the remains of a sparkle she was known for, and her pallor wasn't hers. Upon her neck she had the locket which I recognized, tilted sideways against a breast.

Once you have known a person of true beauty, it is impossible to separate that beauty from them, and especially if it is in the soul, which it was with Letty. Whatever physical beauty a woman has is immeasurably enhanced if she possesses thoughtfulness and goodness of nature. This inner beauty emanating from her depths is the true measure of beauty in a person, after all.

Leticia was gifted with intelligence and a personal loveliness- the way she moved her hands, her direct look, her natural poise and grace. She radiated emotion and thoughtfulness, and a distracting beauty, yet without the slightest intent on her part.

She was open and yet mysterious, simply because there was so much more to her than a moment revealed. Having not lost her trust in others, she was devoid of that guarded aspect some women must have who have been terribly hurt by love. Perhaps she had been lucky.

Letty was one of those rarest of beauties with beauty throughout. In that way, she had everything.

I leaned down and put my arms around her, my face placed within her hair. She raised her arms up, and it was then that I could tell how weak she was. Her breathing was shallow, and quick.

When I finally pulled back, and looked at her face, she managed a smile, and lifted one hand slowly to my face and touched the back of a finger to my cheek. "Cowboy, I'm a dyin'," she spoke barely above a whisper. "I'm sorry."

I was flooded with emotion, and with a mixture of two realities. It was just then that I most wanted to tell them about their daughter, but I must not have thought it was possible, because I didn't do it. Whatever there was, it seemed that Letty had accepted it.

Something inside me was rushing to do something, because I had seen what comes after, but only a knowledge held the two realities together, unable beyond memory to close the gulf of time. There was in that real moment only the slender fragment of life that is mortality, which, beyond its reality, imagines its place in an eternal scheme which does not accept the end of things loved.

For all it was that I knew, I felt an abject helplessness, and looked back at her husband, who was standing by the door, looking down. She had relaxed her arms, and her eyes were closed. Her face and countenance were expressively peaceful. She looked asleep.

Although I was filled with questions about her, I had only asked those which arose from our conversations.

How was this extraordinary woman, who had such poise and grace and intelligence, and genuine goodness, developed from her humble rural beginnings?.. It seems obvious that her parents were as she was: they nourished and raised the daughter that I saw.

Her parents, lacking the means to travel and show her the world, had a mission, and this was to bring the world into her imagination.

I gently let go of her, and backed away from the bed, turning to her husband, who stepped forward and stood next to her. I was about to leave the room, but he glanced over, and made a motion with a hand held behind his back, which I took to mean that he wanted me to stay. He then sat next to her, and took both her hands in his. As he leaned forward and seemed to be whispering to her, I vividly remembered what he had said to a class on Destiny, noted by a student:

Not all the forces in the universe can make you love when you don't love, or keep you from loving, when you do.

We are powerless to override within the mind the true allegiance of the heart. So it has always been, to make us one with our emotions, and to protect that to which we have given ourselves.

As I was watching in full view of them, Fo spoke something to her in a low voice, and she opened her eyes. Then she laughed softly and caught her breath.

Fo looked back at me, something inexpressible in his black eyes, and then looked at her, his head held close: "I was always crazily, madly, hungrily in love with her... Since the first day I saw her... Never changed a whit... Can't figure it out. It was magic."

I didn't know if he was talking to me, but found myself saying. "Yes, it was."

Friends and associates would notice that Fo seemed more resolute after her death. Not sadder, but more resolute. It was his second loss.

LATER THAT afternoon there was a spontaneous memorial and remembrance held by the staff in a conference room on the fourth level which also housed offices and living quarters, and a communications center. There were probably forty or fifty persons in attendance.

It seemed every one had a personal experience, or feelings to relate about the woman they had known as Letty. At one point BJ came to the front, didn't say anything, but played the most hauntingly beautiful and moving number on a violin. A young man who was a resident fellow on a doctoral program- though he didn't look out of high school- pulled a harmonica out of his pocket and joined him, and the effect was spellbinding. I saw for the first time in BJ, beyond the brilliant scientist, a superb musician. It is not uncommon, they say, for genius to encompass other fields.

Perhaps an hour had quickly passed, in an emotional and heartfelt celebration of someone truly loved, when, though not expected, Letty's husband walked through the door, to thank everyone for their kindness and caring. He shook hands and hugged many shoulders, and then stepped upon a dais to speak extemporaneously a few words which turned out to be rhapsodic and lovely, to no one's surprise. His voice was deeply reflective and personal, of course, and I took note of what he said, and hope I can relate it justly, if not in actual sequence. True to his nature, he spoke of greaterness which one must hold against despair. He spoke, in an incomparable loss, of meaning.

"There is a reality that exists beyond the senses, beyond the knowledge that we have, beyond our present understanding, even beyond our imagination, and that reality is filled with possibility and with promise.

"In its potential lies all that we may become, the germ and flower of our significance, the essence of our meaning, the completed circle of our destiny."

He paused for a second or two, and then added simply: "Nothing does not exist."

"Let me show you something reasonable," he continued after a pause, and it was not clear to me if he was speaking to the ones there, or in memory to a classroom, or even to himself. "Just when you feel most alienated is when you are nearest to the heart of meaning: How can that be?

"The sense of estrangement itself posits unity (something to be estranged from)- some tangible ideal which exists despite our feelings otherwise. A remarkable irony is in that even our deep despair is an affirmation of faith, a calling to us from the greater being..."

It did not seem to me that the rationalist was in conflict, but rather that he was in the process of testing a hypothesis, and even a philosophy, against the reality, and had found it sound.

He went on, with resoluteness, in a protest against the mortal dilemma:

"It is not enough to have just one life," he declared with an emphasis on each word, of reasonableness.

"We cannot learn enough in a single lifespan... When we begin to know the improvement called wisdom that life offers us, it is often at the end, when we must take leave and say goodbye, and that seems strange and incongruent.

"Death to the conscious being hides its inevitability in love, to animate our desire, and resolve for more than there seems to be- a deep and silent voice whispering a question, *What do you want, mortal beings!*"

He talked of other things, sometimes speaking quietly, or more strongly, sometimes in a reflection, the last, in a benediction for his wife, read from a little piece of paper he pulled from his pocket: *I always loved you.*

I loved you when you were first conceived, and cheered
When the little whiptail succeeded in pushing his way through
the gentle skin of his delicacy.
I loved you when you were loved and sung to by your mother,
I loved you on the day you were born
I loved you as a little girl, as a lovely young woman,
As a woman growing more beautiful in maturity and experience.
I loved you in the flowering of your maturity, with the slight
appearance of grey adorning your temples.
With the lovely creases of age embellishing your skin,
With the deepening beauty of your eyes as the years
Yielded their wisdom and experience.

I loved you in the mystery of aging, with the splendid colors
Brushed in ephemeral canvasses across the evening of your life,
Which never came because you've left too soon...
I love you in memory and in your constant presence in our dream
Together. I will see you in the morning, when you awaken.

Fo held his hands out, fingers and palms placed together, then rotated them over, as the room responded in applause, which was surely for his little poem and words, for the true love they expressed, and for the irreplaceable object of that love.

Everyone met then in the cafeteria, to enjoy a wonderful luncheon, where BJ rose to introduce 'the man from the outer dimension,' and no one seemed to question the anomaly of my presence. It seems a deal had been struck with the authorities to allow my entrance, and that explained why I was ushered in without ID, but not why the redundant surveillance teams in the grey cars were obliged to trail my journey. Perhaps they were assuring my arrival, or perhaps it was just a show of power.

I remembered Otto telling his friend in Bisbee: "They know things about you. You know nothing about them. That gives them power."

"Perverse," Fo shrugged.

"Okay," Otto conceded. "Perverse power."

BJ kindly ushered me back to Fo and Letty's front door, where I could express my appreciation, and say goodbye. I wanted very much to talk, but told myself there would be another time, soon.

I found Fo in a state of reflection, hands clasped behind his head; eyes closed, and a look of deep tranquility on his face, as if he were listening to something distant- words, or music; or to something within.

Perhaps it was her.

$$* \qquad * \qquad *$$

LEARNING IS impossible without the help of the spirits of knowledge which come from the future to guide and aid human thought. Learning reaffirms the future. By training the mind through education, we learn to open pathways from the spirits to us.
-notebook "15", p43.

THE TRUTH is, we are not one people.
We are the watchers and the watched. And the watchers have the power and means of force. No matter the Constitution and the Bill of Rights, these mischief makers can, with a cursory gesture, take your liberties and wreck your life. They have the ways. Their insistence on a transparent society serves their purpose and not your good. They want control over the lives of the citizens, over your life. Try to imagine what it means, and if you wonder, look at history: They have been in business before.
-Ottolin W. Narstedder, *Government, and Corporate Power*, p347.

"Authority needs its bogeymen, to hide its real agenda, which is control over the people."
-Otto.

BY INJUSTICE all ideals are erased. Justice is the only ideal.
-notebook "18", p9.

I THANKED everyone for their kindness and, with deep feeling, prepared to leave a most extraordinary setting, where the great drama of hope and confidence had been beset by an absurd reality as ancient as the human.

As he accompanied me down the elevator to the parking garage, I spoke briefly with BJ about the matter of Letty, and felt somewhat assuaged by his answers, and more so by his kindness and sympathy.

And, again, I held back another voice that wanted to speak of a reality to come, which must have followed from this day, as a necessity as unchangeable as the moment past. Whatever we trust about the future still cannot replace what we have lost in the present, with only the imagination as refuge from the grasp of the immediate- the imagination, and the certainty of its promise.

BJ, despite my assurance that I would be fine, and my knowing how intense his schedule must be, insisted on walking me over to where my red car was parked by the Volkswagen bus. He shook my hand and gave me an embrace, offering kind words of sympathy, and I remembered our last goodbye upon the landing above the Way of Stone, where a graceful stairway rose to a walkway which led through a splendid courtyard under the shade of flowering trees and a bower of climbing roses which breathed their fragrance into the mist of a fountain. Beyond, and out to where the walkway made a bend, would appear- its graceful roof resting upon a shaded colonnade- a place known long before as home.

For Letty, its reality would be as the next moment, when she awakens before loving intelligences within the Dome of Sky.

The heavy steel door rolled open, and I eased out, seeing last in my rear view mirror the big frame of a brilliant soul I had known before, and who then knew me.

THE TURRETS and guns of the tanks parked in the field across the rail line, barrels raised to line with the windows of the elevator house where the staff was housed in the floors above the library, and Letty would be with her husband, appeared, as I circled around to leave, like a tear in the fabric of spacetime.

The great, thick, circular walls of concrete which wrapped themselves about the scientists and their work, rising skyward to suspend them above the thoughtless contest waged below, seemed warm and organic and living, against the inanimate statues set in place around them.

The guards, fixed and robotic, stared emotionless as some thing from that realm above them moved among them in escape, carrying from it a living piece in trust, shielded in emotion and intellect, transparent and invisible.

A young man in camouflaged uniform with a stubby machine gun strapped on his shoulder raised his arm outward as I approached, signaling me to stop. He walked around to the passenger side window and looked in, asking, "Any guns?"

"I'm not a gun man," I answered. I wanted to say more to him, but he was just doing his job. It wasn't his fault that she died.

He looked again, and waved me forward.

A hundred yards or so farther, where the road entered the compound, there were still assembled perhaps twenty law enforcement vehicles of every type- military, state police, sheriff, unmarked- and a dozen or so uniformed officers and soldiers stood alongside and across the road.

Four suited agents approached, and one ordered me to step out of the Fiero, whereupon the four of them proceeded to conduct a thorough search, pulling up the carpet pads, and looking in all compartments, opening the engine door and hood, and vigorously searching for something, even going through my travel bag.

One, perhaps the senior official, asked tersely, after their search turned up nothing: "Bring anything out of there?"

Choosing among a selection of answers, I said, "No, sir."

"No reading material?" he followed, "A blue manual, about a hundred pages?" I suddenly caught it.

"Not educated enough, by far," I said, adding, "It was there on the internet, I believe."

The agent hesitated in that split second wherein the brain resets itself, and then announced, "You can go."

BJ had told me that my exit was prearranged to be trouble-free, but contracts are made to be broken.

I looked over to my left as I idled out of the militarized zone, just in case there was an old yellow-gold station wagon with a tall driver standing by it, but the place was empty, and I have not seen them again. Likewise, the glass eyed followers in their grey cars.

I followed the paved street which paralleled the railroad tracks until I reached the Dairy Queen, where I treated myself to a sundae, and sat on the bench outside with a heavy heart, trying futilely to absorb the day. At the corner where the street intersected with the highway through town, a sheriff's car flashed its lights, and a portly gentleman somewhat past retirement age with a big mustache walked forward to plant himself outside the driver's window, thick hand resting on the top of the car.

He had a toothpick in a corner of his mouth, which bobbed up and down as he seemed to be choosing his words. I could just see his eyes behind his dark glasses in the late afternoon light.

He cogitated for a minute longer, then calmly asked, "Your friends in there okay?"

I didn't want to divulge anything, so said, "Yes."

"I knew 'em," he said.... "I should say, I know 'em now... Just can't help 'em."

"I understand," I said. He seemed a straight shooter, if you'll pardon the pun, and a likeable fellow.

Then he slapped the top of the car, and hesitated, shaking his big head.

"I spose you're wonderin' who crapped out this idiocy... Shore wadn't me... Some grandstandin' bureaucrats. But that don't worry me. I watch the news, like you. What worries me is why... And who's really behind it."

He stepped back. "Well, you take care now. You're gonna be okay."

I thanked him, and felt better for what he had shared.

*　　*　　*

THE GREAT STANDOFF was to play out for another six weeks, and provide whatever it provided for the administration that staged it, and inestimable "news value" for the media, who enjoyed high ratings for its drama which was most always the lead story, followed by short features on the wars' tragedy, the latest threat of terrorism, or celebrity trivia, and then back to the crisis in Kansas.

Whether by design, or by simple inference and association, just over half of Americans came to believe that the scientists were involved in something connected to terrorism, or were atheists, abortionists, and anarchists. I have since read that 54% of this country believes that science has created more harm than good. Half of those are simply following the preachings of savvy fundamentalist religious and media personalities who have a stake in promoting controversy, and in influencing politics.

Finally, just before Thanksgiving, something happened which brought the whole matter to critical mass, which must inevitably result, and may even be systemic in these provocations. In the scientists' case, there was nothing to settle: It was not a matter of withholding information critical to national security. The book was out there, and could not be recalled.

Perhaps it was to teach them a lesson. To command an ownership over intellectual property, or to divert the rewards to special interests, and thus to control its influence, or as Jerry Falwell had declared, "To punish the godless scientists for taking unto themselves the power of God. For this unforgivable sin they will be stricken down."

The net effect was what happened on Thanksgiving eve, when something joyful, planned in midsummer, went terribly wrong.

BJ, true to his nature, had planned ahead to install a large holiday season peace sign upon the top of the elevator house. This was when the staff was free to roam into town, when construction was being done, and lots of things were going on, and the town was excited about their new industry, though having only general knowledge that it was scientific and technical, perhaps connected to the computer business or artificial intelligence. The project was being promoted and supervised quietly by a well-known builder with Kansas roots, who had chanced to take a couple of lauded classes called Destiny 101, offered by a "Professor Fo" at the University of Arizona, which he worked into his architecture program, to his everlasting benefit.

Four or five of the scientists, led by BJ, used up precious off-hours rummaging from stores and businesses in town for materials to make the rotating sign. Steel banding and rebar were donated by a builder's supply store, and other materials and labor were provided by a welding and fabricating shop in mid-town on the main street. A tractor wheel and axel shaft were rummaged from a farm implement and supply store in town, and all it took was to hoist it all up to the roof of the elevator house, carefully avoiding the array of satellite dishes.

By late summer, just before the arrival of the guns, the frame was assembled, set with blue lights, and fixed above the tractor wheel, complete with hub and shaft, which was belted to a small electric motor so that the whole assembly rotated, swaying the ten-meter symbol slowly across the 360 degrees of countryside. The "Peace Team", as they called themselves, which consisted at that moment of a nano-scientist, a geneticist, a biophysicist, and a specialist in quantum mechanics, congratulated each other and, for three or four nights, instituted a dry-run of sorts, as a preview of the holiday spirit of peace and good will.

As the blue-lit peace sign within a circle turned from the field of view, its lines would narrow and merge until at 90-degrees only a vertical line appeared, curiously like a punctuation mark- or, as a finger, some townspeople were keen to note- although it was a simple manifestation of geometric position, and implied no message, subliminal or otherwise, beyond the traditional greeting of the sign of peace and renewal in the holiday season to come. On the last test night, the peace team stood in the chill upon the roof at the far end of the facility and looked up at the rotating symbol, admiring their creation as the rotating light cast them in variegated waves of blue. They stood proudly admiring the low-tech structure, shaking hands all around and cheering, looking like ghostly blue beings from an alien world.

Then the engineering marvel was set on the back burner, awaiting the start of the season of peace at the feast of Thanksgiving.

Finally, on the eve of the holiday, BJ and one other member of the peace team climbed upon the roof of the elevator house to check out and make a final adjustment to the peace circle before turning it on to begin the holiday season. Perhaps it would even offer good will to the increasingly nervous crews attending the ring of armaments, kept on high alert by the rhetoric coming from officials in Washington.

The news cameras stationed back of the line cordoned off by authorities recorded the stunning event wherein there was no sound beyond the initial crack of the rifle, when the figure first doubled in the shock of the bullet's impact, but recovered itself, arms extended, turning the spirals of a cartwheel.

It seemed a controlled descent to those below, seen in slow motion as he gracefully made two turns in the three and a half seconds occupied in the descent, cradled and held airily by gravity's ghost as he accelerated. Any body of any weight- a pebble, a brick, a boulder, a human- will always fall at the same rate, pushed earthward by the bend in spacetime occasioned by the earth's mass.

A sniper had fired off an unerring round at a man on the roof of the elevator house, just at dusk when the light can be confusing, and shadows can look a lot like guns, and a simple wave of the hand can be easily misread.

BJ was to be the only other casualty of the infamous "Standoff" in Kansas.

*   *   *

CHAPTER SEVENTEEN

GOING HOME.
OTTO

LOOK INTO the faces of the past, and see the ghosts of yourself. The eyes which gaze out of old photographs into your own seem to speak out of a silence from living souls who travel along with the present into the future. The souls who speak silently in the language of emotion.
-notebook "10", p39.

"Some into realms of new existences. Some into peaceful blessed oblivion, the immortality of the once living. And grand untold numbers uncalled to life, rest in the deepest quiet of all, though even that is not a total silence, but in a scintillating state of potentiality audible to the infinite sense."
-notebook "12", p27.

"Certainty is the mind's redoubt, which defends itself against change. It lifts its drawbridge of belief against evidence..."
-Otto (to Jerry Falwell on Larry King Live).

THERE IS SOMETHING different about going home. It does not have to do with direction- home can be anywhere- or velocity of travel, or time in route.

There is an existential difference in going home. Home is more another dimension than a place- until you get there, and then it is a place, and all else, another dimension. For some, it is the place you belong to; for others, it is the search itself, which finally takes the form of that elusive place, to satisfy the human in his remarkable adaptability, substituting for the reality, the ideal.

I was returning south on that road down from Plainville where the scientific facility rose protected within its concrete shell, its community of scientists and researchers engaged in unlocking secrets known to the future.

A return trip is not opposite the going. It is, rather, of another dimension entirely, infused with the experience attending it. We are transformed by that experience, and so the person returning from a place is never the one who came.

I passed through Hays, through Liebenthal, and the famous post rock country, and on to the main street town of La Crosse, where I saw the lighted sign of Nick's Daylite Donuts, and a block down, the little motel managed by the kind lady, where I had slept so soundly on the last night of Letty's life.

It was good to keep moving, to allow the flow of thought to continue as it must when there is so much to absorb, if not to understand.

The juxtaposition of two realities, experienced in the view of death, is as ancient as the consciousness of self, and even other species are known to mourn the loss of life, as the inevitable price of love. But to see a third reality in the *awakening*, to be known as the next moment after death, has been to embellish that inevitable price with hope, and the ageless dream of immortality.

For the first time in the experience of conscious life on Earth, centered within a tower built for another purpose, and besieged by forces of convention with a dark and tendrilous history, the powers of learning were set free in the conception of life into immortality, to complete the circle of thought, the circle of creation.

I had seen her united with them in that other place and time, had walked within the awakening in the Dome of Sky, had witnessed the realness of their experience, the ultimate of this day in theirs, if the mind does not fail its vision in forgetfulness.

I heard the music of the resurrection on an unforgettable day of remembrance, when friends gathered to celebrate the performance of timeless art, and said goodbye to them upon the ancient Way of Stone, where they had walked within the magnificent enfilade to meet a visitor from the past.

One goodbye, as remote as any future, and then this.

We are circumscribed by death, which scatters us in the diaspora of generations, with only the threads of memory to hold us in connection with living thought. There is no memory without emotion, and so it is by emotion that our spirits are given a presence in time.

Emotions are the purest form of memories. They are beyond memory, and apart, reappearing not as interpretations of past states, but as the pure states themselves, carried in a living form, ageless and unchanged.

Without emotion there can be no memory, and no learning. All thought has emotion at its heart, rising first in conscious development, giving birth to self-conscious thought. It is emotion that is shared across species, and is possessed by the unborn child, and makes it human. Emotion is the knowing.

Emotion is thought in its infancy. It is the infancy of thought, and the reason to protect the child. Emotion is the heart of thought; without emotion, thought is hollow. It is also the medium by which we grieve at loss. It's really all about love.

I SLEPT somewhere, having worked through my train of thoughts, and then continued on to that place where, on the flat plains where the settlers' graveyard lay at the end of the road of cypresses, my grandparents were at rest.

In this community of the dead, they had been laid down to sleep around and back from the oldest graves of the first settlers and pioneers set nearest the front gate where the community began, growing outward generation upon generation subtracted from the living, and added one by one.

You cannot walk among them without feeling their presence.

There was no one sitting in surveillance this time, so I was able to stand at their feet for as long as I wanted, thinking their names, and picturing their faces that had looked out from old photographs for as long as I remembered. I also knew other photographs, of their parents, and so could imagine them as children in a time which was modern to them, and held no hint of what was to come down in a lineage of miraculous births to this moment when a grandson they never knew appeared, to draw them gently into remembrance.

I knelt on one knee above them and gazed through the prairie earth that covers their sleep, wanting to see what they looked like, the beauty of their forms, the remnants of their clothing which still lay about them, the color of her dress, the vestiges of her thick hair, pulled upward and back in that final dressing to reveal the elegant shape of her face and head; the salt of the last tears which fell upon her in goodbyes infused with elements in crystals of emotion. Salt, like love, is eternal.

I felt them speak to me through the emotions of their son, the father I knew, through his devotion and conflicts unresolved, because death comes too soon to make peace with all our little wars.

To have any regrets about the past is to wish some part of yourself away, since you are a composite of everything you have experienced. All you can do is to come to understand the past, and turn it into generosity and good.

Every memory is but a seed, which is nourished by each individual into whatever is allowed and chosen, so that any regret is transformed into hope and beauty.

I wondered for them why we should live again, why we should awaken the sleep that stills our yearning. It is because we are not finished yet, because our dreams lie beyond the mere moment of our lives, because we imagine greater realms.

It is not the perpetuation of our selves, but our unfinished business which calls us, the completion of love.

I believed there is a beauty in these people in their houses of dust, whose blood still flows in the veins of their children. But, as well, that there is no fulfillment in death. The purpose of the resurrection is the fulfillment of life: in mortality we are deprived of the secrets which lie beyond the span of life.

There is no meaning in death but to discover love, and no reason, beyond the dream of victory.

THERE IS a reason why we are haunted by the past, since it is a part of us removed in time, reminding us of our past selves. The landscape of personality drawn across by ghostly memories in covered wagons, and voices long silent except in dreams.

The past is the archetype of personality, and we are haunted by it and enamored of its ghostly images in thought which holds our essence in its heart. We are the children of history, and the past inhabits us as a living spirit.

It is because we are not one. None of us is one.

We are the many souls that we were at times and places in our past. The unborn, the newly born, the child creature, the youth. Our selves through maturity, and then old age.

We are the image in our parents' eyes, the memories of us taken with them to their graves. We are the heroes in the hearts of the children. We are the composite of our memories and myths and unfinished dreams.

We are not one; none of us is one.

As I communed with them I became increasingly aware that it was not a matter for me, or for another, to consider their return to life, and when or how it should be. Whether it would be in that zone of immortality I had visited, or in another in that eternal recurrence nearer to the Omega.

It was certain that the "Specialists" I met already knew about them, and indeed, about the events of this day and yesterday, holding, as was said of them, "complete knowledge." The specialist, Robeling, who seemed strikingly like a young Ralph Waldo Emerson, and may indeed have been the famous nineteenth-century intellect's reincarnation, given the phenomenality of that future time, had mentioned cryptically as we sat around the table at the feast of plenty, "We know the immortality document. We have your book."

I took it at the time to refer metaphorically to a "Book of Life", but realize now that he was simply speaking of this writing in the form of a report to the Committee of Safekeepers, which would also speak of my father's parents now resting in this community of the dead. What else they would know of them, to include their DNA sequences and field points of thought and memory, is for the future to reveal, as of the infinite subtleties of their personalities, the emotion of their lives- their unique identities.

For the first time I was beginning to understand more about the business of the Specialists: The work of the resurrection would come naturally out of the conquest over death, which will not be complete until those who have died can be recalled to share in its opportunity-the mortals, called to immortality.

Because the mortal gave rise to immortality, it is most reasonable and natural that the future would hold a special regard for its forebears who paid the sacrifice of death. The *Specialists* talked of justice, and of love, and of the pure meaning of their work, and it was most certainly of this duty that they spoke.

As time passed by in a succession of events to be never ending, the future immortals will take their turn- with the assistance of their "associates" in super-intelligence, and those in the "vanguard" of the resurrected- in bringing into their midst those souls who knew death and its loss. This accomplishment, and its effort carried out in love, was the source of their joy.

It seems to me now that all four of the specialists I knew would have been in the category of the "vanguard"- those who had known death. Hence, they were not strictly "immortals", but occupied in their time a special distinction as having risen from mortality into the realm of the immortal.

The four Specialists seemed extremely interested in matters of our time, and this may have had more to do with having in their presence a subject directly translated from a living past, rather than through the lens of history.

Exactly how the sequence of reincarnation was determined is still a mystery, and it seems the process was less of a redemption than of a practical matter of matching souls with others to arrive at meaning. There was no attitude of punishment or chastisement by delaying a return, as in death there is no time, and so the first knowledge would be of awakening from one moment to the next.

Some were called back, whose lives expressed the desire for more life, whose love exceeded life, whose gifts could serve in the immortal cause, as they had in the mortal one. Those who cared for the Earth.

This is the "light" they spoke of.

It is not that someone sits in judgment, but that the goodness of us shines more fully, to guide the resurrection to us.

I remembered an assurance of the immortal BJ as we sat on the curb of the Way of Stone, where it slipped into the sea, as I had expressed a mortal concern regarding the influence of position and power within the family of humans:

Geronimo and the benevolent chieftains before the train of popes. Mothers and daughters and sons before the kings and conquerors.

Graveyards are places of mystery, hallowed in the presence of what was once living, infused with lingering emotion, and even the less reflective among us is given to wonder, What is the meaning of it all?

Foglesby spoke that evening on the veranda of this meaning:

"Each conscious being is born to Destiny, out of infinite wisdom, toward which that being moves in a process called *learning.* Some progress more in their journey than may others. Some, little at all.

"A few have pulled destiny to them, touched the hem of its garment and extraordinarily claimed its power- never for themselves, but for those and that which they love, for it was love which was the primary cause of their gift and vision.

"In the greater love is greater life... In the greatest love is the everbeing."

ACROSS TO the back of the cemetery I had noticed two young people walking among the tombstones, quietly engaged in some type of activity. During the time I spent with my grandparents they had worked their way closer, and I saw that they seemed to be attending each grave- the young woman entering something in a laptop she carried, while the young man carried a GPS device and a digital camera. It appeared they were doing research, and they would often consult the computer together, visiting about what the information revealed.

As I glanced at them the girl waved, and then both of them walked over to introduce themselves. We visited a minute, and they asked about my family, and about the loved ones I was paying my respects to. When I asked if they were doing a university project, they explained that their work was indeed for class credit, but beyond that they were members of the Poets' Society of Safekeepers, and were entering information about the burial spots of individual souls in a permanent database.

The young man explained that with the passage of time and generations, loyal family members die away, and eventually gravesites may deteriorate and be lost. As far as is possible information and details of the lives of the souls resting there are also placed into record.

There then followed a most interesting conversation which lasted into early evening, although I did not relate to them matters of my future experience, or of the tragedy which passed the day before in Kansas involving a drama everyone was following.

The two young people who called themselves "Poets" were early students in a new field which had expanded in one year to over forty campuses, to change and reveal every discipline, to include education, history, sociology, anthropology, the humanities and philosophy, related with biophysics, nanobiology, quantum mechanics, and other schools of study- in short, with that range of areas elucidated and propelled by the Discovery.

When I inquired discreetly about their work the students confided that they were involved in more than a documentation of record, and that their work had a purpose in the eventual conquest over aging and death.

They spoke of capsules and storage, of GPS documentation of burial sites into a digital memory of personal archives, of "each one a guardian of two," and of "the transformation of lives as prospect of future destiny to imbue daily experience, providing a sense of great meaning and its motives for peace and a changed world."

Most remarkably, these young people mentioned that they were enrolled in graduate and post-graduate programs to be "Specialists". It became apparent that they were not simply technicians recording data, as they spoke of morphic resonances associated with their work, of something awakened by the notice of it, even in death.

They said we had to reform our understanding of the purpose and destiny of life, to enable the resonances which will communicate through time to unify knowledge and understanding, saying, "We have to learn to de-mystify death, if we are to know what to do about it."

It was fascinating to see in these young scholars with their limited tools the forerunners of those who would engage the return to life, some of whom I knew on a day a mere twenty-five decades away, which knew the fruition of their efforts.

Perhaps they will read what the professor told his class, recorded in notebook "12", page 66: "Whatever extreme is conceivable, given motive and opportunity, emerges into reality."

"The past survives most formidably," Fo asserted, "in unconscious memory, and is passed forward from generation to generation in the silent resonances of emotion and conviction, emitted and picked up through the invisible bridges across time's experience.

"All is known that has ever happened to affect the present, in the physical record of the earth and nature, and beyond, in thought and emotion."

Fo continued, regarding a reality engaged by the young Poets here:

There can be no memory unless there is something that is sent out from the source of that memory, from the thing, itself remembered. Memory catches the transmission and translates its patterns into images of the prior form or condition, in interpretations of its physical and emotional states.

As we were seated around the table that day of our first meeting on the veranda, when I had asked about the phenomenal nature of my arrival, the fellow, Robeling, explained enigmatically that, "Thought may be directed backward, and forward, to affect time and alter destiny." He also added interestingly that the destiny of Walt Whitman is changed with each reading of his work.

IT SEEMS irrefutable that if death is to be deprived of its finality, and life of its mortal limitation, then we must adopt a different premise about life and death, in an existential, scientific, and artistic shift which integrates the two states into the same possibility, affirming that there is more potential to life than we know- always more, never less. *More potential than our minds are prepared to conceive.*

At some time before the phenomenal events within the Dome of Sky, scientific and spiritual advances had provided a victory over the sentence of death, and they were the immortals who in a completion of meaning began reaching back to bring into their presence those once claimed by death.

The conquest over death was not to be completed in immortality, but in the resurrection.

The young chroniclers at the cemetery noted ironically that the only resistance to their work so far had come from people of faith, who perceived an interference in the plan of the divine to provide its own resurrection in its own manner and time. It is easier to believe in the divine miracle than in the scientific process.

Foglesby observed it as a trait of the human in conflict to disclaim the visible in favor of the invisible, proclaiming faith in an unbelief which served a purpose in antiquity, until the imagination bore the fruits of advanced realities.

There is a voice, an instinct, which tells you that you can go there, but you cannot return. So we do not go.

But this voice is a timid one, and misunderstanding.

We visit these places of the past, or of the future, but we cannot stay there only because the observer has not yet merged with the observed in the place that time is. This is how Fo explained it.

We will always return in such matters to that emotion which infuses thought, not to provide answers, but to compel their solution at the end of our searching.

I SAT THERE within the low breathing of the vast space which fills the prairie, and listened to their music out of the stillness of time borne across the years unrecoverable now except in the emotion of memory.

For once I could hear emanating from the ground the soft melody played out by slender fingers on the steel guitar laid across her lap, as children stood around and sang with her the music in her heart. The year was 1921.

I could imagine her voice softly leading her children's voices in the spirit of music which flows through them on that last Spring of her life, into time to this day pulsing from the strange recesses of death which sleeps in its illusion until awakened by the desire of life to hear its singing again, in the eternal presence of all that has ever been.

That day exists still, forever as it was, in the moving presence of time, bound outward in light which carries its message undiminished into the knowledge of destiny.

They are with us now, calling to us in exquisite resonances transmitted within the slender thread of remembrance.

As I stood where my grandparents lay there came on the car radio, floating over the graves in the still evening air, that transcendent composition which would become the theme song to honor the scientists.

Called, *Bridge of Tomorrows,* it was the same music which BJ had played on the violin at Letty's memorial service, accompanied hauntingly by the harmonica, here rendered into inimitable beauty in an arrangement by the great Phil Coulter.

As I listened deeply, the strains of silence lifted from the prairie soil to join the refrain of life, and I felt these dead were indeed upon that bridge, awaiting the distant morning of the resurrection.

*   *   *

"WE HAVE to dare new adventures of the mind and spirit in order to know ourselves, because our true dimensions are bounded only by our imagination. In this, we are each and every one called to our destiny."
-Foglesby, at the Biden hearings, U.S. Senate, Jan. 2005.

"We are at our least, not when we are estranged from a metaphorical deity, but when we forget our humanity."
-"Specialist" BJ, on the Way of Stone.

*"Christ thunder, man! The law isn't an icon... Written laws have enslaved more people than they've ever kept free. Dictators rule by law, and if the law isn't reasonable or arguable, then it becomes a dictator to once free men, misused and hated.
"When people cry Freedom! it is against the law they are crying- someone else's law.. What did you think?"*
-attorney Gerry Spence, to Rev. Falwell on
Larry King Live.

Freedom smiles in question: 'Do you have a protest? Does anyone disagree?' Pity the poor society that has silenced all protest.
-Otto, *in conversation with Foglesby.*

SOMETHING HAPPENS when we let go of the moment and move into time. We are strangely most comfortable there, imbued by that dimension which gives perspective and meaning to the passing moment. Perhaps it is because the present cannot in itself provide understanding which only comes in reflection. As creatures of imagination and reflection, we are most at home in realms of time.

We borrow from the infinite to construct that sliver of time we call the moment. And yet it is a moment which vanishes with its arrival, whose passage is no broader than the dimension of a single thought, moving across time, which creates all past and future. We linger in the present for a blink, and then we abandon it as an illusion, uncertain that it was.

In order to know if this is truly the present, we must be assured that the moment we know rides at the outermost edge of time, expanding its reality at the speed of light against the void of nothingness. That there has been nothing before that can be called this future- no thought, no imagining, no anticipation, or plan, or dream, or hope.

But we already know this not to be so, since we have called the future by its name, merging it with the past to create that continuum of conscious presence through which reality is born and kept.

We are not denizens of the moment. The conscious presence is of time.

The era of my grandparents a century ago is completely familiar to us still, despite the history that has intervened- the wars, trips to the moon and planets, politics, art and science and technology- and life would still be recognizable to the human returned from the century or millennium before us, because the nature which connects us is basic: When do you plant your seeds? What is your child's name? Are you well?

Beyond all that are the abstractions which refine our humanity, the concepts of knowledge that tell us who we are and to where we are bound- knowledge enveloped by the same concern: When do you plant your seeds? What is your child's name? Are you well?

The future can only be strange or frightening if the demons and saints within us prevail- or indifference- and we lose our humanity.

ALTHOUGH I had constantly associated him with Fo and Letty, I did not ask about Otto on my visit to the facility. I had only inquired discreetly about the professor and his wife upon my return from the future, and only looked for them in places marked for my discovery, even carefully measuring my thoughts so as not to trade upon their privacy. In the case of their friend, it was not my place to inquire at all, and I was not to hear from Otto directly until the letter arrived at the farmhouse under the logo of the Safekeepers with its sky blue image of a lotus flower.

Something changed after the firestorm which resulted from the death of the staffmember scientist, BJ, shot by a federal sniper as he attended to a peace sign upon the elevator house on Thanksgiving Eve.

The Attorney General called a hasty press conference to present the government's side, saying that the constant tension of the siege had frayed the nerves of his agents and troops, and this was the fault of the rebellious scientists who, by refusing to accede to the demands of the Department of Justice, had brought their problems on themselves.

The nation and the entire world, who had been following the dramatic and inscrutable sequence of events since the drama began, didn't buy it.

Within the facility there was extreme shock and grief at the loss of a beloved friend and colleague, and anger at the feigned sincerity of the attorney general, who was scrambling to cover his flank. Foglesby had told his class, though with no reference to a particular individual, "No soul, with mere words, can lie. Even the most shameless deceiver is servant of the truth."

The professor of history, less generously, had called political deceit, "The image on the shroud of authority."

After his wife's death Fo had seemed to set about a discipline, pouring himself even more fully into his work, though he did not change outwardly. With the loss of BJ less than a month later his resoluteness remained, though those who best knew him could tell how the second tragedy had affected him. In the end it would not change the outcome of his work.

The death of the scientist had cast the drama in a different light, and a group of legislators led by Senator Joseph Biden called for special hearings immediately upon the return of Congress from recess. The governor of Kansas launched her own investigation, and there were calls for the Attorney General's impeachment.

Within five days of the tragedy, in a full-hour program of Larry King Live, an elderly fellow with bushy eyebrows and a large brow made even more prominent by a rim of wavy white hair appeared as the main guest. He was known to be connected with the subject of "The Great Standoff", as a friend and colleague of long standing. What he was to tell his host and the world audience came as a mystery wrapped in the enigma.

After the meeting in Bisbee which I happened to witness most tangentially, wherein his friend revealed to Otto an outline of the matters surrounding the Discovery while seated in the dining room of The Copper Queen Hotel, augmented by a further discussion in the courtyard of the older professor's house where stood the giant saguaro, the unmarked car that Letty noticed crossing back and forth in the street below remained on duty, its occupants looking through the arched opening in the rock retaining wall, where the high steps rose to the enclosed deck.

The information shared by Fo with his friend that day, conveyed in minimal outlines for the purpose of eliciting advice, came to haunt the old professor like a skeletal ghost who possessed no form or identity, while wielding enormous significance incapable of being fleshed out for ordinary perception. Nothing Otto could have told them about his friend or his discovery could have elucidated the matters already revealed and published with the equations and Code in the blue book with a hundred pages.

But some things defy logic, as everyone learned in the first few minutes of King's interview with the noted Ottolin W. Narstedder, Professor Emeritus of History, and long-time supporter of high causes, caught up in "the times of which the prophets spoke."

Otto appeared thinner than when I had last seen him, his face a bit drawn, and his large eyes, dark and intense, seemed deeper set. When his guest entered the studio, King, wearing his signature suspenders over a blue shirt, rose to his feet to reach across the desk and shake his hand. Otto still managed his broad smile and sense of humor:

"TONIGHT, WE are privileged to have with us as a guest for the full hour a distinguished professor emeritus of history, noted author of numerous books and articles, and life-long advocate for peace, the environment, justice, and the rights of man, woman, and child on planet Earth.

Praised by Nelson Mandela, and called by President Carter the modern Tom Paine, the professor considers it a privilege to have served jail time with the likes of Martin Luther King, the Berrigan brothers, and others in the rank and file of fighters for justice and equal rights. Besides his intellectual and academic achievements, he has found time to protest against wars and their mindset, nuclear proliferation, the arms industry, land mines, the destruction of our forests, the pollution of rivers and oceans, poor health care for children and mothers- you name it, whatever is bad.

"Otto, what happened? It has come to our attention that you have been on an extended vacation you didn't plan: Can you tell us about it?"

"Well, not much, Larry. A funny thing happened on the way to the Forum." (Otto managed a wide smile.)

"How long have ya been gone?"

"I was getting ready to board a flight to return from a conference in Beirut on the 15th of September when three unsavory types persuaded me to board another plane where I was blindfolded and bound, and flown to a base in Kazakhstan and placed in a concrete box underground about four by five feet whose ceiling was ample for a pigmy person to stand, but not a short American, like I am. It was an intelligent design which doesn't allow a human to stretch out, Larry."

"How long were you held there?"

"Well, from the 16th of September, or thereabouts, until about five days ago, when I was flown to Damascus, and set free. The exact number of days is scratched there on a wall of the rathole, where I could review them in Braille...seventy-one, if you care to go verify.

"I thought a lot about John McCain, and began a game to try and remember everything I knew. Good exercise. Luckily, I've done a lot of reading, and a fair amount of living, so there was enough to think about."

"Damascus? They kidnapped you in Beirut and returned you to Damascus?...Why?"

"I wasn't complaining, Larry. And kidnapping is a bad word: 'extraordinary rendition' sounds better, doesn't it?"

"Did your release have anything to do with the tragedy in Kansas- the killing of the scientist?"

"I knew nothing about Kansas until I was returned to the Middle East, and yes, I'm assuming it had everything to do with it."

(Larry King rested his face between his thumb and forefinger, seriously studying that answer and its implications, as the station cut for a commercial break.)

"Otto, what did they accuse you of? Was there any mention of the situation with your friend, Professor Foglesby?"

"I asked that first question repeatedly, What am I being accused of?.. Finally, one of the goons who spoke American English, snapped, 'We snatch the agitators. You, sir, are an agitator.' It was only after we arrived at the base that I was accused of being a terrorist. The interrogations that followed centered on that theme."

"Terrorist."

"Yeah. Terrorist."

"I have to ask you, Professor... Did they use torture?"

"Larry, when you take away someone's liberty, when you imprison without charges, and allow no defense, and threaten with death, that is torture. Injustice is the torture of the mind and soul. Injustice is torture."

"Rumsfeld was asked about that- about making prisoners in Gitmo stand in place for ten hours- and he replied that this was no punishment, since he was often on his feet for more than ten hours at a time."

"Rummy didn't have a wife and children, or aging parents somewhere, not knowing if he was dead or alive. He didn't have to worry impotently if his loved ones were alive, or suffering, or starving, or killed by a clusterbomb. He didn't have to worry if his life was over. He didn't have to suffer the indignity of soiling himself as he was forced to stand for hours. He didn't have a soul in torment- though he should have."

"What if the prisoner is guilty?"

"What if he is not? These prisoners have not been charged.

"It is the mind which is free or slave, Larry. Not the body. The great travesty of servitude is what it does to conscious existence, wasting the right to, and opportunity of free expression, which issues from the autonomous self. Whatever starves and steals from another the potential for greaterness destroys as well its own destiny, so that nothing is left free.

"One cannot declare oneself free while another is imprisoned unjustly, because in the presence of injustice all ideals are erased. Justice is the only ideal, from whose insistence and transcendence was conceived the Bill of Rights."

"So we're doing it the wrong way, in this war on terror?"

"Larry, you can't wage a war on terror because war *is* terror. Violence given is an equal measure of violence received: the abuse of childhood simmering in anger and frustration until it lashes out in equal abuse. The individual mistreated by society responding in punishment and retribution- an eye for an eye- in a continuation of the cycles. Death avenged by death, murder by murder...Violence is a way of life.

"Even in war, which trades in violence begot by other violence until every warrior has a reason and justification for mayhem. Spies and counterspies, police and suspect, prosecutors stretching the truth, and defenders covering and coloring the truth...The battle begins at birth, with the assignment of a name wherein the subject is shackled by duty, honor, and country in the terms prescribed by someone else whose interests are vested in power...Lies and counterlies and the religion of authority which orders your conversion to its way, or else- the dictatorship of law made by lawyers for lawyers in a game called consequence, played across a graveyard of deceased freedom by agents in dark glasses who scurry across the night, watching over rebellion."

"Makes you wonder about our collective sanity, doesn't it, Professor?"

"If you use 'mental health' as a reference point, or datum line, and then diverge from that place to society's obsession with legality, crime, violence- and its lack of focus- then what you see is the 'normalization' of abnormality... I've had some time to think about it, Larry, especially lately." (King laughed silently.)

"What have you figured out?"

"We believe in violence: that's what we believe in. We think we believe other things, but it really comes down to violence. Violence is our religion... It's not the peace sign on the elevator house, proclaiming itself over the countryside- Good Will to Man. It's the crack of the rifle, and the bullet smashing the chest. It started when we were kicked out of Paradise for disagreeing with the authority, and it's continued ever since, and every now and then a peacemaker would appear, lifting up a peace sign and talking about love, but he would be sacrificed... You know why, Larry?

"Because he interfered with our business, which was violence."

"That's grim."

"Yes, it is, Larry, but let's try and change it."

("Let's break now for a commercial, and when we return I want to bring on some more guests to round out this fascinating and important discussion with the great scholar and activist Professor Emeritus of History of the University of Arizona, Dr. Ottolin W. Narstedder. Perhaps I should add, 'agitator' and accused terrorist just returned from rendition in a third country...whew! And, longtime friend and colleague of the famous and controversial Professor Foglesby- we'll get to that important matter soon.

We'll have in our studios another famous guest, and renowned defense attorney from Wyoming, Mr. Gerry Spence, and seated next to him, the Reverend Jerry Falwell, while we'll call in on the screen another well-known religious personality, the Rev. Pat Robertson... This should be interesting, folks! Don't go away.".")

"Welcome Counselor. Welcome, Reverend. Before we start this off I'd like to ask the professor, Have you spoken with your friend, Professor Foglesby, since your return?"

"Yes, I spoke with him at length from Damascus, and a number of times since."

"How's he doing?"

"We spoke of his work. It's going very well."

"Didn't talk of personal matters- the death of his wife, and then of Dr. Smith?"

"Didn't talk about that. Didn't talk about his legal situation, or the siege either. He spoke of the achievements coming out of the Discovery, and of what they portend for human life. Fantastic science he is sharing with colleagues everywhere. Truly revolutionary."

"Counselor, what about this? Just about everyone is confused... What's at stake with the National Security Agency in a scientific discovery that opens frontiers of learning? I don't get it."

"There are vested interests, Larry. People who want a stake, and don't want others to have a stake. Others who fear scientific advance, fear changes which cause them to lose control. The fundamentalist religious right commands an influence on the White House, and this is a factor."

"Reverend Falwell, science has always endeavored to discover new things, to advance knowledge. I had successful heart surgery, and am alive today, with millions of others, because of science. Are you against the advancement of science?"

"That doesn't matter. Professor Foglesby is choosing to disobey the law."

[Spence] "The professor has no choice but to ignore a law morphed out of a questionable edict. First, you declare something which is self-serving and unreasonable, if not unconstitutional. Then you hide behind the fallout, letting the law do your dirty work for you.

"This matter didn't start with the law: it started with a bureaucratic edict of prior restraint. You devise a rule, or concoct one to fit a situation, then you promote a liaison with some or other law. Your miscegenation produces an offspring which you hope will most resemble the law than your self-serving rule. You hide behind the mask and let another do your monkey business... It's an old trick, known to authoritarians for ages, and refined since. If you can turn your rules into laws, so much the better for you.

"If not, there are other ways. The law politicized is nasty."

[Falwell] "This country was founded on the basic laws of the Ten Commandments of God. This is why we have prospered. When we turn away from this morality, then we will suffer God's wrath. The law is the glue that holds us all together...The scientist Foglesby wants to choose the laws he will obey, and he must pay the consequence. The law's the law, and must be enforced. We can't just choose to ignore it. The counselor should know that."

[Spence] "Christ thunder, man! The law isn't an icon.. Written laws have enslaved more people than they have ever kept free. Dictators rule by law, and if the law isn't reasonable or arguable, then it becomes a dictator to once free men, misused and hated.

"Many Jews escaped Europe and the Holocaust by forging false papers- *which was against the law.* The law facilitated their extermination...Slavery was instituted and protected by law. When people cry Freedom! it is *against* the law they are crying- someone else's law... What did you think?

"Every despot, every lame government, every control freak uses the law as a cover: If the law doesn't suit him, he adapts it to his purpose. He manipulates it; he distorts it; he plays with it...The great brilliance of America is its Constitution and its rules regarding law."

[Spence turns to King]

"The reverend sees God as a prosecutor... Now there's the ultimate nightmare for an old country defense lawyer like me, Larry. A prosecutor with infinite powers and little mercy... No, I see the god or power who created the universe and all its creatures with better things to do. I see her, or him, or it, as the ultimate defender... Your God is a little scary to me, Reverend."

[Falwell] "You need to get right with the Almighty, Counselor, and then you won't have anything to fear. God loves you, Gerry."

[Spence] "Oh, I just cast my lot with the creator and creation of life, so I don't have to fear. Each time I defend a soul I'm just doing a little bit of the Lord's work in the court of Man. That's how I see it... God is a concept, and is not the same for everyone.

"Your god is hungry for retribution, and mine is full of understanding and compassion. Unfortunately, when men who are hungry for retribution claim they are acting for their god is when we are all in trouble, as we have learned."

[Falwell] "In this country we're all equal under the law. This is what's great about America."

[King] "What about it, Gerry?"

"It's a nice story, Reverend, but in no country is everyone equal under the law, and in no time. The law is different for you if you are rich and powerful, and if you are poor and powerless. Laws are made and used and bent by interests who have the resources, the 'big guys.' It is the little guy who is often bent and excluded in the process. It is not the law that Ashcroft is following in the siege in Kansas; it is an ideology, and special interests who have influence over the White House and Congress and the attorney general."

[Falwell] "Shame on you, Counselor, for questioning the integrity of our Attorney General, who is a godly man and is God's servant in his job. He is chosen by God to do his important work."

[Spence] "Ashcroft was appointed by God?"

[Falwell] "God acts through his servants. The president prays and seeks divine guidance in his appointments, so, yes, I would say that this righteous man was placed there by God to do his work, as was this president."

[Spence, smiling to King] "So God was behind that business in Florida. He must have a fine sense of humor, Reverend."

[King] "Professor, what do you say?"

[Otto] "My own opinion, Larry, is that religion is metaphorical, and morality is literal, and the two have nothing to do with one another. When religion defines morality it becomes the thief of liberty, and the murderer. Morality is debased when religion touches it because religion does not allow the rights of consciousness. You disagree with its version of the truth at your peril, and freedom- your right of determination- is lost."

[King, to Falwell] "Does religion have an influence in the contest staged in Kansas? Why has the temperature risen so high in a matter that seems like science. What's wrong with science?"

[Falwell] "There's nothing wrong with science. The problem is that Dr. Foglesby and his scientists are claiming unauthorized knowledge. They are claiming knowledge which is not given by God."

[King] "What knowledge is that?"

[Falwell] "Everyone has heard the rumors, Larry- that within the 'key' of the code discovered by Professor Foglesby there is the knowledge of resurrection and immortality. The end of death."

[King, squinting his eyes at Falwell] "Seems like that would be the greatest discovery ever, Reverend. *The end of death...* Your faith has been prophesying it for two thousand years."

[Falwell] "Yes, the resurrection is a key of our faith- not of a code discovered by a scientist. The Resurrection will come at the sounding of the last trump, when the dead will rise from their graves, and be caught up to meet the Lord in the air."

[King] "What do you say, Otto? Can the last trumpet be sounded by science?"

[Otto] "I cannot argue with what the reverend believes. People believe many things, and their beliefs are important to them. The 'last trump' is presumably a metaphor. Is it a metaphor for the awakening? Is the awakening to be accomplished by man's knowledge, by understanding, by science? Do we achieve things as a payment for learning, for growing, for effort? Will the victory over death be one of those things we have to earn as a species, in order to merit its reward? Imagine the things that will have to be fixed first! Is there to be herein the 'savior' in Man?

"In the end, Reverend Falwell's reliance on belief in an interpretation of scripture will probably have nothing to do with whether our knowledge expands to encompass even the mortality which has beset us since the beginning. The scepter will be passed to us when we have earned it- not through belief alone, but through discoveries in learning.

"Unfortunately, Larry, through most of history the shaman, the priest, the prelate, the sorcerer, the king, have dictated the boundaries of knowledge, have instituted superstition and unthinking faith as a medium of their control over the thought and lives of others, killing their possibility.

"These powers have always claimed to speak for 'higher powers,' or that 'higher powers' speak through them. Old King Henry the Eighth declared that 'the King's law is God's law,' making it handy for him to wield brutal and dictatorial control over his poor subjects. Any dissent was deemed 'traitorous,' and prisoners passed under the bridge through Traitor's Gate, to enter the Tower of London, where thousands were executed. When people lose control to rampant power, they are led like sheep to the slaughter, Larry- or left to languish in waiting. 'Henry VIII's Court,' someone said, ' had nothing to do with God, and everything to do with power and money...' The perversion of justice is with us still, and must be understood and guarded against in all its degrees."

[King] ("We're going to have to give some time to our sponsors now. Don't go away, because we've got another guest, and we're going to hear more from the 'country lawyer,' Mr. Gerry Spence, and his perspective on matters of the Standoff in Kansas, and what it's all about- weird, folks, and this is America! The Reverend Pat Robertson will join us with his reaction, and we'll hear more from the distinguished professor about his experience in rendition, and his understanding of what's going on: the times, they are a'changin', Otto... Stay tuned, folks.")

[Larry King] "We're back, and boy what a confrontation! Rev. Robertson, thanks for joining us..."

"Thanks for having me, Larry. Good to be with you."

"Reverend, as Jerry Falwell has said, there are rumors floating around that the scientists in Plainville are dealing in matters related to the conquest over mortality. Suppose they are. Suppose that mankind has reached a threshold whose crossing will afford at last the opportunity to extend life indefinitely- the gateway to a new humanity: Are the scientists dealing in the Black Arts? Is this forbidden ground?"

[Robertson] "Larry, there is no more blasphemous sin than to usurp the powers of the deity. These scientists are treading on dangerous, dangerous ground, and I think God has given a warning to Professor Foglesby by taking the one closest to him, and to the others by permitting the death of Dr. Smith to happen as it did. These were wake-up calls to these people who think they can go anywhere with science in defiance of spiritual realities."

[King] "That's strong, Otto. How would you answer Reverend Robertson?"

[Otto] "I'm not surprised at the reverend's statement. There has long been a conflict between established religion and free thought, between the church and science. Beginning five hundred years before the birth of Christ, at a time when there were great thinkers who were aware of the atom, of math and physics, and the nature of the solar system, of the circulatory and nervous systems, who had developed great concepts of ontology, science, politics and philosophy, and this inestimable and hard-won knowledge was recorded on scrolls and placed into a central temple of knowledge and wisdom called the Library of Alexandria, Falwell's and Robertson's people came and burned that glorious refuge to the ground, and returned on occasions later to burn it again and again, until it was destroyed, along with its knowledge, for two thousand years, the last epoch of which was called appropriately, The Dark Ages, a time of unspeakable brutality, ignorance, and suffering, until, slowly and painfully, knowledge was regained in The Enlightenment, with its brightness to civilize the mind and heart.

"It was the best that had ever been, and they killed it out of ignorance. I'm still mad as hell about all that."

[laughter, as King quips] "Two thousand years, and you're still mad?"

[Otto, with a big smile] "I'm a historian, Larry. Historians have a long memory! I want to know what more Socrates and Plato and Euripedes wrote, and every voice in the Pinakes documents, that ignorance came and torched. Yeah, I'm mad. I'm hoping that the counselor here won't defend the arsonists if I sue.."

[Spence, winking at Otto] "Don't count on it. I pick my cases, Professor. Right now, I'm busy in Kansas... However, I can attest with certainty that neither of our reverend friends here were near the deeds in Alexandria. Wrong culprits this time."

[King] "Pat, let me return to what you said about the tragic deaths in Kansas: Do you really think that God kills people to punish others? Isn't that crazy?., and criminal? Wouldn't that make God not only brutal, but insane?"

[Robertson] "Larry, we can only rely on the word of God in his Holy Book. I have this to say to the vanity of the scientists: What you call your claim to possibility is false. You can't have a resurrection without Jesus Christ. The trump will sound and the Lord God will call his chosen from their graves, and those who haven't lived in truth will spend eternity in Hell."

[Otto] "I understand that is your belief."

[Falwell] "But you don't believe."

[Otto] "I believe in the metaphorical and the metaphysical and the ghost of a flea. They all exist."

[Falwell] "But you don't believe in the divine and heroic sacrifice of Christ, which paid for our redemption?..."

[Otto recognizes a ploy. King cups his chin in his hands, smiling.]

"Larry, humanity is full of heroes and sacrifice. The story of the Christ is repeated an untold number of times in each generation... What I want to know about the theological Jesus in the midst of his sacrifice is, Was he depressed, or was he on fire? Did he burn with the moment?.. For if he did then the forsaking of his life for a cause was not a sacrifice, and it wasn't divine: It was supremely human.

"We have taken the human in the Christ, and made it divine, and the suffering he endured was largely misinterpreted, and wasted."

[King] "Wow! What do you say- either of you? Who wants to take this on?.. Gerry, you can sit this one out, if you prefer."

[Spence, adjusting his cowboy hat, and smiling] "Okay... The better part of valor."

[King] "Reverend Robertson?"

"Larry, all I can say is, with that kind of comment the professor joins the ranks of the sinners and blasphemers. It doesn't matter how many books he's authored, or what his stature is among men, he's going to face the judgment of God Almighty. Christ is risen, and every sinner of every stripe will be called to account, and the unbelievers will be eternally punished."

[King] "Otto, that means you. What do you have to say for yourself?"

[Otto, smiling] "Larry, I have never seen where Jesus said anything like that. Anyway, I have just returned from two and a half months of being hauled from a hole in the ground, beaten and interrogated under blinding lights by men in suits and dark glasses whose eyes you never saw, and then jammed back into the pitch dark hole, with no assurance of ever regaining my freedom. The preacher here is probably picking the wrong person to threaten with the wrath of his God. There was the beginning of eternity in that hell, too, though there are many,

many others who have endured a hundred times more, and death. I enjoyed the novelty for about a minute: eternity is a whole different matter."

[King] "I get the feeling the reverend is angry at something... Reverend?"

[Robertson] "Like the Lord God, Larry, I'm angry at unbelievers, who are causing so much trouble in the world. People who think they can stand alone, without God. The scientists need to forsake the Devil of doubt."

[King] "Otto?.. Are you causing trouble?"

[Otto] "I think the Reverend is a better person than his words imply. I guess I'm 'an unbeliever' in piousness, but the Reverend Robertson is a victim of his belief, which excludes the rights of others to think differently. He sees his religion in a contest with the devil, so those who are not of his religion- which include the great majority of humankind- must be on the side of the malevolent- the Beelzebubians."

[King, grinning] "Beelzebubians?... But there *is* good and evil, you agree?"

[Otto] "The Reverend- pious man that he is- assumes his religion to be against the influence of the devil Satan. What if he is wrong?..

"When the devil is made incarnate, he will not be *against* religion: He will be *of* religion, for therein is the power. True evil, exceeding the human, is mythological in proportion, and conjures its gods and demons to inspire and justify its crime. This is the great, dark mythological secret that organized religion has struggled to keep- its inherent flaw.

"The reverends here would like to impose a theocracy in this country. It's worked so hunky-dory in other places. Hey, why not adopt it here...A religious state. They see no conflict, or irony."

[King] "Which of you would like to answer?.. Those are pretty strong charges. Would you like to end the separation of church and state?"

[Falwell] "There can be no legitimate government without God. In Chapter 26 of the book of Matthew, verses 51 through 53, the Bible holds that government authorities are appointed by God."

[King] "We're going to have to move along.. I want to get back to the baffling situation in Kansas, and we are going to have you all back soon, to discuss this further.

Professor, what is your response?"

[Otto] "As I like to explain it, science eats the fruit of the tree of knowledge. Established religion has been antithetical to science because religion declares its truth, and science is a method of learning new things. Both are dealing with mysteries, but differently.

"Not all religions are dogmatic, but dogmatic religion claims truth and demands belief, and so runs into conflict with the nature of learning and freedom. It says, we will substitute belief for knowledge, and we will tell you what to believe. We will declare unauthorized knowledge a sin, and enshrine belief as a virtue.

"For eating the fruit of the tree of knowledge you will be cast out of Eden into darkness, and pay the penalty of death: For the virtue of belief and unquestioning faith you will be promised immortality, and what you cannot believe you must accept by faith. In this inverted reality lie the seeds of power for the long-reigning authority, from which the human soul has suffered extreme distress.

"Most remarkably for its profession to the contrary, religion has never had a claim to morality. In the name of religion the worst cruelty has been carried out by humans upon one another. We've seen history's savage fanaticisms: darkness masquerading as light, and evil as righteousness. Religion is metaphysical; morality is literal, and the two have little to do with one another. When religion is allowed to define its version of morality, awful things happen. Liberty is sacrificed, and the end result is murder... There is no salvation here."

[King] "Those are powerful charges. I want to ask either, or both, of the reverends with us what they think- and then I'll come back to the barrister, to get his reaction in these matters, and then more on Kansas."

[Falwell] "The professor is speaking as an individual who denies God, who is lost from God. He is a liberal who thinks he doesn't need God... He is defending his own kind among the scientists there in Kansas, who deny the Creator, while usurping the power of the Almighty to effect the resurrection of life. They are messing with nothing less than the soul, the spirit of life, and they will suffer retribution."

[King] "Otto?"

"Larry, I don't claim to speak for God. I have done well in my life just to speak for myself, though I have tried to speak up for my fellow beings also, who cannot speak for themselves. Contrary to the reverend's fantasy, I am not qualified to deny God. Is any one?

"I have a great respect for people of true faith. My mother was one of those true and dear souls whose faith sustained her through life. She was not pious; she was not religious. She believed in the goodness of God, in the basic goodness of the human. Her faith was very private; she did not believe in preachers who lie down with politicians, or in politicians who lie down with preachers. Her faith was real. I tried to be like her, but couldn't be, even though I was trained as a Jesuit priest in my young days..."

[King] "Really! What happened?" "I fell in love with a beautiful woman."

[King] "Not compatible with priesthood."

[Otto] "No. Love defies belief, among other things- the ultimate rebellion of the spirit, in favor of the spiritual."

[King] "You don't believe the spirit is subject to a church?"

[Otto] "..Or to a state, or government, or to any order of authority."

[King] "The spirit is free."

[Otto] "The spirit is nothing if not free. It is synonymous with the spirit of Life, which precedes all knowns, and so does not bow to ideologies or traditions, which are bound things."

[King] "Where is the spirit of life; what does it consist of?"

[Otto] "I think the spirit of life is life's essence and meaning and fullest potential. It abides everywhere, and calls from Destiny. It is the object of all creation, and is the potential of matter and energy to create knowing: to know its own creation."

"Why?"

[Otto] "Oh, that is the question, isn't it?... Is it the thought which wants to know itself- a kind of cosmic vanity? Or something infinitely greater?.. A cosmic necessity."

[King] "But what good does it do to have all this infinite potential and Destiny when a third of humanity lives in abject poverty and suffering- downtrodden, and abandoned? Where's the dream in that? Why injustice? Why so much malice?"

[Otto] "Are you asking the Jesuit, or the ethicist?...Larry, all malice is from a kind of ignorance born, and willful neglect, the same. But the Potential is in the dream, which, when enacted, will save the human species. And the ideal is the enticement to advance. And the reward is in the mind, in the measure.

"Joy is a measure of life, as is pain: they all tell us how precious life is. That it can't be wasted, and that we cannot continue to allow tragedy and suffering to consume us- that we must do something about it. The potential is in *us;* it is our common spirit, which suffers when one suffers, and is lifted up by the lifting of another."

[King] "We are our brothers' keepers."

[Otto] "Our sisters' and brothers' keepers, and keepers of the planet and its creatures, and of the ideals of knowledge."

[King] "Humm... Believing something doesn't necessarily make us better..."

[Otto] "Or save our souls... But, becoming better humans nourishes the spirit- the common spirit of humanity on Earth."

[King] "The Golden Rule: Do unto others..."

[Otto} "A precept of sentience, the survival of conscious life, the simplest rule."

[King] "Why so difficult then? Why so much conflict and suffering and malice? Why are the habits so hard to break?"

[Otto] "Because the human doesn't realize who she is. She does not have a vision of her destiny, and common necessity... Only a faint intimation rewarded in love. The human species stands fatefully poised before the last step, awaiting the will to follow through with its freedom."

[King] "What other steps are there? Where has man been so far?"

[Otto] "The steps have been few, actually, since the beginning- and long- retraced in each individual as an archetype of the race: First, consciousness, then self-consciousness- the reflective mirror of reality wherein she could see herself. But she still does not know who she really is, because religions- of state, of faith, of politics, and prejudice- have kept her divided against herself, and alienated from her connections with the greatest thought, the Destiny of Life, and its cosmic purpose... There is a seminal book, Larry, written in 1902 by Dr. Maurice Bucke, called *Cosmic Consciousness.* Einstein spoke of the 'cosmic religion' of artists and scientists.

"The spirit of Life is a learning of the real and untried, a thinking of the unthought, of the new. It infuses us, and is who we are."

[Robertson] "Larry, if I can respond here... By denying God, the professor, and the scientists, are lost souls who have no legitimacy in their thought or ideas. What they speak are abominations, and their discoveries are godless as well, and for this society has to clamp down on them. Our Attorney General has taken a lot of heat for his courage, but he is on God's side."

[King] "Professor, what about it?"

[Otto] "Contrary to the reverend's trade in the saving and losing of souls, never does one 'lose the soul'. The soul is unalienable. One may lose touch with the core of one's being, and feel the isolation, but the soul, the purpose, is there with the inner being, waiting for its reunion with the self."

[Spence] "Larry, if you'll let an old defense lawyer get in here... I would say that the good reverends here are jumping the gun in passing righteous judgment on Dr. Foglesby and the scientists. I have met everyone there at the facility in Plainville, and have spoken with many of them at length. They appear to me to be diverse, and open, consisting of ordinary people who share a love of learning and discovery. Some are people of faith, but faith is not incompatible with science. All believe that science has a role in the liberation of the human to seek its destiny... They are brilliant in their fields, but otherwise, ordinary folks who need freedom to work and explore... Isn't knowledge the revelation of God?"

[Otto] "I agree with Brother Spence. The reason we declare unalienable rights is that we ourselves may need them, and those we care for. Some people don't need a lot of freedom; some need a great deal. Some are content to be ruled. Others enjoy being rulers. It is all about what people want for their lives- people are even known to vote for their own servitude, becoming, as Robert Ingersoll observed, 'a democracy of the unfree.'

"The modern human, if he allows it, will be disposed of his rights. He is merely allowed the exercise of them, to whatever degree is convenient to the established order. He is tethered. Nothing as regards this person is unalienable. He maintains a myth of freedom, but the fence and guard towers are there, just behind that hill.

"The right to keep and express, to learn or disavow ideas, to have and express thoughts must be unalienable, if the human is to have freedom and progress. The people did not vote to bring on the Renaissance. Advancement was not subject to a plebiscite: the Renaissance was effected for the most part by solitary work and thought, and by individuals who swam against the tide of tradition and dogmatism toward an ideal of the future."

[Spence] "Larry, the knowing human has always had a decision to make in the course of his or her life: Will I be a slave, or will I be free? Wherever people have been bound to slavery, other people have readily served to act as enforcers of that servitude, always in sufficient numbers and with sufficient ingenuity to make the recovery of freedom difficult, even bloody.

"The scarcity of a thing increases its value. When freedom is scarcest, people will die for what little is left.

"I worry now, Larry, that when a misbehaving government loses its legitimacy, then its rulership is *by* law, and not *of* law, and the merit of legitimacy is lost in the corruption of power. In America now, freedom must not become an illusion maintained by the authority which can recall it. True freedom cannot be recalled. These rights that we hold are our truths, and are *inalienable*."

[King] "What's your prediction about Kansas?"

[Spence] "The science isn't a problem. Foglesby is in the right. The mixture of politics and religion in a matter of science is what becomes explosive. I have faith that even in our damaged system of justice we can work it out."

[Falwell] "Larry, the problem is not with science, but with what science is trying to do. The resurrection will come on that day of the Lord God Almighty, and not at the hands of unbelievers who are playing God. They have been warned."

[King, to Otto] "Professor?"

[Otto] "Reverend, what if the God is the ultimate scientist, and shares the purpose of the workers in science?.. The purpose of the Resurrection is inherent in life's meaning. Meaning comes from understanding- the opposite of simple belief. What if you are misunderstanding your God?"

[Falwell] "I consult with the Lord God daily. I pray for truth, and He answers. I don't always like the answers I receive, but I accept them."

[Otto] "I listen to different voices, and do not assume that they always speak the truth. Thus I am free to change my mind, and anyone is free to question me.

"Larry, the reverend is saying what he honestly believes. The 'forbidden zone' of fundamentalist doctrine is its infallibility. Its God can't be wrong, so in the absence of evidence, it demands faith. In the absence of faith, it intones retribution, and demands repentance.

In the absence of repentance it promises the punishment of suffering. It wishes suffering upon those who do not agree with its established truth. Religious- or political-authoritarianism, for their acknowledged certainty, have not been humane forms.

"Certainty is the mind's redoubt, which defends itself against change. It lifts the drawbridge of belief against evidence."

[King] "Whew! Well, I feel like we've barely scratched the surface of these matters related to the drama unfolding in Kansas. One hour is not enough, folks!

"We're going to invite everyone back to discuss this further, and next time we'll make room for questions from the audience...I've got to ask Gerry Spence: Counselor, do you think you and your team are going to get this thing resolved soon? Looks to me like the corral gate is open and the horses are gone.."

[Spence] "Sure. As regards the ideas, Larry, the corral is empty. You can shut the gate, and guard the barn, but the horses are out on the open range, and they ain't coming back. I have every confidence that justice and reason will prevail in the end, and that science will go forward."

[King] "Otto, where do you go from here?... By the way, how did you know that you were in Kazakhstan? Rendition is supposed to be a matter of secrecy, and deniability."

[Otto] "When you're a historian it helps to be a linguist. Unfortunately, I didn't glean much from them that was useful, or edifying, beyond knowing where on this pale blue dot was pinpointed my being- and I would never have imagined what a solace that one bit of knowledge is. It is intensely personal to the human: 'Great Spirit, I am *here!*'

"Larry, if I may add one thing, which Foglesby's discovery affirms: Thanks to the influence of our French friends, and the brilliant insight of the Founding Fathers, we made a Declaration of Human Rights- the Rights of Man. It is time to complete that declaration with its missing half: the Declaration of Human Potential as a right. This is where our final liberation as a species lies, and where we must go. It is our true value and our explanation. It is our necessity. It signals our destiny."

[Larry King] "Thank you for that, Professor. We've got lots more to talk about.

My thanks to Reverend Falwell, to Reverend Robertson, and to the Don of trial lawyers, Mr. Gerry Spence, for joining us. And a special

thanks to Professor Ottolin Narstedder, who agreed to join us so soon after his return from captivity. There is much, much more we did not have the time to discuss, but I hope we have a better understanding now, at least, of the complexities inherent in 'The Great Standoff.' Thanks to everyone and good night."

*   *   *

BEFORE THE END of days which were to play out in the unfathomable drama acted out in a zone of discomfort between science and a world of politics; before the Supreme Court, in a five to four decision, invalidated the Justice Department order of restraint, which had precipitated the crisis in Kansas, and would ineluctably witness the deaths of two invaluable and irreplaceable souls- one death having been senseless and preventable; the other, merely tragic, as death is in love's presence- I had made my way, filled with emotion, and anticipation of the future promise, south through the center of Kansas, and across the flat plain of Oklahoma's panhandle, where my grandparents lie at rest.

Water cuts itself deep into the topsoil of Kansas, so creeks are narrow and deep with trees overarching. In those dark moody waters, if you look down into them, children were told, you can see the ghosts of your ancestors.

Out on the plains there was much that reminded one of the forebears- the great empty spaces, and winds which sing through the tall grass and cry, sometimes, through the branches of trees planted by the settlers.

We are circumscribed by death, which scatters us in the diaspora of generations, with only the threads of memory to hold us in connection with living thought. There is no memory without emotion, and so it is by emotion that our spirits are given a presence in time..

I crossed the plains of the panhandle of Texas, and entered New Mexico, which had known the lives of four generations of my family. Crosses along the road mark, from place to place, the site where an accident took the life of a loved one. There is a name for these hallowed markers in Spanish, and many were of men- young, and middle aged- who drove recklessly, and paid the price.

One would sometimes see a white wooden cross in a bar ditch, anchored by cement or by stones, a woman's dress placed lovingly upon it, surrounding it in a sensual embrace, its folds lifted by the winds, to express in anguished undulations the reminiscence of love.

No matter how close we are, we never get that close, do we?

That space we call identity separates us one from another- even the parent from the child, the child from its parent, the lover from the loved.

We are separate in our selves, and this is the mortal price for *being,* which notes its presence in a name we call our own. It is the only way we can distinguish ourselves from the infinity around us... Our identity is our separateness.

We are circumscribed by death, held by the threads of memory in connection with living thought. There is no memory without emotion, and no learning, and no imagination. Emotion is thought in its infancy. It is also the medium by which we grieve at loss.

It's really all about love.

As I returned home through New Mexico, illumined by a perspective which crossed the boundaries of time, from the past into a future which knew all these matters of which you are reading now, I visited places I had known in youth, looking for times I remembered. The adobe ghost village resettled by "hippies". A flower painted bus sitting in the yard, a young mother in a long dress holding a child, the pony-tailed, bearded father, watching me.

For a moment I saw them again- they were there, and the smell of a wood fire and bread baking in an iron stove, the rustle of cottonwood leaves, a dog barking in the distance.

And then I lost them.

The old bus was rusted, its hand-painted skin faded, a stack of blocks at each corner, wheels long ago robbed, tattered curtains which once lent privacy dangling over some windows in the dusty interior.

They were there, so real, and then they were gone.

A place cannot recreate its past. It is time that moves on, across places like the wind, weathering them slowly, inexorably, then erasing them.

Tattered curtains which once offered privacy, faded flowers painted in love and idealism of youth are ravaged by time, and only memory reclaims them.

Each era is rendered into meaning by memories, and into immortality by love. We who create this moment borrow from the past and invest in the future to sustain the fragile dream which is our living reality. Despite the call to the hereafter, we cling tenaciously to life, unwilling to trade a moment for all of eternity unknown.

This is the best that was, and will ever be, the time of love and ideals and dreams, and babies, and flowers. The time that *is.*

*   *   *

CHAPTER *EIGHTEEN*

OSLO

*The ancients once placed great stones in perfect alignment
with the sun and stars. For modern man it is knowledge
by which we align ourselves with the stars.*
-Dual-Pad notebook "4A", p47.

"Love must be taught, and learned, in each generation."
-Letty.

*LIFE is a near-death experience, whose reality should
awaken every mind into a perpetual awareness.*
-red Top Flight notebook "36", p25.

"That future will be waiting for us which we create."
-Motto of Destiny 101 class.

ON THE FLIGHT to Oslo, six miles above the glistening Atlantic, Fo abstractedly rehearsed the speech in his mind:

"Ladies and Gentlemen of the Committee, esteemed hosts, guests and friends, it is with near infinite humility that I stand before you today..."

In his mind, the speaker gazes across the august body, a mischievous smile widening his lips, his dark eyes sparkling with the humor that springs from irony, spoken to lighten the occasion, though the response is delayed a few seconds, and then muted into smiles and light stirring.

It is possible that someone among them would know that 'near infinite humility' was a theme which had challenged and entertained his classes on Destiny over a sum of years, and the thoughtful pause came from a reflection that someone who knew him would have probably laughed audibly had she been there, breaking the ice of formality- and of solitude- that such moments compel in the individual standing before history.

This was the reason for the pause in his thoughts, which came into presence from far away. He felt the slightest scent of something familiar, and a touch from within and without, of the soul who enveloped him.

Fo had always known the woman as essential, not above or below or beside the man, but folded around, surface against surface in an alter image, rather like the womb that gave him birth, flesh upon flesh and within flesh, not a merging, but an intimate and lasting contact. Man is born of woman and this is his fact, and all of nature is Mother as begets her name.

And so with the soul, which does not merge into oblivion, but remains individual, the mirror image of another, nestled upon and within it by their kindred being, some small part of which we call love- the unfathomable and 'infinite humility,' which accepts and relishes its necessity.

Without love we are exposed, absent of the image which reflects back from within and without the boundaries of our selves, which do not shine of their own light, but are cast in illuminations granted by others.

Fo rested his head on the reclined seat, eyes closed.

Behind him, two rows back, in dark suits, sat two security men provided by the government around the clock since the attempts on his life by religious zealots in the days which followed the siege. The preacher, jailed without bond, had promised the vengeance of God upon the scientist, but apparently grew impatient with the delay and took it upon himself to do his god's work.

Six weeks after the failed attempt another man, with pious anger on his face, stepped out of the shadows, hands behind his back, and encountered the professor as he walked home early one morning. The scientist, hearing his name, politely answered his assailant, who was uttering a verse from the Holy Bible, saying then, "Do you believe in the true and living Christ?"

Fo stopped and studied the man's face for a moment, and then answered, "I believe millions believe that, and it gives them hope."

The man seemed confused by the answer. His shoulders flexed. He seemed to take on an authority: "Only the one true God is the creator of life. You, sir, are a traitor to God."

275

Fo instinctively raised his hands to protect his face just as a flask of acid was emptied upon him. After the initial agony, graftings of his own skin grown from stem cells whose cloning had offended the espousers of life had, within a few weeks, largely reversed the damage, and Fo seemed none the worse, his spirit unaffected. He never became angry or anxious. His mind was occupied with the vastness of greater things.

When someone spoke harshly of the matter, Fo responded simply, "They're mistaken. We're told the Christ Jesus taught peace and love."

There were conversations around the hospital bed in the first days of the treatment in which colleagues and old friends quietly debated the issues inherent in religious anger, noting among them the anomaly that the same proponents of the sanctity of life are often advocates of the death penalty and war. "Thou shall not kill," noted one participant, is interpreted opportunely.

Fo had many times addressed these matters in his classes, and always measured them against mankind's potential, and its ever upward struggle to fulfill its destiny. And so he did not speak again, though he listened intently, but also for the tight pain that stretched the skin of his hands and face.

"The devil has a religious face," commented one, regarding the immense tragedy of religious conflict throughout history.

"As may great goodness," thought the man lying covered in bandages.

Fo never climbed a ladder to be above others, preferring to walk his distances in circumferences of what life had taught him, and so he never had to worry about falling, as climbers may.

It had seemed to Otto such an admirable solution to the presumptions about social success. Fo simply had no sense about it, only those personal rewards handed over to the discoverer in new thought and ideas, and in the growing connections with the reality of existence which seemed undifferentiated from love itself- the creation shaping itself about the soul, to welcome it into unity.

Foglesby had come to that place where great and deep thought reveals a mysterious and hallowed presence which permeates the eternal, where all is transcribed by awe into spirit, and the journey, begun in self-knowing, became a spiritual one.

Once he had described it to his class, speaking poetically of life and science and the delight of learning as a *recognition,* where the mind sees a reflection in what is learned, saying to reality, *I know you. I know you!*

Reality expanded before him, and, like Blake, his senses "discovered the infinite in everything."

*   *   *

"WE HAVE COME from across the world to receive this recognition for some thing done, or made, or realized," (Fo was to continue), "but it is not the 'we' who have accomplished something, because the creation was made in the absence of the self, in its forgetfulness.

When we turn our sights deeply and beyond to the grand reality then the little candle that is our self-consciousness is dimmed to our notice, and we become participants in the light which illuminates the answers we search for in vain in the dim, close reflection of the self.

We live in a modern age, gifted with new knowledge and revelations, but technology has not changed thought. The ancient text may be fragile with age, or the stone worn away with time, but the thoughts are as fresh and real as they were at the writing, because thought is timeless. Only understanding advances.

The ancients once placed great stones in perfect alignment with the sun and stars, integrating death and destiny in symbols of the afterlife.

For modern man, it is knowledge by which we align ourselves with the universe. It was only knowledge that the ancients lacked, and understanding, to complete the vision inherent in thought, for the highest possibility of the human is latent in our brains. Destiny, at some deep level, is ordered and known by the mind, and intimations of it lift upward in tiny, imperfect voices that we call inspiration, out of whose evidence have been born the greatest creations of art and music and thought, none of them consciously made- reflected upon, yes- but translated without conception into knowing.

As we learn, we discover how things are- finding truth in the knowledge. But because we can never have all the knowledge, we can likewise never have all the truth. More of reality always lies before us, and in infinitely greater volume than the known. What we can do to avail ourselves of the unknown reality is never to declare ownership of the truth. The only idea which is disallowed is the idea that other ideas are disallowed, that we alone have the answer.

The most persistent conflicts in the past have been waged, not over the known, for the extent of knowledge was small, but over that vast region of the unknown conceived in imagination, to which our prejudice lays claim.

The great writer, Alexander Solzhenitsyn, who won this chair but was forbidden to occupy it, in a lecture read in his absence at this podium, noted poignantly, 'The heart is especially at ease with regard to that exotic land about which nothing is known.'

At ease, and profoundly disquieted, for we are beguiled by mystery, by that unknown knowledge that lies before us. Called 'the darkness of the unknown' by someone who wished us to fear it, it is, rather, composed of light, and draws us to discovery as a distant traveler to the warm lamp of his door. In learning, we are 'going home.'

And yet, we are none of us originators of a thought or idea. There is nothing we recognize but that was known before and forms in the future day its own image to be reborn in the thought and memory of recognition. Every particle in Nature's repertory of existence is defined by every other; every void, by its potential to arise into being in a form inherent in a continuing creation- circles and spheres and shapes and spirits of existence which touch and surround and define one another in a ghostly structure of realities springing into being, and receding into the everbeing.

That great sum which has never existed in this universe is never to be known, for all things that will exist *are*. Their discovery, in an eternal event, is a harvest of reality into the known. Learners are the avid harvesters of reality.

It is the premier profession and responsibility of each generation to the next, in the flow of history, to reveal the ideals of destiny, which is the highest reach of the human to compel its immortal presence in unity with creation.

No less is the mission of the parent and teacher to inspire the child.

Do teachers know what it is they are teaching, its essence and spirituality- that knowledge is eternal? The final secrets of the universe, when they are known, will be found within the structures of thought and language. They will appear as revelations within the mind, or as its creations, in parameters no grander than the beholder. They will not appear as mystical revelations of supreme powers, to be interpreted and portioned by cloaked guardians of the occult, and protectors of the past, who for long have kept humanity divided against itself.

We were the half-men who did not know that we could declare our humanity and be whole again, because we gave a part of it away to those who said, *You have the favor of the gods, and righteousness to pursue your enemies into victory!*

The fields are strewn with the harvest now, and innocence laid waste by holy winds has left its shadow in stains of blood across the landscape of a gentle Earth. We were the violence that tears this world apart because we shaped it by habit into the image of our worship, and taught it to our children.

In this future time, of power of one to affect and condemn another, we cannot continue to be half-human, divided against ourselves and against nature, the other half possessed by angry gods who manipulate their primeval territories in the mind. We must heal the damage they have done in their tenacious business and free the soul of the darkness that clings weightily against it, embracing at last, and joining the complete and infinite creation which holds our salvation in unity.

No idea is the human's to prosecute in judgment of another. The only measure of truth is, Is this idea free; does it promote freedom and learning and humanity? And if it does not then it does not matter that we think it is spoken by an authority, human or divine: The authority is mistaken, and has misled us.

The authority, my dear friends, of divisiveness is mistaken!

The historic artist and mystic, William Blake, spoke words that were personal, but may be applied to peoples and societies who have endured the orders of conflict and exclusion laid over them by vested powers who designate themselves to rule: 'You must,' he said, 'create your own system, or live as a slave to another.'

It is time for the world to build a new system devoid of conflict and exclusion, in a unity of vision and understanding, to visualize a desired future and bring it into being for the generations to follow, for our salvation lies ahead of us, in our creation of it.

We have looked to the ancient deities and called upon them to help us, and in vain, as the world disintegrates, because they are not there in the past.

Do you wonder where the real gods are? Have you seen them yet?

It is because these gods are yet to be born. They are of the future, and shall be as we make them.

But how do we create our own new system? How do we create the changes that will free us? By what transforming, unifying experience can we be directed to address our destiny?

If we can live intensely enough, we can be of one soul- one in our differences and in our uniqueness, co-participants in our gifts of memory and understanding and imagination.

We are all of us sprung from a common ancestry, but changed by the darkened knowledge of rebellion against the eternal sameness which would keep us as we were. We are, at our best, children of the forbidden angels who celebrate our condemnation to the light of change and growth and humanity which flows in brilliance from the deep cell of our banishment from innocence.

For freedom, the soul's necessity, is not a condition achieved, but a continuous willing to overcome the forces which resist it, and so the spirit of the human finds its wings, beyond the vaunted idea of freedom, in the freeing itself, which must continue generation to generation, and age to age.

We are, more clearly than ever before in history, designers of our own intelligence. We will become as a species what we want to become, the object of our own desires, the products of our unequivocal need for love and understanding and freedom, or else we create the hell of our worst dream, the misbegotten paradise.

If we do not choose freedom, my sisters and brothers, and choose it personally, and as cultures, we will have condemned ourselves and our children to a lesser future where fear and doubt in a repetition of sorrows strangle the dream of life which is the plenipotentiary of the greatest gift which comes with the reality of conscious existence, and that gift is the potential to know and fulfill our greatest possibility, and claim it with each moment of our lives. To find and fulfill our purpose we must design new wings to thought, and learn to use them, and then teach their art of flight to new generations.

The greatest challenge to the human mind, as noted by Balzac, is not to drift into sleep- which is to say, into death- to constantly awaken the will to know and learn, to challenge the order. We must in our modern societies surpass a culture of things which traps its patrons by their self-consciousness, from which many cannot escape. We must surpass a culture of supervision which subjugates a citizenry by self-conscious controls which obviate the responsibilities of freedom, and benefit the controllers.

We must learn to think differently. To develop our humanity we must learn *the art of thinking.*

Once you have ever known that reality beyond the pale of common thought, you can never safely return to the 'sane and normal.' You may countenance the ordinary, but smile secretly and murmur, *but I know the other world,* the furtive glance at the forbidden which indulgingly sweetens the accepted view, if even noted, then not admitted by others.

What *is,* imbued by what *may be,* is the radiance of the spirits of thought and sentience. And if its pleasure be the birthright of the advanced species, *then why not now,* if we deem it desirable! We claim, at any given moment, what we may imagine.

A DOORWAY has opened to human history, to the human condition, to the possibility of our species, as wide as our imagination and will to enter it, to bring into fulfillment the oldest and greatest dream of consciousness. People, with great trepidation, have confused the revelations of the Discovery with the denial of faith and tradition, and sought to censure them, not understanding that the process of science is a quest as well for spiritual knowledge. They see science as a possession of forbidden knowledge, but do not ask themselves, *When was this knowledge forbidden, and by whom?*

They see new knowledge to be in conflict with creation and the nature of man, as if all truth were known and revealed in the past, and that there were no *new creation* necessary to the survival of the conscious species. But *the creator is within us,* and so to avow the creator is to avow life, and to diminish life is to erase the thought by which the creator exists.

And so to the world which harbors life, for to deplete the world is to diminish life, and erase the thought.

'You shall not kill' is not an edict from on high so much as an axiom inherent in the phenomena of existence, breathed in every thought sustaining it. Extinguish the thought- of the human, of the earth and its habitat, of the irreplaceable mystery- and the blackness of the unconscious void descends.

We are not different from the one-celled creature who is drawn to the light in an ancient memory of its birth, for we are all creatures called out of the darkness. Our destiny is in the direction of the light, and we resist from the center of our being its fading.

Learning is the unfolding of reality within the mind, whose process forever changes the human and its world.

If you have found a core of meaning, if you care about something, then your life, beyond a contemplation, is a responsibility and a service, and you are bound by duty to leave the world a better place. If you have tasted freedom, then you have a duty to share it, and sow the seeds of freedom for others. As individuals of a species of unknown and perhaps unimaginable rarity, we must be protectors of one another, and of life.

And so with knowledge, which you must achieve, but which is not yours alone.

And so with peace, which does not fall upon you without casting its healing light upon the world touched by you.

Learning is creation, and creation is a continuing relationship between the creator and the created sustained by the reality of their mutual existence. Neither is god nor servant to the other.

Is that what we have missed in the hierarchies of power- that none is god, and none is servant?

SOME WOULD say that all man can know or understand is held within the limits of the lifespan. That all knowledge is mortal, all thought, mortal. And so there can be no greater source available to man, that there is no cosmic spirit beyond the elaborate confines of the brain, that all is a mind-creation.

Some others hold that only religion can fulfill a vital need in the human, by providing a reason in the scheme of mortal life. They say the release from mortality comes at a price of obedience, that we must believe in a creed or other to be saved.

But the human is *imaginer,* and so it is an audacious and natural extension of the power of thought that it aspire to the everlasting. Haunted by its sense of greatness, the creation lays claim upon the future. The same boundless mechanism of thought which conceives of life and its reality may also just as validly conceive into being its immortality.

We are not destined to oblivion so long as desire provokes will, and will, desire. We are the stuff of our dreams and actions.

Beyond the physical, we live in a dreamworld, a world of dreams and ideas, out of which we construct that agreement among us that we call reality. And then upon this creation we base our lives and thoughts and emotions, and design our freedom.

The conscious being will never be able to find ultimate meaning so long as it is constrained by death. The most important things, the deeper things, cannot be understood in the context of a lifetime. To understand them, one must go beyond life, beyond mortality.

What meaning the human knows comes out of the hope and faith and trust that there is an everlasting, the intermediaries to which have throughout history turned the purest intimation into conflict and calumny for their ends, to keep the dream contained. But now at last we know the thought that brings us into connection with the purpose of our being, and that is to know our unity with the spirit to which we are born, to return home from the shadow of the abyss which is death's false claim.

There is no meaning in death, but to discover love, and no reason, beyond the dream of victory.

Though we do not now live within the fulfillment of the dream, we have already given birth to children who will not have to die. That is our profound new reality. That is our fact. Now, what are we to do with it?... Look forward, my fellow spirits, and see the end of death.

The victory over death is not possible at this moment, nor in any time before. The technology of the resurrection lies before us, born of those supreme intelligences we will create from our will and desire. We will engender the minds that will resolve our dilemma, because it is ordained within our destiny, for we were born to fulfill the glorious imagining. We are like the uprooted cactus that, unknowing that it is dying, emits its flowers, to seed the ground anew.

Sometimes we almost make the connection. We almost understand... And so powerful is the reality that its mere shadow cast upon us for an instant lingers bright as the sun, because for a brief moment we feel the power and presence of the Source, and know that it is within us.

We are the mortal, possessed by the immortal idea. We are dreamers bound by love, and guided to a destiny we imagine in its reality. As creatures of spirit, we are also children of the known, unsure whether we might discover ourselves at last, not in a place, but in a thought, and in the idea of beauty find beauty itself."

*   *   *

POSTSCRIPT

AS I COMPLETE these words to the Committee of the Safekeepers, and as well to any who may read them, the sun has risen enough to cast the mountain range in variegations of light. Mist hangs against those slopes most exposed to the morning light which streams through openings in a bank of low clouds, making this place a kind of composite of beauty everywhere.

The mountains and low hillsides are splashed in patches of yellow and gold, with wildflowers whose petals are wrapped about themselves in the morning chill. Later, in the warmth of the nearby star, they will unfurl their glory in splendid color and rotate their faces in unison to follow the sun's arc across the sky.

How does each know that the other is there, and rotating its face in spontaneous emulation, but for that knowing throughout Nature they spoke of as the cosmic knowing, the liberation of thought by learning, named by the senses into reality?

All of this was meant to be revealed. We are one with all of it in the knowing. Billowed by the sacrifices and accomplishments of the exceptional few who saw knowledge as the birthright of the human to be won at all costs, the veil of mystery was pushed back as the unknown spoke in a familiar voice, of things long hidden but destined by thought into being in a continuing creation.

On this morning visiting birdwatchers with their colorful hats and garb donned long before daylight stood spying on the creatures of flight and song, beginning with the first light of day. I had seen them over the years at this place which is well known to birders, and something about them always evoked an admiration. They, unlike me, were capturing still shots of life as it passed.

Now, as I rounded the curve and saw them there engrossed in their peaceful fascination I understood for the first time this aspect of their lives, and smiled to myself as I caught the receding image of them in my mirror, for I too, at long last, had become a contemplator of life.

I passed around the grounds of the clubhouse there above the lake, where actors and artists from Hollywood once gathered to celebrate friendships, and then one day in another still shot of life leaned together with Letty's mother, arms across shoulders in a color image, smiling into the future in a moment which, like all others, would come only once in forever.

Absent for some months now, although worlds had passed in that interval, I was curious to see once again the spot where the immortal being appeared out of a moment in time to befriend the human.

The scene looked much the same as it moved into view beyond the pasture with its tufts of yellow grass, except that the great cottonwoods after a hundred summers had taken ill and yielded their turn to others growing in limber shoots upon the river's banks. The great skeletons had taken on a whiteness whose outlines were etched upon the blue sky in an architecture of their memory a painter could render into art.

A sculpture made from solid polished timbers of salvaged ironwood stood just before the concrete bridge which had never rated a name. I stopped and smiled to read the words cast into a bronze plate and then painted a deep turquoise. They announced, **THE BRIDGE AT KINO SPRINGS,** and then below in smaller letters, **"A modern bridge, of ordinary design."**

A spot had been filled in at the roadside to make a parking space and a car was there beside which stood a little girl and her father, both looking toward the center of the bridge to where a woman stood, hands touching the railing, looking westward up the riverbed through the morning light. As I slowly passed by I caught a glimpse of her face, lifted slightly upward, her countenance peaceful and serene, though infused by energy as if she were breathing life.

Up the road aways I turned around, and then recrossed the bridge. This time the woman whose deep trance of meditation I had not at first interrupted turned her head and for an imperceptible instant our eyes met in the knowledge beyond explanation of a shared world.

I do not know if her memory carries that meeting as mine does, in a medium of kindred souls. Perhaps it does, and she will one day read this story which seeks to reveal in the humblest way what it was we knew.

I glanced once more as I passed, at the remains of the great trees whose memories of a century's seasons are written in concentric rings into the architecture of their deaths, vividly silhouetted against the sky by the mind that perceives them. Beyond that elemental trust, by the sweetest irony, they do not exist.

I SAW THE PROFESSOR for the last time that universe away in events compressed against the invisible separation of them from the touch of understanding.

Awakened from slumber the night the winter turned to spring, I heard a familiar voice apologizing politely for its intrusion and then proposing a meeting on short notice.

"I'm in flight. Would like to touch down in a place you know. Can you meet us in two hours?"

"Of course! Of course," I replied, dampening my excitement in a repetition of the response. "I'll be there."

"Wonderful. See you there." And then the line dropped.

Needless to say, I sprang upward and in what seemed a single motion dressed and readied myself for a meeting I had hoped for, though not expected. I put on a coat, and actually contemplated taking a change of clothes, then found the presumption amusing, and simply carried a book I had been reading, and a small notepad. Within an hour I was at the airport with time to spare, and pumped with energy and anticipation I could not simply wait, and so struck off across the ramp area where the old DC-3 had sat luminous in the starlight on that incomparable morning, then strode briskly down the taxiway into the darkness, listening to the rhythm of my footsteps upon the cold asphalt.

The sound at first was indistinct, a soft undulation just at the edge of hearing, as if the night were speaking in whispers from the distance all around. I stopped and listened intently as the disturbance steadily shaped itself into a direction far into the darkness, signaling the approach of a jet. As the sound grew I turned and began jogging back up the dark taxiway toward the dimly lighted ramp area, but stopped once to look again into the distance just as two sabers of light stabbed outward rotating their shafts as if probing the darkness in a search. Almost simultaneously lines of blue lights snapped on to mark the adjacent runway, which sloped upward diminishing to a point a mile and a half in the distance.

The descending behemoth screamed by in a wind and touched down to the prolonged skid of its tires upon the asphalt, and then to the blast of its thrust reversers which would slow the velocity of landing into a sedate turn somewhere up there where the blue lights merged and the taxiway returned.

The plane had been at rest just briefly as I arrived, its interior lighted, and I could see through the long row of rounded windows the figures of some people rising to stand, and the heads of others who sat reclined in their seats. Some looked outward to where I stood, and I caught a wave or two, but all was quiet.

I suddenly noticed a whir behind me and a motorized stairway eased into place against the base of the doorway just back of the pilots' cabin in the nose high above. The door loosened and twisted open and around, leaving a solitary figure standing against the light within, tall and slender, a hat upon his head.

Fo stepped forward and then down the stairway, flexing his arms outward, fingers intertwined in a motion which I had seen a time or two before, when he was about to do business.

He looked good, and rested. He shook my hand vigorously, reaching a long arm around my back to give me a couple of slaps in his familiar style.

I felt emotion in his voice as he spoke. But really he just said that he was stopping to say goodbye.

I felt there was so much to talk about, and yet very little. Everything had been said, and the notebooks I still held contained guidance I needed, if I could just discern it.

We stood in silence for a moment and I knew that it had to do with Letty, and nothing could be said, or needed to be.

He told me that a country had extended an invitation to him and a team of world class scientists and engineers and scholars- *crème de la crème,* he called them, the finest minds available- to pursue the greatest project of discovery in the history of humankind.

I knew a small amount about its context, and a great deal about its future, but suddenly was struck by an unexplainable need to say nothing more, perhaps out of deference to matters of self-consistency, though I had been assured that there was not a way its rule could be violated.

We stood for a moment longer and then he clasped both my shoulders between his hands and shook them slightly, a smile appearing, his eyes sparkling under the brim of his felt hat.

"So long," he said, turning to climb the stairway, "Better get going. It's midnight."

And then I heard him call me by my childhood nickname.

I raised my hand quickly and almost called, "Wait!" Then I smiled as the figure climbed the steps.

"...Destiny," is all I offered.

The following morning headlines stunned the world, announcing that Flight 1000 was blown out of the sky in a blast photographed by an American satellite.

An intense and prolonged search for debris turned up nothing, not a trace of the airliner or its passengers and crew. One hundred and ninety eminent souls on board.

Further searches found only the emptiness of a vast ocean, and the silence of its deep.

*   *   *   *   *

The Beginning.

In a violation of our destiny, something is killing every one of us.

The judge of ignorance has long sentenced every living being to death, has sentenced you, and I, all our ancestors, and our children to death. In a relentless holocaust, there are no survivors.

Hope has not been enough to win an appeal, nor the visions of faith, nor the dream of justice and beauty, not even love.

To the heartless judge of ignorance, these mean nothing.

We will be saved in the end by knowledge.

We will learn to overcome aging and death by engendering the noble and supreme intelligences. We will create the gods who will call us back to life, or we will not return at all. It is in our hands.

It is time to inspire and begin the ultimate scientific, moral, and spiritual quest.

The end of death.